Apache Mahout Cookbook

A fast, fresh, developer-oriented dive into the world of Apache Mahout

Piero Giacomelli

[PACKT] PUBLISHING
open source
community experience distilled

BIRMINGHAM - MUMBAI

Apache Mahout Cookbook

First published: December 2013

Production Reference: 1181213

Published by Packt Publishing Ltd.
Livery Place
35 Livery Street
Birmingham B3 2PB, UK.

ISBN 978-1-84951-802-4

www.packtpub.com

Cover Image by Faiz Fattohi (faizfattohi@gmail.com)

Credits

Author
Piero Giacomelli

Reviewers
Nicolas Gapaillard
Vignesh Prajapati
Shannon Quinn

Acquisition Editor
Usha Iyer

Commissioning Editor
Llewellyn Rozario

Lead Technical Editor
Amey Varangaonkar

Technical Editors
Sharvari Baet
Mrunal Chavan
Venu Manthena
Amit Singh

Project Coordinator
Shiksha Chaturvedi

Copy Editors
Alisha Aranha
Janbal Dharmaraj
Deepa Nambiar
Karuna Narayanan
Kirti Pai
Adithi Shetty
Laxmi Subraminian

Proofreaders
Ameesha Green
Maria Gould

Indexer
Mariammal Chettiyar

Graphics
Ronak Dhruv

Production Coordinator
Nilesh R. Mohite

Cover Work
Nilesh R. Mohite

About the Author

Piero Giacomelli started playing with computers back in 1986 when he received his first PC (a commodore 64). Despite his love for computers, he graduated in Mathematics, entered the professional software industry in 1997, and started using Java.

He has been involved in a lot of software projects using Java, .NET, and PHP. He is not only a great fan of JBoss and Apache technologies, but also uses Microsoft technologies without moral issues.

He has worked in many different industrial sectors, such as aerospace, ISP, textile and plastic manufacturing, and e-health association, both as a software developer and as an IT manager.

He has also been involved in many EU research-funded projects in FP7 EU programs, such as CHRONIOUS, I-DONT-FALL, FEARLESS, and CHROMED.

In recent years, he has published some papers on scientific journals and has been awarded two best paper awards by the International Academy, Research and Industry Association (IARIA).

In 2012, he published *HornetQ Messaging Developer's Guide, Packt Publishing*, which is a standard reference book for the Apache HornetQ Framework.

He is married with two kids, and in his spare time, he regresses to his infancy ages to play with toys and his kids.

Acknowledgments

I would like to thank my family for supporting me during the exciting yet stressful months in which I wrote this book.

Thanks to my wife Michela, who forces me to become a better person everyday and my mother, Milena, who did the same before marriage. Also thanks to Lia and Roberto who greatly helped us every time we needed their help.

A special acknowledgment to the entire Packt Publishing editorial team. Thanks to Gaurav Thingalaya, Amit Singh, Venu Manthena, Shiksha Chaturvedi, Llewellyn F. Rozario, Amey Varangaonkar, Angel Jathanna, and Abhijit Suvarna, as they have been very patient with me even when they had no reason for being so kind.

While I was writing this book, I also moved to a new job, so this is the right place to thank Giuliano Bedeschi. He created SPAC and now, with his sons, Giovanni and Edoardo, leads one of the few companies I am proud to work for. SPAC's people really helped me during this transition period.

About the Reviewers

Nicolas Gapaillard is a passionate freelance Java architect, who is aware of the innovative projects in Java and the open source world.

He started his career working at Linagora (`http://www.linagora.com`), an open source software company, as a developer in the security business unit. This business unit aimed to develop open source software that revolves around security, such as certificate management, encrypted document storage, and authentication mechanisms.

Next, he worked for an open source software integrator named Smile (`http://www.smile.fr`), where he held the roles of a developer, trainer, and technical leader in Java technologies.

After several experiences as an employee, he decided to create his own company named BIGAP (`http://bigap.fr`) to do missions as a freelancer. This gives him the freedom to manage his time in order to work on and study innovative projects.

One of the missions was to work for a French startup named Onecub (`http://www.onecub.com`), which aspires to automatically classify e-business e-mail using categories for the customers. At that time, only Mahout provided some out-of-the-box algorithms that threats about these problems. Since then, Nicolas started to make a deeper research into the Mahout project and data mining/data learning domain.

One day, Packt Publishing saw his article (`http://nigap.blogspot.fr`), and asked him to contribute to the review of the book, so he accepted this offer with pleasure.

I want to especially thank the author of this book who has worked very hard to write the book with a concern for quality. I would also like to thank Packt Publishing who trusted me to contribute to the review of the book, and manage the processes very carefully, and permitted me to synchronize the review with the redaction of the book.

I would like to thank the other reviewers who have helped for the redaction of the book and the quality of the content and also thank my wife, who let me have some free time to work on the review.

Vignesh Prajapati is working as a Big Data scientist at Pingax. He loves to play with open source technologies, such as R, Hadoop, MongoDB, and Java. He has been working on data analytics with machine learning, R, Hadoop, RHadoop, and MongoDB. He has expertise in algorithm development for data ETL and generating recommendations, predictions, and behavioral targeting over e-commerce, historical Google analytics, and other datasets. He has also written several articles on R, Hadoop, and machine learning to produce producing intelligent Big Data applications. He can be reached at `vignesh2066@gmail.com` and `http://in.linkedin.com/in/vigneshprajapati/`.

Apart from this book, he has worked with Packt Publishing on two other books. He was the author of *Big Data Analytics with R and Hadoop, Packt Publishing* (`https://www.packtpub.com/big-data-analytics-with-r-and-hadoop/book`) and has also reviewed yet to be published *Data Manipulation with R DeMystified, Packt Publishing*.

I would like to thank Packt Publishing for this wonderful opportunity, and my family, friends, and the Packt Publishing team who have motivated and supported me to contribute to open source technologies.

Shannon Quinn is a candidate of the Joint Carnegie Mellon University-Pittsburgh Ph.D. program in Computational Biology. His research interests involve spectral graph theory, machine vision, and pattern recognition for biomedical image recognition, and building real-time distributed frameworks for biosurveillance with his advisor Dr. Chakra Chennubhotla. He is also a contributor for Apache Mahout and other open source projects.

I am a big fan of the Mad Men TV series where I heard the song "Going out of my head" for the first time performed by Sérgio Mendes and Brasil 66.

I think my feelings for you, Michela, are best represented by the following verse:

Goin' out of my head over you

Out of my head over you

Out of my head day and night

Night and day and night, Wrong or right...

Being a father these days is becoming a very tough task; Enrico and Davide, I hope you will appreciate my efforts on this task.

— Piero Giacomelli

Table of Contents

Preface

The rise of social network websites coupled with the new generation of mobile devices have drastically changed the way we handle data in the last 10 years.

To give you an idea of what is going on, we refer to a study done by Qmee in 2012 that shows what usually happens on the Internet in 60 seconds. The results shown at `http://blog.qmee.com/qmee-online-in-60-seconds/` tell us that Twitter received 2,78,000 tweets, Facebook received 41,000 posts every second, while YouTube gets 72 hours of video uploaded. These are the biggest websites, but even for national or international websites it is common to have millions of records, collected for logging purposes.

To manage such large volumes of information, new frameworks have been coded to basically allow the sharing of the computational tasks via different machines. Hadoop is the Apache solution for coding algorithms whose computational tasks can be divided between various hardware infrastructures.

When one deals with billions of data records to be analyzed, in most cases the purpose is the information extraction to find new relations between data. Traditionally, data mining algorithms were developed for this purpose. However, there is no way to compute, in a reasonable time, the data mining tasks when dealing with very large datasets. Mahout is the data mining framework created to be used, coupled with Hadoop, for applying data mining algorithms to very large datasets using the MapReduce paradigm encapsulated by Hadoop. So Mahout offers the coder a ready-to-use framework for doing data mining tasks using the Hadoop infrastructure as a low level interface.

This book will present you with some real-world examples on how to use Mahout for mining data and will present you with the various approaches to data mining. The key idea is to present you with a clean, non-theoretical approach to the ways one can use Mahout for classifying data, for clustering them, and for creating forecasts. The book is code-oriented, and so we will not enter too much into the theoretical background at every step, while we will still refer the willing reader to some reference materials for going deep into the specific arguments. Some of the challenges we faced while presenting this book are:

- From my experience, Mahout has a very high learning curve. This is mainly because using an algorithm that uses the MapReduce methodology is completely different from the sequential approach.
- The data mining algorithms themselves are not so easy to understand and require skills that in most cases a developer does not necessarily have.

So we tried to propose a code-oriented approach to allow the reader to grasp the meaning and the purpose of every piece of code suggested without the need of a very deep understanding of what is going on behind the scenes.

The result of this approach should be judged by you and we hope that you find pleasure in reading it as much as we had in writing it.

What this book covers

Chapter 1, Mahout is Not So Difficult!, describes how to create a ready-to-be-used development environment in one machine. A recommendation algorithm will be coded so that all the pieces involved in a data mining operation as the presence of Hadoop, the JARs to be included, and so on, will be clear to the reader without any previous knowledge of the environment.

Chapter 2, Using Sequence Files – When and Why?, introduces the reader to sequence files. Sequence files are a key concept when using Hadoop and Mahout. In most cases, Mahout is not ready to directly treat the datasets that are used. So before entering in the code algorithm we need to describe how to treat these particular files.

Chapter 3, Integrating Mahout with an External Datasource, details recipes to read and write data from an RDBMS using command-line tools as well as code.

Chapter 4, Implementing the Naïve Bayes classifier in Mahout, tells us in depth how to use the Naïve Bayes classifier to classify text documents. How to convert document terms into vectors of numbers counting the occurrence will also be fully described. The use of the Naïve Bayes classifier and the complementary Naïve Bayes classifier from the Java code will also be presented.

Chapter 5, Stock Market Forecasting with Mahout, deals basically with two algorithms: Logistic Regression and Random Forests. Both of them will show you the possibility to analyze some common datasets to obtain forecasts on future values.

Chapter 6, Canopy Clustering in Mahout, starts to describe the most used algorithm inside the Mahout framework, the one involving cluster analysis and classification tasks of Big Data. In this chapter the methodology for using canopy cluster analysis to aggregate data vectors around common centroids will be described with real-world examples.

Chapter 7, Spectral Clustering in Mahout, continues with the analysis of the clustering algorithms available in Mahout. This chapter describes the ways to use spectral clustering, which is very efficient in classifying information linked together in the form of graphs.

Chapter 8, K-means Clustering, describes the use of K-means clustering, both sequential as well as MapReduce, to classify text documents in topics. We will explain the use of this algorithm from the command line as well as the Java code.

Chapter 9, Soft Computing with Mahout, describes an old literature algorithm named the Frequent Mining Pattern. It allows you to forecast the items that should be sold together moving from the previous purchases made by customers. The Latent Dirichlet algorithm will also be presented for text classification.

Chapter 10, Implementing the Genetic Algorithm in Mahout, describes the use of the Genetic algorithm in Mahout to solve the Travelling Salesman problem and to extract rules. We will see how to use different versions of Mahout to use these algorithms.

What you need for this book

We will cover every software needed for this book in the first chapter. All the examples in the book have been coded using Ubuntu 10.04 Lucid release and a virtual machine created with Oracle Virtual Box.

Who this book is for

Apache Mahout Cookbook is ideal for developers who want to have a fresh and fast introduction to Mahout. No previous knowledge of Mahout is required, and even skilled developers or system administrators will benefit from the various recipes presented in this book.

Conventions

In this book, you will find a number of styles of text that distinguish between different kinds of information. Here are some examples of these styles, and an explanation of their meaning.

Code words in text, database table names, folder names, filenames, file extensions, pathnames, dummy URLs, user input, and Twitter handles are shown as follows: "In the same way you could also use Eclipse to access the `svn` repository and compile everything using the Maven Eclipse plugin."

A block of code is set as follows:

```
File ratingsFile = new File(outputFile);
DataModel model = new FileDataModel(ratingsFile);
CachingRecommender cachingRecommender = new CachingRecommender(new
  SlopeOneRecommender(model));
```

Any command-line input or output is written as follows:

```
wget http://www.grouplens.org/system/files/ml-1m.zip
```

New terms and **important words** are shown in bold. Words that you see on the screen, in menus or dialog boxes for example, appear in the text like this: "Click on the **Add** button and after a few seconds, you should be able to see all the Mahout jars added."

> Warnings or important notes appear in a box like this.

> Tips and tricks appear like this.

Reader feedback

Feedback from our readers is always welcome. Let us know what you think about this book—what you liked or may have disliked. Reader feedback is important for us to develop titles that you really get the most out of.

To send us general feedback, simply send an e-mail to `feedback@packtpub.com`, and mention the book title via the subject of your message.

If there is a topic that you have expertise in and you are interested in either writing or contributing to a book, see our author guide on `www.packtpub.com/authors`.

Customer support

Now that you are the proud owner of a Packt book, we have a number of things to help you to get the most from your purchase.

Downloading the example code

You can download the example code files for all Packt books you have purchased from your account at `http://www.packtpub.com`. If you purchased this book elsewhere, you can visit `http://www.packtpub.com/support` and register to have the files e-mailed directly to you.

Errata

Although we have taken every care to ensure the accuracy of our content, mistakes do happen. If you find a mistake in one of our books—maybe a mistake in the text or the code—we would be grateful if you would report this to us. By doing so, you can save other readers from frustration and help us improve subsequent versions of this book. If you find any errata, please report them by visiting `http://www.packtpub.com/submit-errata`, selecting your book, clicking on the **errata submission form** link, and entering the details of your errata. Once your errata are verified, your submission will be accepted and the errata will be uploaded on our website, or added to any list of existing errata, under the Errata section of that title. Any existing errata can be viewed by selecting your title from `http://www.packtpub.com/support`.

Piracy

Piracy of copyright material on the Internet is an ongoing problem across all media. At Packt, we take the protection of our copyright and licenses very seriously. If you come across any illegal copies of our works, in any form, on the Internet, please provide us with the location address or website name immediately so that we can pursue a remedy.

Please contact us at `copyright@packtpub.com` with a link to the suspected pirated material.

We appreciate your help in protecting our authors, and our ability to bring you valuable content.

Questions

You can contact us at `questions@packtpub.com` if you are having a problem with any aspect of the book, and we will do our best to address it.

1
Mahout is Not So Difficult!

This chapter contains the following recipes:

- Installing Java and Hadoop
- Setting up a Maven and NetBeans development environment
- Coding a basic recommender

Introduction

Mahout is basically a set of machine learning Java libraries meant to be used for various tasks, such as classification, evaluation clustering, pattern-mining, and so on.

There are many good frameworks that are user-friendly and fully equipped with more algorithms to do these tasks. For reference, the R community is much bigger and in the Java world we have had the RapidMiner and Weka frameworks present on the scene for many years.

So why should we use Mahout instead of the aforementioned frameworks? Well, the truth is that all the previous frameworks are not meant to be designed for very large datasets. When we refer to very large datasets we refer to datasets, no matter the format, whose records require an order in the scale of a hundred million records.

The power of Mahout lies in the fact that the algorithms are meant to be used in a Hadoop environment. Hadoop is a general framework that allows for an algorithm to run in parallel on multiple machines (called nodes) using the distributed computing paradigm.

The key idea behind Hadoop is that instead of having a single juggernaut server that handles the computational and storage task of a very large dataset, Hadoop divides the whole task into a set of many subtasks, using the divide and conquer paradigm. After all the single tasks have been done, Hadoop is responsible for managing and recombining all the single subsets once their computation is over and the output is generated. In this case, it is possible to divide heavy computational tasks into many single node machines even if they are not so powerful, and obtain the results. The idea is not far from the first distributed computing example such as **SETI@Home** (`http://setiathome.berkeley.edu/`) and the **Great Internet Mersenne Prime Search** (GIMPS) (`http://www.mersenne.org/`), but in this case we distribute machine learning algorithms. We will cover the details in a better manner over the course of this book with the help of various examples.

Installing Java and Hadoop

The first part of this chapter will be dedicated to setting up a working environment in a single node Hadoop machine, so as to get the reader ready to code in the easiest and fastest way.

As we said before, we are interested in guiding coders to install a development machine to be able to test their Mahout code quickly. We will not go too much in detail on how to deploy the code on a production Hadoop cluster. That is out of the scope of this book; it involves a more detailed and sophisticated approach and configuration.

We only need to let the reader know that for all our recipes we use a single node cluster, so even if in various recipes we describe the parameters needed for an algorithm to be run in many clusters, in our case, the internal computation will be always forced to use one node cluster. For reference on how to configure Hadoop clusters, we refer the reader to another good book, *Hadoop Operations and Cluster Management Cookbook, Packt Publishing* by *Shumin Guo*.

Using `cygwin` it is also possible to test Hadoop and Mahout in a native Windows system but we will not cover this argument; we point out only to the related wiki on the Apache website (`http://hadoop.apache.org`).

Considering that Hadoop can also run in a cloud environment, the willing reader could also use Amazon EC2 to set up a single node Hadoop cluster for testing purposes. The reference for using these configurations can be found in the Amazon EC2 wiki (`http://wiki.apache.org/hadoop/AmazonEC2`).

At the time of writing, Microsoft released a Hadoop implementation that can be run in Azure Cloud but we have not tested it. A simple Google search could help you.

It is also possible to download Hadoop from the Cloudera website (`www.cloudera.com`)—a VirtualBox 64-bit image of a complete installed Hadoop system.

Nevertheless, configuring a minimal system from scratch could greatly help you to understand how Hadoop and Mahout interface together.

At times, it is also possible to configure Mahout without Hadoop to test the code. However, as a matter of fact, since Mahout gets the most of its advantages in terms of performance and scalability from Hadoop, we think that this second option is less learning focused.

So, we are going to install Hadoop and Mahout on an Ubuntu 32-bit machine. We will use a virtual machine so as to have a fast replication development environment available.

With an open source approach, we prefer to use the VirtualBox machine emulator; for those not familiar with VirtualBox, please go through *VirtualBox 3.1: Beginner's Guide, Packt Publishing* (`http://www.packtpub.com/virtualbox-3-1-beginners-guide/book`).

In our case, since we use a VirtualBox virtual machine hosted by a Windows 7 Professional Edition and we do want to have a possible fast reply from the guest machine, we decided to use the Ubuntu Desktop 10.04 32-bit. Considering that we use mainly Debian-based commands, it is possible to replicate Ubuntu on a Debian-based distribution.

Hadoop and Mahout are not meant to be run as a root user, so we create a user called `hadoop-mahout` to install and run everything.

Our installation strategy will follow the given points:

- Installing JDK 1.7u9
- Installing Maven 3.0.4
- Installing Hadoop 0.23.5
- Installing NetBeans 7.2.1
- Compiling from sources Mahout 0.8-SNAPSHOT

The reader could also download the latest Mahout binaries, including the correct jars into his/her example project, but using Maven helps the reader to control the Mahout releases better, and the versioning of jars. In this case, all the Mahout jars' dependencies should be downloaded manually and this could be a very time-consuming and boring task.

Maven will also be used for our test code. We will not cover the features that Maven has to offer; we only point the reader to a good Packt book: `http://www.packtpub.com/apache-maven-3-0-cookbook/book`.

Before moving to the coding procedure, we need to install everything, so let us start with the downloading phase.

This is the first introductory chapter that will permit the reader to see how to create a single node Hadoop development environment.

> We advise the reader to follow the next recipe very carefully, as all the other recipes in the book depend on its correctness for compiling and running properly.

Getting ready

We begin by downloading the JDK. Hadoop and Mahout need JDK 1.6 or higher and we use the JDK 1.7u9, which can be downloaded from the Oracle website: `http://www.oracle.com/technetwork/java/javase/downloads`.

Hadoop could also be run with the OpenJDK implementation of the virtual machine but we prefer to use Oracle's implementation.

Maven 3.0.4 can also be downloaded from one of the mirrors of the Apache website; in this case, we use the following terminal command:

```
wget http://it.apache.contactlab.it/maven/maven-3/3.0.4/binaries/apache-maven-3.0.4-bin.tar.gz
```

Then, you could also download Hadoop 0.23.6 using a similar command as follows:

```
wget http://apache.panu.it/hadoop/common/hadoop-0.23.6/hadoop-0.23.5.tar.gz
```

Now that you have everything downloaded in one folder, in our case `/home/hadoop-mahout/Downloads`, you should see the following screenshot:

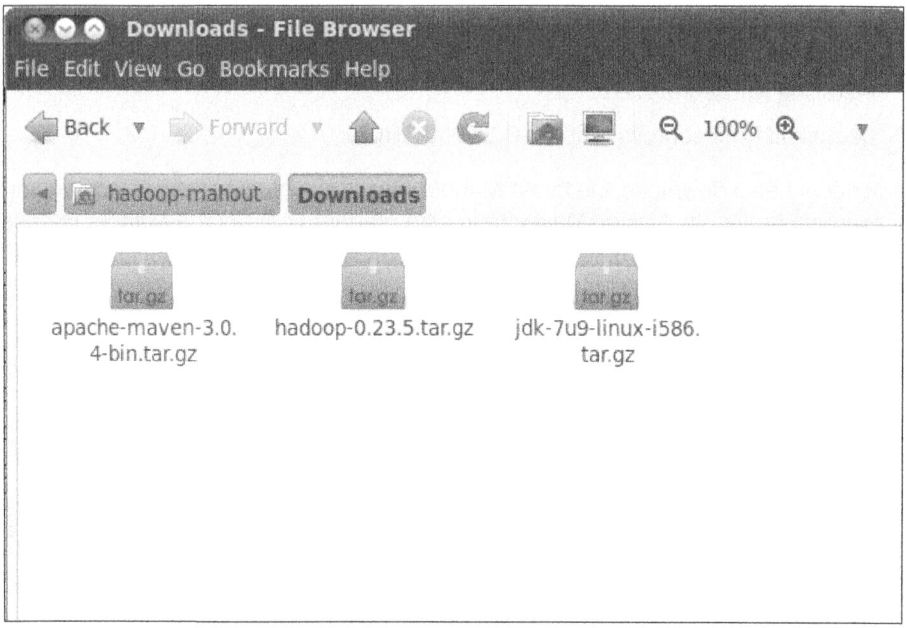

How to do it...

In this recipe we will finish the setup of our environment for the Java, Maven, and Hadoop parts. The steps for all three frameworks are always the same:

- Decompress the archive
- Add the correct console variable
- Test the correctness of the installation

Now, we will decompress every archive and move the resulting folder from the `/home/hadoop-mahout/Downloads` folder to the `/home/hadoop-mahout/` folder. This is because the `Downloads` folder is meant to be erased or used by other software, so we want to save our installed procedure:

1. Decompress everything in the terminal window to the `Downloads` folder by typing:

```
cd /home/hadoop-mahout/Downloads
```

2. Then give the following commands:

```
tar -C /home/hadoop-mahout/ -xvzf jdk-7u9-linux-i586.tar.gz
tar -C /home/hadoop-mahout/ -xvzf apache-maven-3.0.4-bin.tar.gz
tar -C /home/hadoop-mahout/ -xvzf hadoop-0.23.5.tar.gz
```

3. This will decompress the three archives into the folder `/home/hadoop-mahout/`. So the appearance of the `hadoop-mahout` folder should look like the following screenshot:

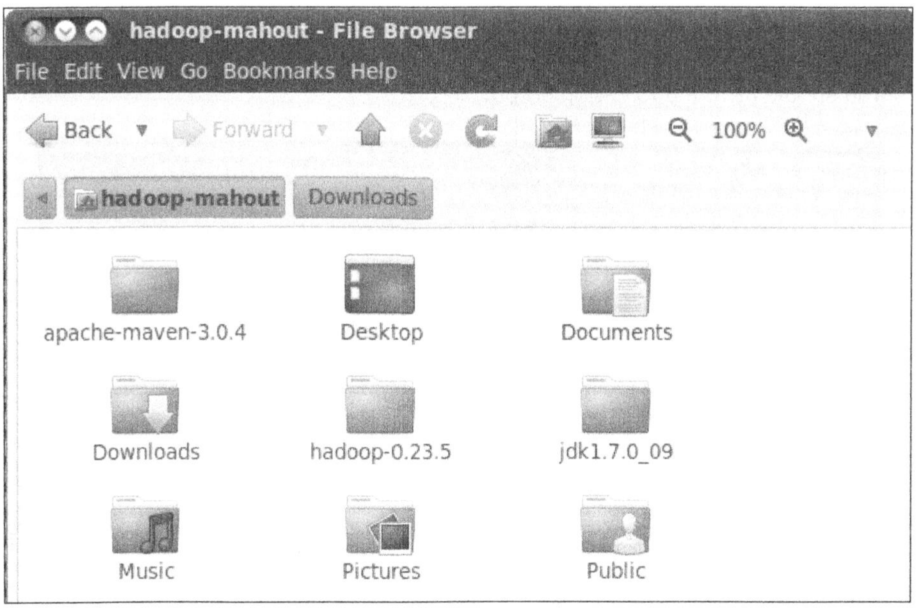

4. We have everything we need to create and set up some environment variables. This is because Maven, Hadoop, and Mahout need to have a configured variable named `JAVA_HOME`.
5. We also need to have the `mvn` command—the Hadoop command accessible from every terminal. To have this variable fixed even in case of a system reboot, we will save them in the `.bashrc` profile as well. This is an easy way in Ubuntu to set up variables for a single user.
6. To accomplish all these settings you need to:
    - Open the file named `.bashrc`, which is located in the `/home/hadoop-mahout/` folder, with your preferred text editor
    - Add the following lines at the end of the file:

      ```
      export JAVA_HOME=/home/hadoop-mahout/jdk1.7.0_09
      export HADOOP_HOME=/home/hadoop-mahout/hadoop-0.23.5
      export MAVEN_HOME=/home/hadoop-mahout/apache-maven-3.0.4
      export PATH=$PATH:$JAVA_HOME/bin:$MAVEN_HOME/bin:$HADOOP_
      HOME/bin
      ```

    - Save the file and return to the console
7. The first three lines create the user variables: `JAVA_HOME`, `MAVEN_HOME` and `HADOOP_HOME`.
8. The last line adds the variables coupled with their relative `bin` locations to the `PATH` variable.
9. To test JDK and Maven, now type the following command:

   ```
   java -version
   mvn -version
   ```

   You should have the following output:

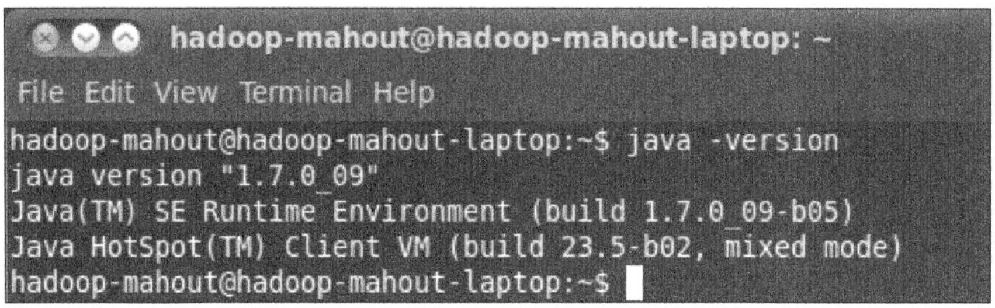

You should also have the output seen in the following screenshot:

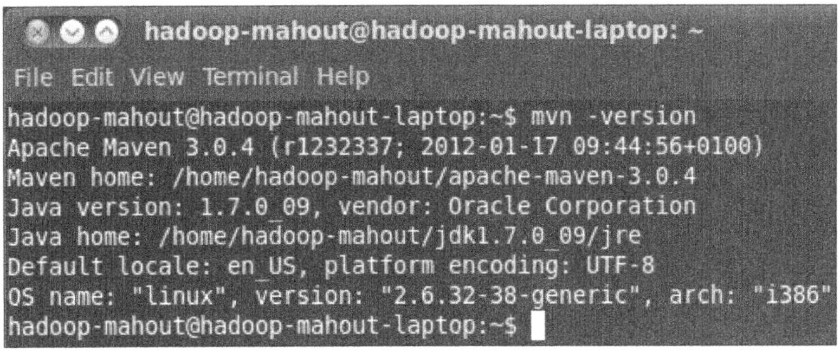

10. To test the correctness of the Hadoop installation, we will compute an example that comes from the Hadoop distribution, which computes the value of pi using 10 MapReduce jobs on a standalone installation.

11. So type the following command from the `HADOOP_HOME` folder:

    ```
    hadoop jar /home/hadoop-mahout/hadoop-0.23.5/share/hadoop/
    mapreduce/hadoop-mapreduce-examples-0.23.5.jar pi 10 100
    ```

12. Do so from a terminal prompt and you should see the 10 MapReduce jobs that start and end with the following lines:

    ```
    Job Finished in 8.983 seconds
    
    Estimated value of Pi is 3.14800000000000000000
    ```

So, here we have successfully set up a single Hadoop standalone node for testing. We are now ready to download and compile the Mahout sources using **Subversion** (**SVN**) and Maven.

Setting up a Maven and NetBeans development environment

This is a fundamental recipe and should be followed very carefully, as all the other settings explained in the rest of the book depend on the successful installation of Maven and NetBeans. If you are more comfortable using Eclipse instead, we suggest you to take a look at the guide provided at `http://maven.apache.org/eclipse-plugin.html`. However, as the whole book is based on the assumption of using NetBeans as the IDE, in case Eclipse is used, every configuration on it should be re-checked.

Getting ready

Now we are ready for the last part, which is installing and configuring Mahout, to be used with NetBeans.

For coding purposes, we decided to use NetBeans as an IDE instead of other IDEs such as Eclipse, because this last version at the time of writing was not fully compatible with all the Maven 3.0.4 specifications. Again, it is possible to use Eclipse or IntelliJ, but the configuration is more difficult than this one. For using Eclipse with Maven, refer to `http://maven.apache.org/eclipse-plugin.html`.

We will compile the latest Mahout snapshot using SVN in order to have the latest release. Nevertheless, you could also download the `binaries` file and link the jars once needed.

We will use NetBeans for compiling the sources, so before proceeding we need to download the file `netbeans-7.2.1-ml-javase-linux.sh` from the NetBeans website (`www.NetBeans.org`).

Once downloaded, the `Downloads` folder should look like the following:

Now to install NetBeans, simply move to the `Downloads` folder and type the following command in the terminal window:

```
/home/Hadoop-Mahout/Downloads/sh netbeans-7.2.1-ml-javase-linux.sh
```

Then, follow the procedure till the end.

Now the `hadoop-mahout` user folder should look like the following screenshot:

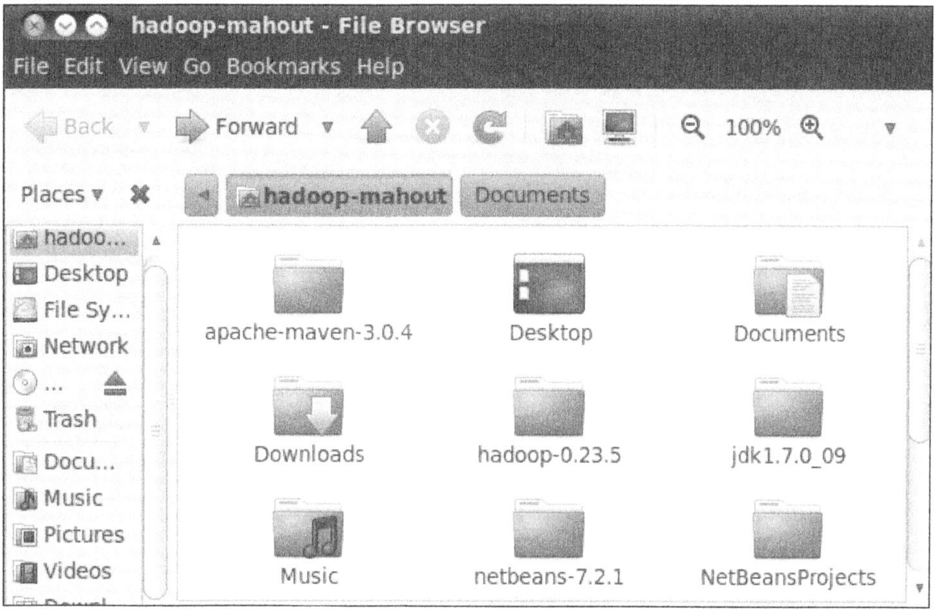

The `NetBeansProjects` folder will contain our Mahout sources and our code. We are now ready for the interesting phase that is the Mahout source-code compilation from NetBeans. Now that we have NetBeans installed, we are ready to compile Mahout's latest snapshot using NetBeans.

How to do it...

At the time of writing the latest Mahout snapshot, the version is Version 0.8. We invite the reader to follow the releases because apart from bug fixes, new algorithms and features that arrive are constantly being released by this vibrant community.

1. We need to download the Mahout sources from Subversion, import the Maven-related project into NetBeans, and finally install everything.
2. Fortunately, the NetBeans IDE offers all this action integrated into various GUI interfaces. Simply using the main menu, go to **Team** | **Subversion** | **Checkout** and complete the field repository URL using the following link: `http://svn.apache.org/repos/asf/mahout/trunk`.

Click on **Next** and complete the form as shown in the following screenshot:

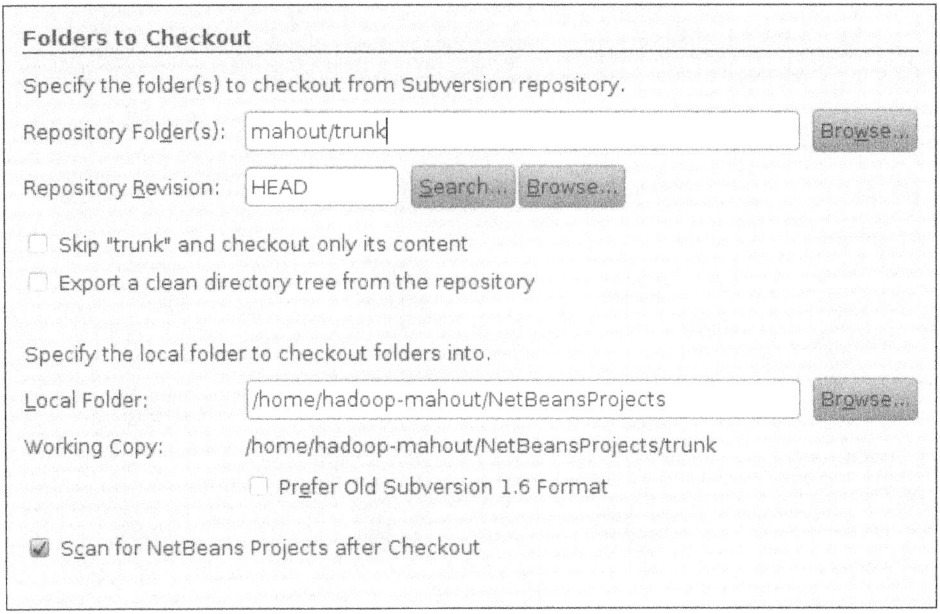

3. Once NetBeans finishes downloading the whole package, it will ask if you want to scan and open the project. So click on **Ok** in the information window and let the IDE import the Maven project. Now, in the **Projects** tab you should see the following structure:

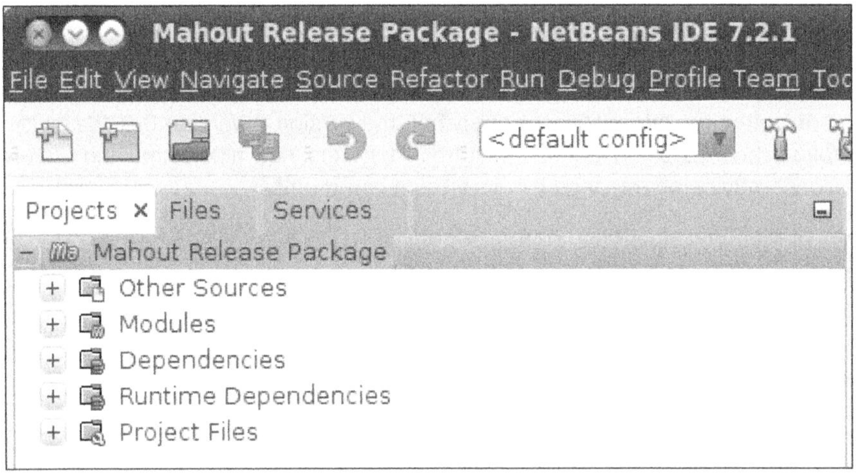

4. The sources have been downloaded and can be found in the `NetBeansProjects` folder.

5. Now for compiling these sources using Maven, right-click with your mouse on the **Mahout Release Package** icon and choose **Clean and Build** item.
6. Time to take a break. Surf the Internet, check you emails, or drink a cup of coffee because the compiling procedure could take a while. When you return from your break you should see the following output:

```
Reactor Summary:

Mahout Build Tools ................................ SUCCESS [1.876s]
Apache Mahout ..................................... SUCCESS [0.457s]
Mahout Math ....................................... SUCCESS [11.356s]
Mahout Core ....................................... SUCCESS [12.909s]
Mahout Integration ................................ SUCCESS [2.262s]
Mahout Examples ................................... SUCCESS [14.978s]
Mahout Release Package ............................ SUCCESS [0.009s]
------------------------------------------------------------------------
BUILD SUCCESS
------------------------------------------------------------------------
Total time: 44.187s
Finished at: Thu Nov 21 10:54:51 CET 2013
Final Memory: 47M/128M
------------------------------------------------------------------------
```

Eureka! We now have all that we need in order to test Mahout.

If you expand all the dependency icons from the NetBeans project structure, you should see all the jars and dependency jars that have been downloaded from the Apache website, as shown in the following screenshot:

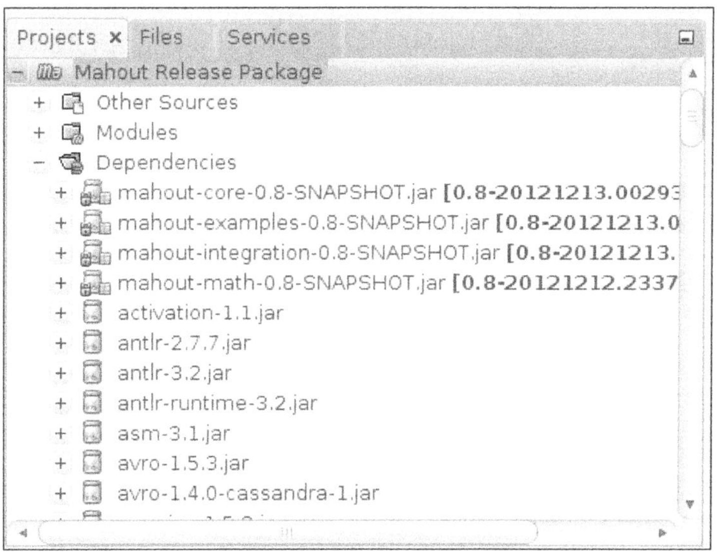

How it works...

The **Subversion** plugin, used by NetBeans, downloads the latest source code from the official Mahout `svn` repository. Once finished, NetBeans recognizes the `pom.xml` file on the source-code repository, so it deals with a Maven source code and then compiles everything, tests it, and in the end creates the jars based on the folder structure.

There's more...

NetBeans gives you only the interface to control the Subversion Maven process. But you could also directly use the command-line interfaces, if you find it difficult to code using a single text editor.

In the same way, you could also use Eclipse to access the `svn` repository and compile everything using the **Maven Eclipse** plugin.

Do not forget that once you have downloaded the sources and before importing the Maven project into Eclipse, you need to be in the root folder of your sources to run the following command:

```
mvn eclipse:eclipse
```

This creates an Eclipse ready-to-use project import file.

> If you do not follow the preceding step, you could have version problems or compiling errors in your code.

Coding a basic recommender

Now that we have a fully configured IDE with the latest release of Mahout compiled from the sources, we can finally run our first example code.

In an effort to code less and get more from the user's perspective, we will see an example on how to code a recommender using Mahout.

As the name suggests, a recommender is a software that is able to make suggestions on new or existing preferences from previously recorded preferences.

For example, the recommender system on purchased items is able to give you suggestions on what you should buy next, based on your previous buys.

There can be various types of recommenders, depending on the complexity of the type of dataset they analyze. In our case we will use **Slope One recommender,** which is based on Collaborative Filter methodology.

Automatic software recommender systems are one of the first problems in the data mining history. Basically, the problem can be divided into two steps:

- Read a huge amount of data that maps a user with some preferences for an item
- Find an item that should be suggested to the user

Everyone that has bought something on an e-commerce website such as Amazon must have seen the site suggestions for new books or stuff to buy. We will simulate the same result using movie suggestions given by some users to mine them and find other movies that have not been seen previously.

Getting ready

Data miners are hungry for data, so the more data you have the more precise your output will be.

Before continuing, we need to download a set of data for testing purposes. We will use the **GroupLens** dataset for movie recommendations.

The GroupLens dataset is a dataset freely available created by the Department of Computer Science and Engineering at the University of Minnesota, which consists of 1 million ratings from 6000 users on 4000 movies.

The data is available in a text file format, which is the simplest way for Mahout to read data. To download the data, simply type the following command into a terminal console:

```
wget http://www.grouplens.org/system/files/ml-1m.zip
```

Unzip the file and you should see that the archive contains four main files:

- `users.dat`: This contains 6000 users
- `movies.dat`: This contains the name of the movies
- `ratings.dat`: This is the association between the users and the movies with a number for determining how much the user liked the movie
- `README`: This is the format explanation

If you open the `ratings.dat` file, which is the one that will be used, you should see the following lines:

```
UserID::MovieID::Vote::datetime
1::1193::5::978300760
1::661::3::978302109
1::914::3::978301968
```

For every line you have a movie rating that can be interpreted as follows: user `1` gave a vote of `5` (out of `5`) to the movie *One Flew Over the Cuckoo's Nest* and gave a vote of `3` to *James and the Giant Peach* and to *My Fair Lady*. The last long number is the long date/time of the rating itself.

Unfortunately, even though Mahout is able to manage some file format as input, this one is not in the Mahout ready-to-use format. This is because in our case the delimiter is `::`. This first easy example will demonstrate some of the common problems when dealing with the non-standard format.

In this case, we will transform the original file into another that has the following format:

```
UseID,MovieID
1,1193
1,661
1,914
```

Basically, we will read the original file line-by-line and copy every line to a new one, removing some unessential information to obtain the final format.

The original file also contains the vote assigned to the movie. For this recommender, we are not interested in the vote given to the movie by the user, so we remove it. We also remove the information on the date of the rating.

As we stated before, we will use Maven to create our example during the whole book. So, we need to create the Maven project in NetBeans. Our steps will be:

- Create the Maven project structure with a `main` class
- Add the Maven dependencies to the Mahout Maven project previously compiled

Fire up NetBeans and from the NetBeans main menu, choose **New Project** and from the window that appears, choose **Java Application** as seen in the following screenshot:

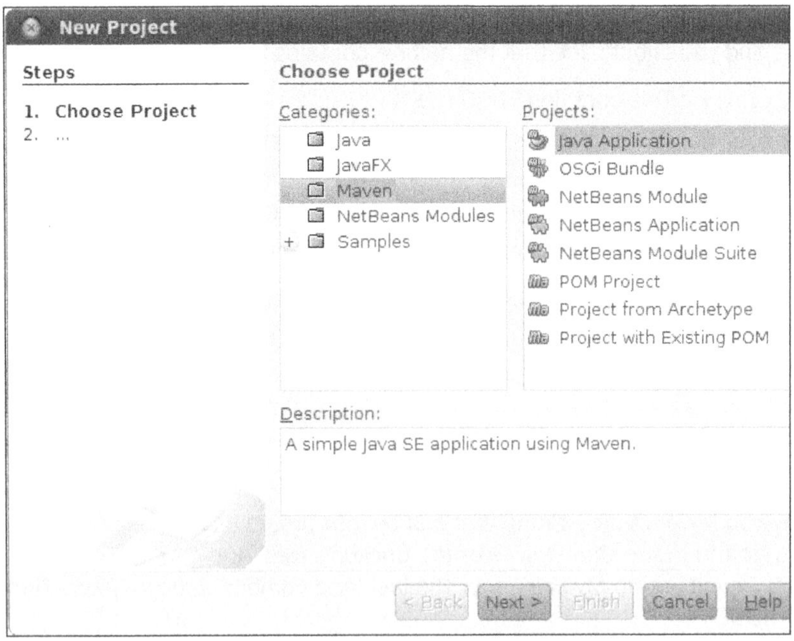

Then complete the following forms as shown:

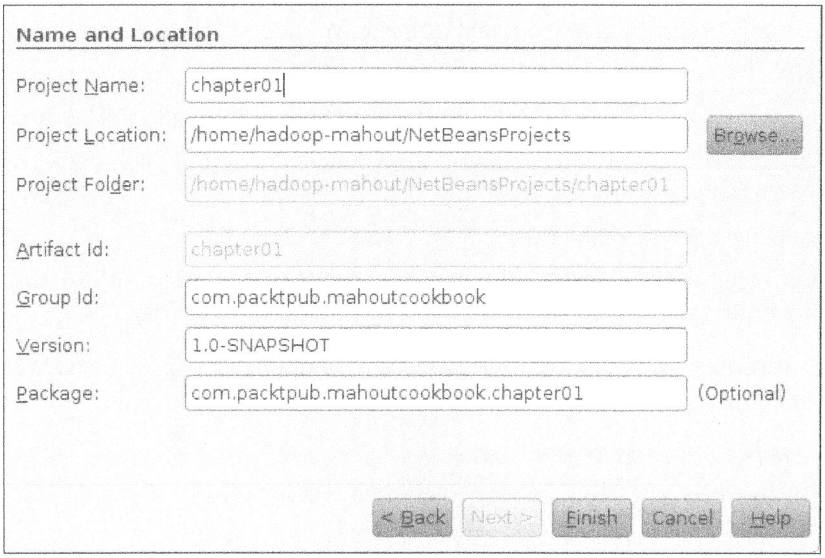

Now, we need to add the dependency to the previously compiled Mahout Maven sources. To do this in Maven's project folder structure, right-click on the dependencies icon and choose the item **Add dependency** from the pop-up menu. Choose the dependency to add as follows:

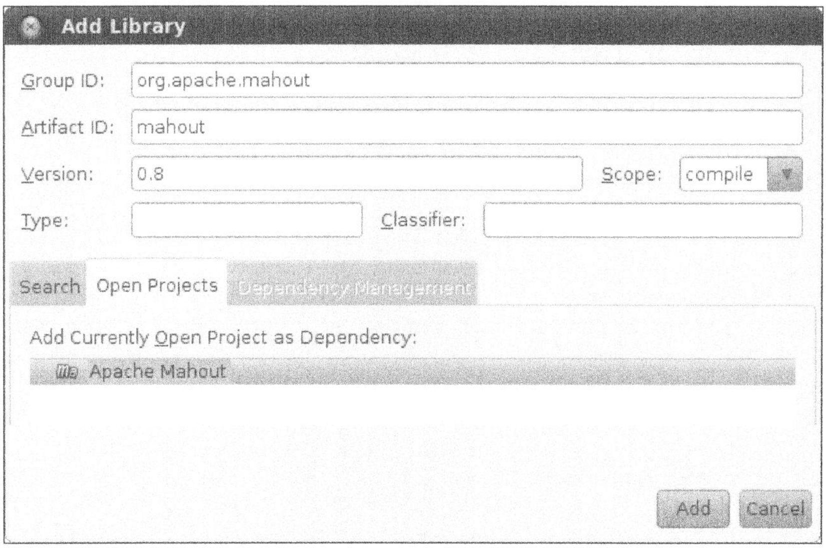

Click on the **Add** button and after a few seconds, you should be able to see all the Mahout jars added.

How to do it...

Now, we are ready to code and test our first example. We need to carry out the following actions:

1. Transform the `ratings.dat` file from the GroupLens format to the CSV format.
2. First, we will create a `Model` class that will handle the format of the new `ratings.csv` file that we will use.
3. Create a simple recommender on this model.
4. Then, using a cycle to extract the entire user's list contained on the `ratings.csv` file, we will see the recommendations on the titles for every user.

Following the previous steps, the code will mimic it. Before proceeding, let us do the necessary imports:

1. The imports are added as follows:

```
package com.packtpub.mahoutcookbook.chapter01;

import java.io.BufferedReader;
import java.io.BufferedWriter;
import java.io.File;
import java.io.FileNotFoundException;
import java.io.FileReader;
import java.io.FileWriter;
import java.io.IOException;
import java.util.List;

import org.apache.commons.cli2.OptionException;
import org.apache.mahout.cf.taste.common.TasteException;
import org.apache.mahout.cf.taste.impl.common.
LongPrimitiveIterator;
import org.apache.mahout.cf.taste.impl.model.file.FileDataModel;
import org.apache.mahout.cf.taste.impl.recommender.
CachingRecommender;
import org.apache.mahout.cf.taste.impl.recommender.slopeone.
SlopeOneRecommender;
import org.apache.mahout.cf.taste.model.DataModel;
import org.apache.mahout.cf.taste.recommender.RecommendedItem;

public class App
{
    static final String inputFile = "/home/hadoop-mahout/
Downloads/ml-1m/ratings.dat";
    static final String outputFile = "/home/hadoop-mahout/
Downloads/ml-1m/ratings.csv";
```

Moving to the main method and the core of our code we first code a method to transform the original MovieLens file into a csv file without the vote as explained before.

```
    public static void main( String[] args ) throws IOException,
TasteException, OptionException
    {
        CreateCsvRatingsFile();
```

The full method is shown as follows:

```
private static void CreateCsvRatingsFile() throws
FileNotFoundException, IOException
{
  BufferedReader br = new BufferedReader(new
FileReader(inputFile));

  BufferedWriter bw = new BufferedWriter(new
FileWriter(outputFile));

  String line = null;
  String line2write = null;
  String[] temp;
  int i = 0;
  while (
    (line = br.readLine()) != null
    &&
    i < 10000
    )
{
  i++;
  temp = line.split("::");
  line2write = temp[0] + "," + temp[1];
  bw.write(line2write);
  bw.newLine();
  bw.flush();
  }
  br.close();
  bw.close();
}
}
```

2. Then, it is time to build the model based on the **comma-separated value** (**CSV**) file shown as follows:

```
// create data source (model) - from the csv file
      File ratingsFile = new File(outputFile);
      DataModel model = new FileDataModel(ratingsFile);
```

3. Create the SlopeRecommender:

```
  // create a simple recommender on our data
  CachingRecommender cachingRecommender = new
CachingRecommender(new SlopeOneRecommender(model));

        // for all users
for (LongPrimitiveIterator it = model.getUserIDs();
it.hasNext();)
{
  long userId = it.nextLong();
```

4. At the end, we simply display the result recommendation:

```
  // get the recommendations for the user
  List<RecommendedItem> recommendations = cachingRecommender.
recommend(userId, 10);

  // if empty write something
  if (recommendations.size() == 0){
    System.out.print("User ");
    System.out.print(userId);
    System.out.println(": no recommendations");
  }

   // print the list of recommendations for each
  for (RecommendedItem recommendedItem : recommendations) {
    System.out.print("User ");
    System.out.print(userId);
    System.out.print(": ");
    System.out.println(recommendedItem);
  }
  }
}
```

Let us take a look at what this code does by analyzing it.

> **Downloading the example code**
>
> You can download the example code files for all Packt books you have purchased from your account at `http://www.packtpub.com`. If you purchased this book elsewhere, you can visit `http://www.packtpub.com/support` and register to have the files e-mailed directly to you.

How it works...

Following the code, we have the `import` statements. All the imports are from the jars linked using the dependencies from Mahout Version 0.8.

The first method is called for data transformation purposes, and it is the `CreateCsvRatingsFile` method. This piece of code basically transforms the original file into the comma-separated values. As you can see, we chose to convert only the first 10,000 rows of the file. This choice is made to reduce the computational time when the recommender actor will enter the stage, and to avoid a Java heap memory exception on one single machine.

Once we are done with this, we enter the interesting stuff contained in the following three lines of code:

```
File ratingsFile = new File(outputFile);
DataModel model = new FileDataModel(ratingsFile);
CachingRecommender cachingRecommender = new CachingRecommender(new
  SlopeOneRecommender(model));
```

After creating a `DataModel` class based on the CSV file, we create a `CachingRecomender` object using `SlopeOneRecommender`.

Mahout comes with different recommenders even if you can build your own. The default recommenders are as follows:

- **User-based recommender**: This recommender basically couples the users using a similarity or neighborhood measure
- **Item-based recommender**: This recommender, instead of using only users as proximity measure in preferences, takes in the variables as the similarity between the items chosen
- **Slope One recommender**: This uses a linearized function to couple users and items together to evaluate proximity

In our case we use the simplest one—that is the Slope One recommender—that is effective.

Then, we cycle through every user that is present on the new file `ratings.csv`, and for every user, we extract the first 10 recommended items.

After a build and compile, the first run should output a suggestion as seen in the following screenshot:

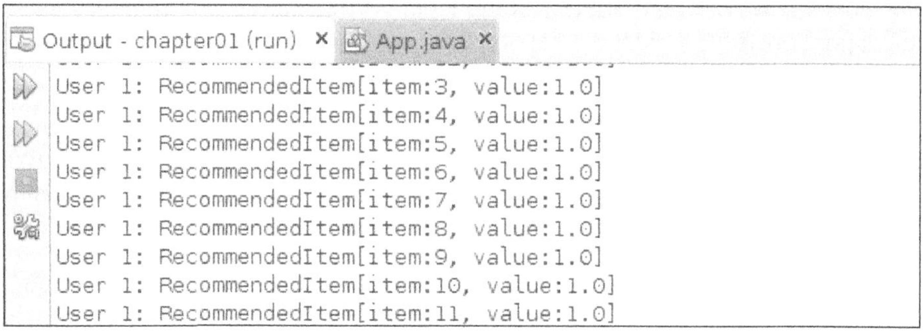

As we can see for user `1`, the recommender suggests the movie with the ID `3461` with a probability of `1.0`. (The probability is always `1` for a Boolean recommender such as the Slope).

If we take a look at the user ID `1`, we can see that the user is a woman who is above 18 years old according to the `users.dat` file. For her, for example, a suggested movie is `3461` according to the `movies.dat` file:

```
3461::Lord of the Flies (1963)::Adventure|Drama|Thriller
2::Jumanji (1995)::Adventure|Children's|Fantasy
```

It is interesting to notice that both the films' plots revolve around the adventures of children. So, it seems that the suggestion given is a good one considering the age of the user, even if the title of the movie *Lord of the Flies* could be updated.

The reader could try to give a different run to the program by using 100, instead of using 10,000 ratings. This can be done by substituting the line, `i < 10000`, with `i < 100`.

In this case, what we observe is that the software outputs no suggestion as we can see in the following screenshot:

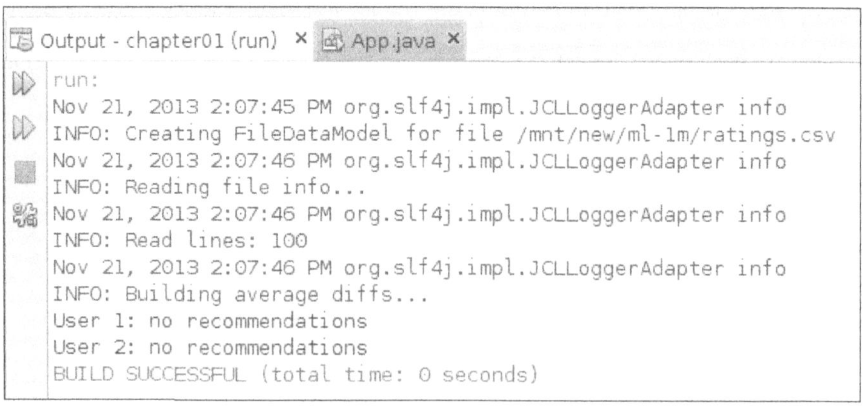

So, the results are greatly affected by the size of the `ratings.cvs` file and obviously the more data you have, the better the suggestions are that the recommender can give.

See also

Now that we have coded a basic recommender, you could also try to see the other type of recommenders provided within the example code. In fact, there is a ready-to-use GroupLens recommender that uses the preferences of the user settings as well. This more sophisticated approach could be more useful for the willing reader to understand how Mahout recommender implementations work.

For a more formal approach on how recommenders work, refer to the introductory article at `http://dl.acm.org/citation.cfm?id=245121`. For additional datasets to test recommenders, you could use the Jester dataset available at `http://eigentaste.berkeley.edu/dataset/`.

For datasets related to e-commerce recommendations, you could take a look at the datamarket website, `http://datamarket.com`.

2

Using Sequence Files – When and Why?

The purpose of this chapter is to show you the use of sequence files. In particular we will cover the following recipes:

- Creating sequence files from the command line
- Generating sequence files from code
- Reading sequence files from code

Introduction

In the last chapter, we were briefly introduced to Mahout and we created a fully working example to be used for demonstrating how to code with Mahout.

At a higher level, the Hadoop MapReduce algorithm works as shown in the following figure:

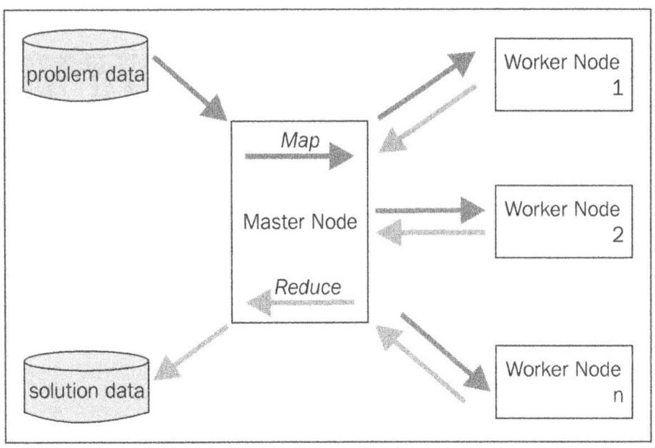

From a coding point of view, we have two stages:

- **Mapping**: In this stage, the original computational problem is taken by the master node and divided into smaller pieces. Every computational piece is then sent to different worker nodes called mappers.
- **Reducing**: In this stage, the output of every mapper node is collected and reassembled using the same key index for all the nodes.

To give a simple conceptual example, we consider Hadoop WordCount that counts the number of words there are in a single text; the output is a set of key/number values, where `key` is the word and `number` counts how many times a word appears in the text. We divide the text into smaller pieces and we assign every piece to a mapper that records the occurrences of the word in that piece of text. At the end, once every mapper finishes its job, the whole set of key/number values is summarized by summing the count of the repeated words. This approach allows you to parse very big datasets, with the only limit being that each mapper should not exceed the memory capacity of the node where it is running. The power of this framework is the possibility to have parallelism in computing the map job, so you can have the advantage of different nodes working at the same time on different smaller pieces of the original input. This parallel approach has been demonstrated to be, in general, five times faster than the sequential approach, even for very simple algorithms such as merging and sorting. You can view the related documentation at `https://www.vmware.com/files/pdf/VMW-Hadoop-Performance-vSphere5.pdf`.

We are aware that such big numbers must be handled with a lot of caution. This kind of approach has been demonstrated to be a winning one in many contexts, both theoretically and practically. Above all, as the databases grow in magnitude, this is the only practical approach.

Nevertheless, the advantage of using the parallel programming approach against the traditional sequential one is limited to the fact that you cannot use the same sequential algorithm. This is why there can be lots of differences in the same algorithm as we consider them from the sequential and the parallel side. A number of machine-learning and data-mining algorithms are based, as we will see further, on the calculation of vectors and matrices that are entities, and that can be easily integrated in a parallel way.

So let's now move on to our first recipe.

Creating sequence files from the command line

Before proceeding with our recipe we need some data to be tested. We chose to use the Lastfm dataset.

Getting ready

We will start by creating a new folder to work with. Choose a folder (in our case, `/mnt/new/`) and type in the following command:

```
mkdir  lastfm
mkdir ./lastfm/original
mkdir ./lastfm/sequencesfiles
export WORK_DIR=/mnt/new/lastfm
cd $WORK_DIR
```

So we create a `lastfm` folder to store the data we want to work with. For the sake of simplicity, we use an environment variable to store the absolute path (in our case, `/mnt/new/lastfm`). Change it accordingly for your examples to work.

The Lastfm dataset is freely available and can be downloaded using the following command line:

```
cd $WORK_DIR
hadoop-mahout@hadoop-mahout-laptop:/mnt/new/lastfm$ wget http://static.
echonest.com/Lastfm-ArtistTags2007.tar.gz
```

To untar it, use the following command:

```
hadoop-mahout@hadoop-mahout-laptop:/mnt/new/lastfm$ tar -xvzf  Lastfm-
ArtistTags2007.tar.gz
```

Now you should have the following folders inside your `$WORK_DIR` folder:

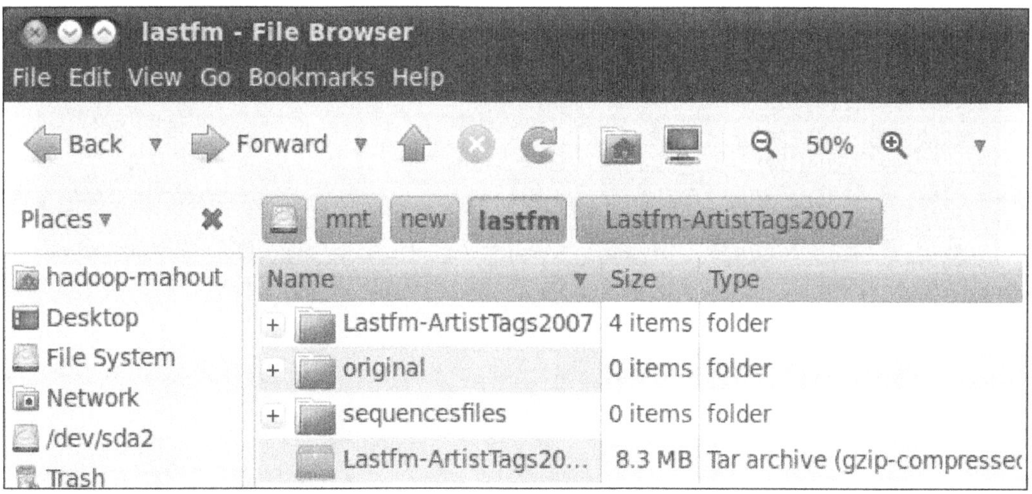

Now we can have our original files in the folder `$WORK_DIR/original` with the following command:

```
hadoop-mahout@hadoop-mahout-laptop:/mnt/new/lastfm$ cp /mnt/new/lastfm/
Lastfm-ArtistTags2007/*.* /mnt/new/lastfm/original/
```

Before proceeding I invite you to take a look at the following files that build this dataset:

- `Artists.txt`: This contains the artist's registry
- `Tags.txt`: This consists of all the tags in the dataset
- `ArtistTags.dat`: This lists all the associations between tags and artists

How to do it...

Now it is time to convert our first file from its original format to the Mahout's sequence format.

The command is pretty easy, as follows:

```
mahout seqdirectory -i $WORK_DIR/original -o $WORK_DIR/sequencesfiles
```

The output of the console is shown in the following screenshot:

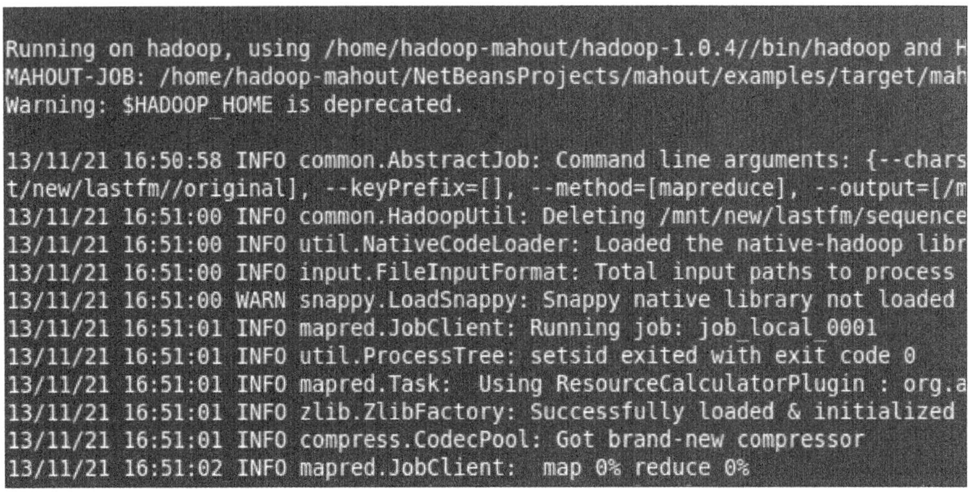

The result can be seen on the `$WORK_DIR` output folder that consists of two files as shown in the following screenshot:

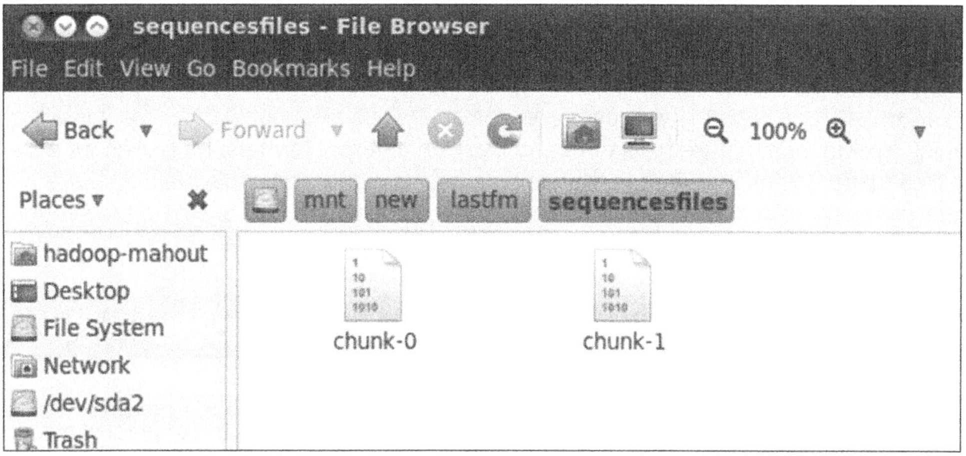

How it works...

Sequence files are binary encoding of key/value pairs. There is a header on the top of the file organized with some metadata information which includes:

- Version
- Key name
- Value name
- Compression

To look at the generated file we could use the following `seqdumper` command:

```
mahout seqdumper -i $WORK_DIR/sequencesfiles/chunk-0 | more
```

The output is as follows:

```
Input Path: /mnt/new/lastfm/sequencesfiles/chunk-0
Key class: class org.apache.hadoop.io.Text Value Class: class org.apache.
hadoop.io.Text
Key: /tags.txt: Value: 440854 rock
343901 seen live
277747 indie
245259 alternative
184491 metal
158252 electronic
```

At the top of the output we can see how the `Key` class and the `Value` class are bound to the Java object (in this case, both are bound to the `org.apache.hadoop.io.Text` class).

By default, without any specification, the parsing is done using plain text format.

Another useful option is the `-ow` command, which overwrites the existing destination files.

The `seqdirectory` option is very useful when parsing text files, but in this case it is without meaning, considering that we have different files with different formats. Moreover, we also have files that are in the required format as their association with the key/value pairs is already uniquely defined. So it is time to move to the code to see how to create the sequence file using a more structured Java approach.

Generating sequence files from code

In this example we will take the file `Artists.txt` and create a sequence file using the unique ID in the file and the name of the key/value pair. The format of the original file looks like the following:

```
25231 Radiohead
20372 Pink Floyd
20251 The Beatles
19600 Red Hot Chili Peppers
18867 System of a Down
18671 Metallica
18671 Coldplay
18143 Nirvana
17629 Death Cab for Cutie
17507 Muse
16268 Green Day
16057 Franz Ferdinand
15306 Nine Inch Nails
15258 Led Zeppelin
15114 Tool
```

We would like to use the same format for creating a sequence file.

Getting ready

Before proceeding to the `netbeansprojects` folder, start your terminal prompt and type in the following command:

```
hadoop-mahout@hadoop-mahout-laptop:~/NetBeansProjects$ mvn
archetype:create -DarchetypeGroupId=org.apache.maven.archetypes -
DgroupId=com.packtpub.mahoutcookbook -DartifactId=chapter02
```

As an output you should see the following screenshot:

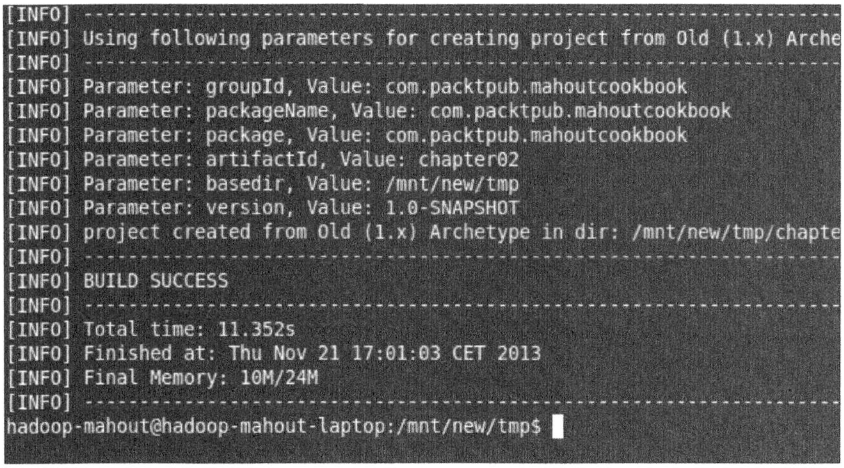

Now fire up NetBeans and from the **File** menu, choose **New Project**; the following window will appear:

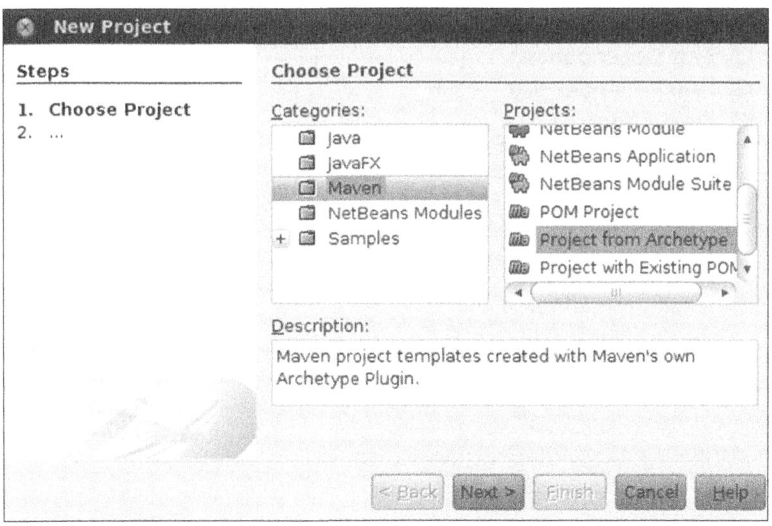

Next you will see the folder created by the preceding `mvn` command:

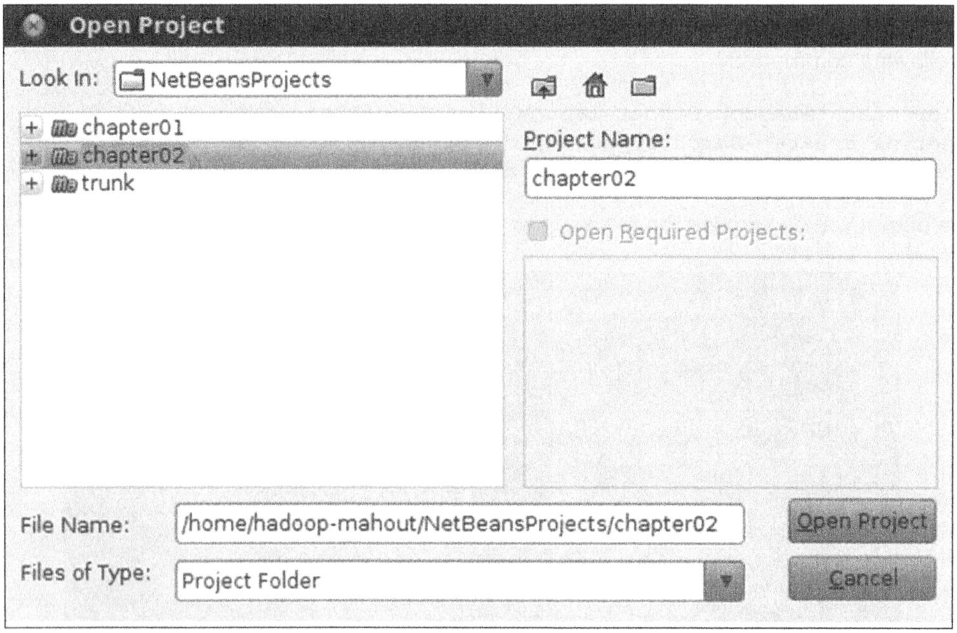

Once you click on the button **Open Project**, you should be able to see the final outcome of your import as shown in the following screenshot:

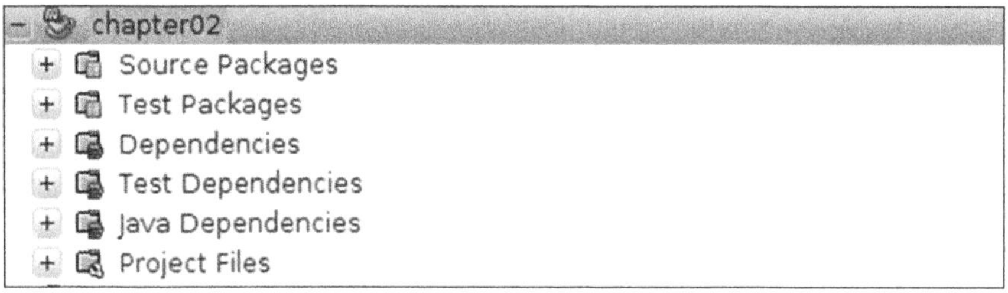

By default when you use the `mvn` command, an `App.Java` file is created. You need to remove it from your project by right-clicking on the project icon and selecting the **Delete** option from the pop-up menu. Now, add a new main class object called `CreateSequenceFileFromArtists` to the project.

You should have the following project structure as the output:

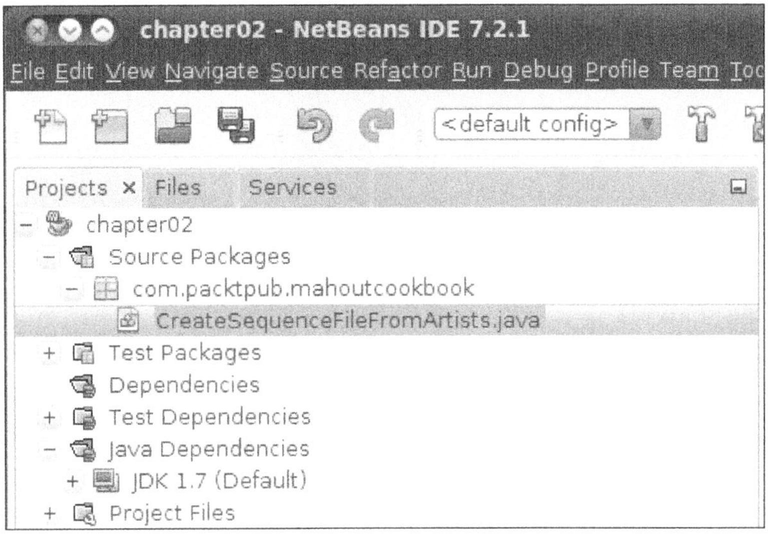

This project needs to run using Hadoop, so you need to link the jars containing the Hadoop interfaces and classes for the **mapreducer** job. The Maven project we created can use the online Hadoop repositories to download the required files.

We need to make everything work to add the jar dependencies. To do this you need to right-click on the `Dependencies` folder from the NetBeans project, choose the **Add dependency** item from the pop-up menu, and enter the following search field in the forms:

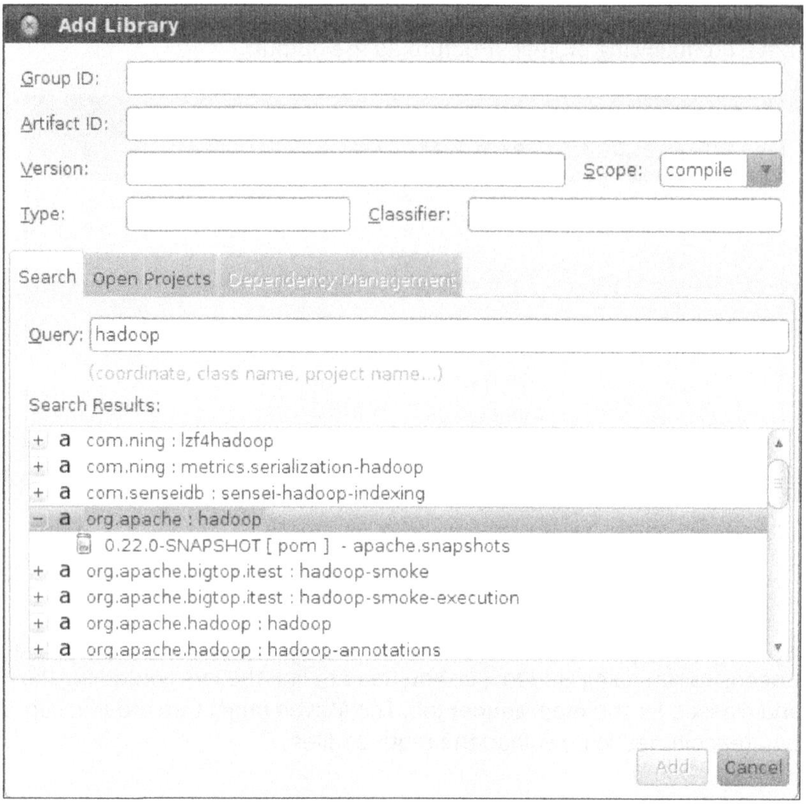

In the same way, add the `hadoop-core` Maven package to have the dependencies installed as shown in the following screenshot:

How to do it...

The code for the class `CreateSequenceFileFromArtists` is as follows:

```
package com.packtpub.mahoutcookbook;

import java.io.BufferedReader;
import java.io.FileNotFoundException;
import java.io.FileReader;
import java.io.IOException;
import org.apache.commons.beanutils.ConvertUtils;
import org.apache.hadoop.conf.Configuration;
import org.apache.hadoop.fs.FileSystem;
import org.apache.hadoop.fs.Path;
import org.apache.hadoop.io.LongWritable;
import org.apache.hadoop.io.SequenceFile;
import org.apache.hadoop.io.Text;

/**
 *
 * @author hadoop-mahout
 */
public class CreateSequenceFileFromArtists {
  public static void main(String[] argsx) throws
    FileNotFoundException, IOException
  {
    String filename = "/mnt/new/lastfm/original/artists.txt";
    String outputfilename =  "/mnt/new/lastfm/sequencesfiles/part-
      0000";
    Path path = new Path(outputfilename);

    //opening file
    BufferedReader br = new BufferedReader
      (new FileReader(filename));
    //creating Sequence Writer
    Configuration conf = new Configuration();
    FileSystem fs = FileSystem.get(conf);
    SequenceFile.Writer writer = new SequenceFile.Writer
      (fs,conf,path,LongWritable.class,Text.class);


    String line = br.readLine();
    String[] temp;
    String tempvalue = new String();
    String delimiter = " ";
```

```
        LongWritable key = new LongWritable();
        Text value = new Text();
        long tempkey = 0;
        while (line != null) {
          tempkey++;
          line = br.readLine();
          temp = line.split(delimiter);

          key = new LongWritable(tempkey);
          value = new Text();
          tempvalue = "";
          for (int i=1; i< temp.length;i++) {
            tempvalue +=  temp[i] + delimiter;
          }
          value = new Text(tempvalue);
          System.out.println("writing key/value  " + key.toString()
            + "/" + value.toString());
          writer.append(key,value);

        }

        writer.close();
        bf.close();

      }
    }
```

The output of the code is as shown in the following screenshot:

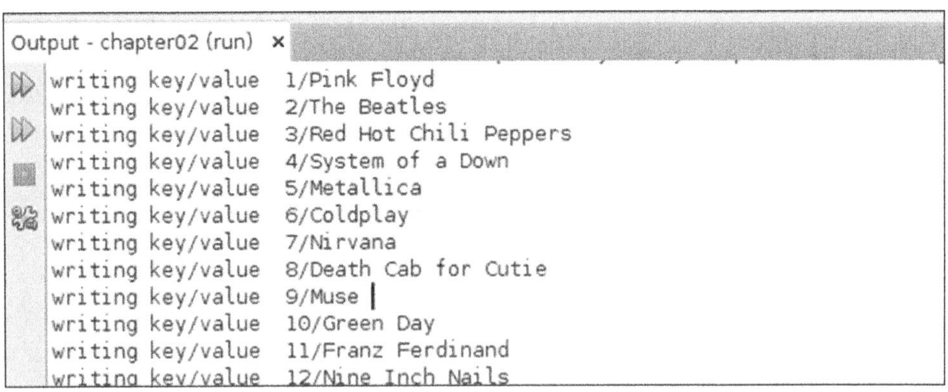

The same output could have been displayed using the `hadoop` command as follows:

```
hadoop-mahout@hadoop-mahout-laptop:/mnt/new/lastfm/sequencesfiles$ hadoop
dfs -text part-0000
```

This is analogous to the Mahout `seqdumper` command, but does not require a target output file.

The output should be displayed as follows:

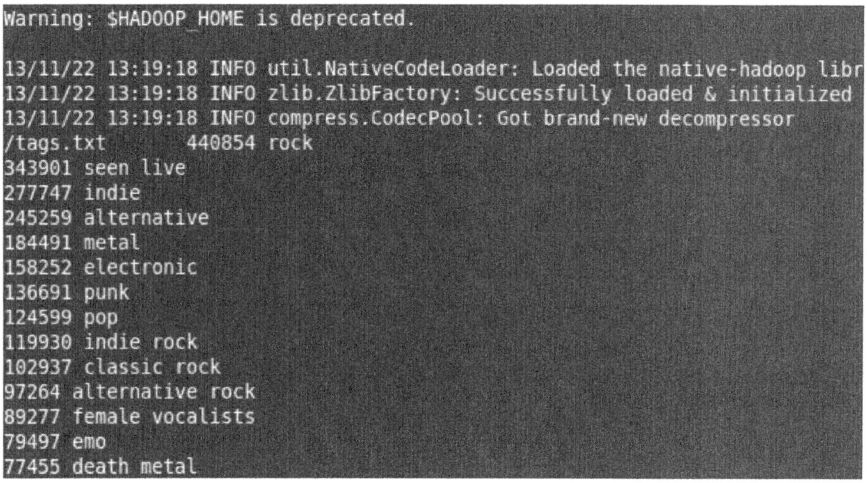

```
Warning: $HADOOP_HOME is deprecated.

13/11/22 13:19:18 INFO util.NativeCodeLoader: Loaded the native-hadoop libr
13/11/22 13:19:18 INFO zlib.ZlibFactory: Successfully loaded & initialized
13/11/22 13:19:18 INFO compress.CodecPool: Got brand-new decompressor
/tags.txt       440854 rock
343901 seen live
277747 indie
245259 alternative
184491 metal
158252 electronic
136691 punk
124599 pop
119930 indie rock
102937 classic rock
97264 alternative rock
89277 female vocalists
79497 emo
77455 death metal
```

How it works...

As we have seen earlier, the format of a sequence file consists of keys/values pairs. Basically, the algorithm performs the following actions:

1. Open the `artist.txt` file and read it line by line.
2. For each line use a counter to create a unique index for the key.
3. For each line read the artist on that line and create the value class.
4. Write the key and the value pair to the sequence file.

We open the file using the `BufferedReader` Java base object. The creation of the `Sequence.writer` object is a bit trickier as we can see in the following code:

```
//creating Sequence Writer
Configuration conf = new Configuration();
FileSystem fs = FileSystem.get(conf);
SequenceFile.Writer writer = new SequenceFile.Writer
  (fs,conf,path,LongWritable.class,Text.class);
```

To create a sequence file you need to declare the Hadoop `Configuration and FileSystem` type, and the class of the key and value pair. In our case we use the predefined Hadoop classes, the `LongWritable` and `Text` classes, corresponding to the `long` and `string` types in Java. In this case as the original file `artist.txt` have the space as separator, we need to split and separate every line to find the artist's name.

The appending of the key/value pair is done using the following code:

```
writer.append(key,value);
```

Finally, we close the `Writer` object using the following code:

```
write.close();
```

Reading sequence files from code

After learning how to create sequence files, it is now time to learn how to read a sequence file. Mahout gives the possibility of reading a sequence file and converting every key/value into a text format. The command is pretty easy. For example, to stream out the file we created in the previous recipes, we could type the following console command:

```
mahout seqdumper -i $WORK_DIR/sequencesfiles/part-0000 -o
/mnt/new/lastfm/sequencesfiles/dump
```

This command writes a file called `dump` in the `$WORK_DIR` folder from the file `part-0000` generated in the previous recipes.

However, this utility can be used only to display the content of a sequence dumper without working on it.

Considering the fact that sequence files are generated to be parsed and used by Hadoop mappers and reducers, we will demonstrate how to read a sequence file from Java code to be able to work with the sequence file. In particular we will read a sequence file and create a CSV file based on it.

Getting ready

To be able to work, you only need to add a new class to the existing Maven project. In the same NetBeans project we created before, we need to add a new Java class as illustrated in the following screenshot:

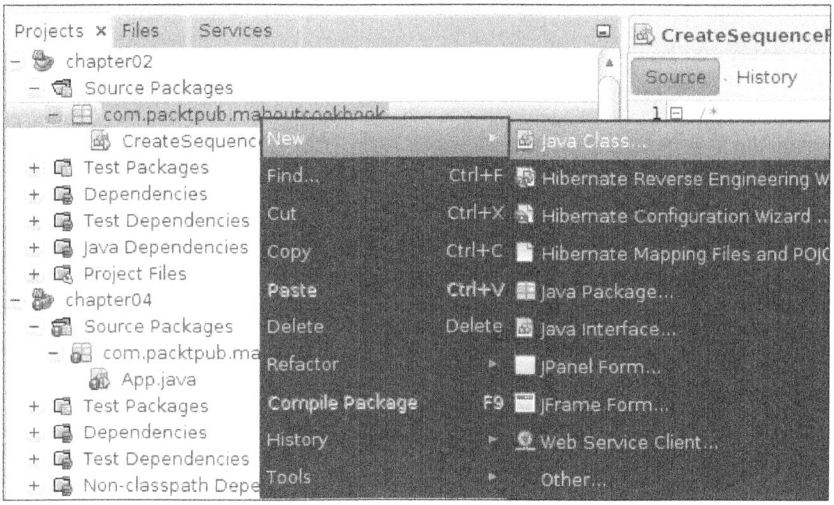

A window will appear, and in the input name text field one should just enter the name of the class, in this case `ReadSequenceFileArtist`, and click on the **Ok** button.

How to do it...

Now that we have our class ready, we simply need to add some code to the main method with the following steps:

1. First, we need to import the used classes as shown in the following code:

```
/*
 *
 */
package com.packtpub.mahoutcookbook;

import java.io.FileWriter;
import java.io.IOException;
import java.io.PrintWriter;
import org.apache.hadoop.conf.Configuration;
import org.apache.hadoop.fs.FileSystem;
import org.apache.hadoop.fs.Path;
import org.apache.hadoop.io.LongWritable;
import org.apache.hadoop.io.SequenceFile;
import org.apache.hadoop.io.Text;
```

2. Now add the following code in the `main` class:

```
public class ReadSequenceFileArtist {

  public static void main(String[] argvs) throws IOException
  {
    String filename  = "/mnt/new/lastfm/
      sequencesfiles/part-0000";
    Path path = new Path(filename);

    String outputfilename =  "/mnt/new/lastfm/
      sequencesfiles/dump.csv";

    FileWriter writer = new FileWriter(outputfilename);
    PrintWriter pw = new PrintWriter(writer);
    String newline = System.getProperty("line.separator");
    //creating header
    pw.print("key,value" + newline);

    //creating Sequence Writer
    Configuration conf = new Configuration();
    FileSystem fs = FileSystem.get(conf);
    SequenceFile.Reader reader = new
      SequenceFile.Reader(fs,path,conf);

    LongWritable key = new LongWritable();
    Text value = new Text();

    while (reader.next(key, value)) {
      System.out.println( "reading key:" + key.toString() +
        " with value " + value.toString());
      pw.print(key.toString() + "," + value.toString() +
        newline);
    }
    reader.close();

    pw.close();
    writer.close();


  }
}
```

3. Once run, the output folder should contain the file `dump.csv` as shown in the following screenshot:

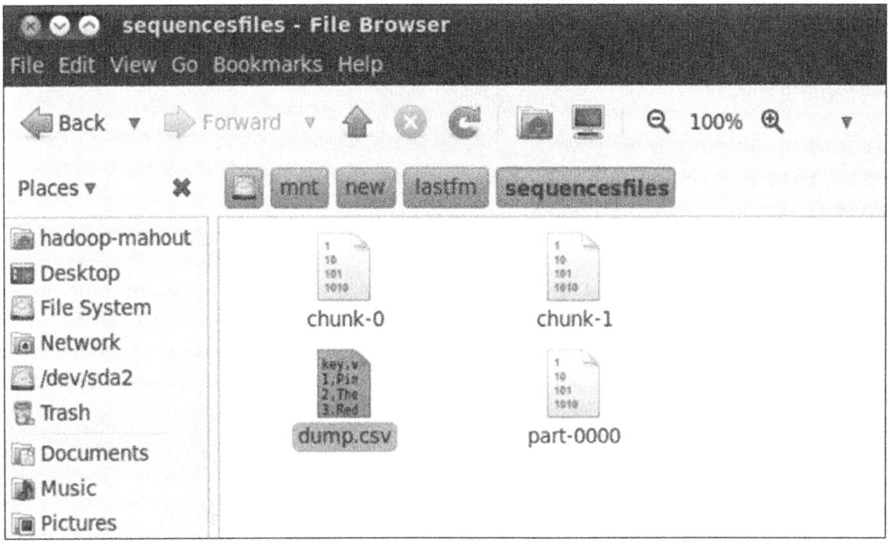

4. On opening this file with OpenOffice we have the following content:

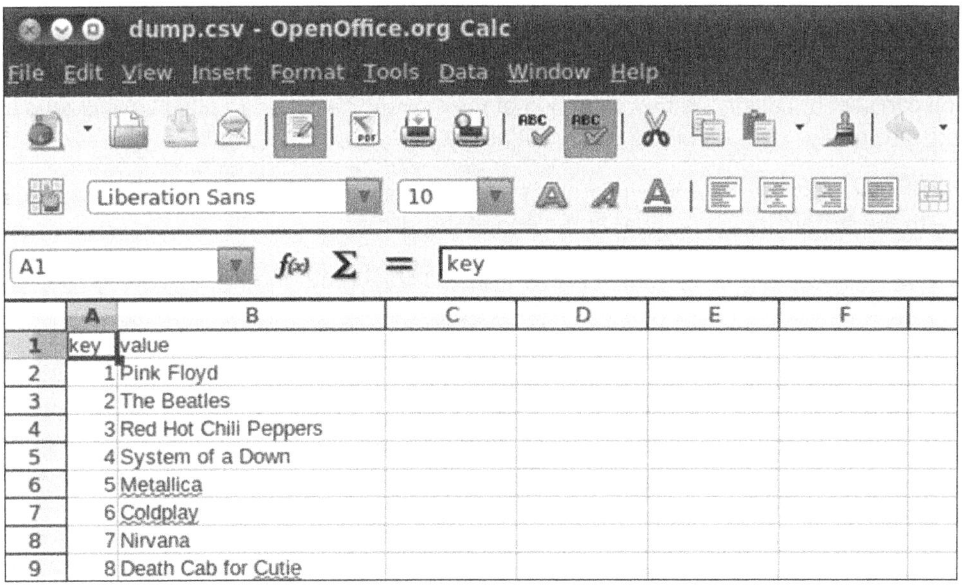

How it works...

The creation of a `PrintWriter` object class to handle outputs is pretty easy. The interesting part is the `Sequence.Reader` creation. The use of the reader class is symmetrical to the writer, except that in this case we need to read the key/value content. The following is the code for creating this:

```
//creating Sequence Writer
Configuration conf = new Configuration();
FileSystem fs = FileSystem.get(conf);
SequenceFile.Reader reader = new SequenceFile.Reader
  (fs,path,conf);

LongWritable key = new LongWritable();
Text value = new Text();
```

We also separately declared two objects for storing the key and value types. We already know which type they were. In case you don't, now it is possible to cast classes types.

To read the file till the end we use the following `while` loop:

```
while (reader.next(key, value)) {
  System.out.println( "reading key:" + key.toString() + "
    with value " + value.toString());
  pw.print(key.toString() + "," + value.toString() + newline);
}
```

As you can see, by calling the `next` method of the `Sequence.Reader` object, every time it is called, a new `key value` objects pair is initialized.

In this case we use the key/value pair only to generate a new CSV line separated by a comma and with the system `newline` char at the end of the string.

Finally, we close every `reader` and `writer` involved object with the following code:

```
reader.close();
pw.close();
writer.close();
```

Using the preceding code is a very bad programming practice as if the `writer` object is null for any reason, we will have a `NullPointerException` error. A better approach would be the following one:

```
if (reader != null) reader.close();
if (pw != null) pw.close();
if (writer != null) writer.close();
```

3

Integrating Mahout with an External Datasource

In this chapter we will cover the following:

- Importing an external datasource into the **Hadoop Distributed File System** (**HDFS**)
- Exporting data from HDFS to RDBMS
- Creating a Sqoop job to deal with RDBMS
- Importing data using Sqoop API

Introduction

Till now we have seen how Mahout works both in a standalone as well as a distributed manner. But basically we have only worked with files, those being datasource files or sequence files generated by some MapReduce job.

Any real-world coder, however, knows that apart from some embedded applications, 90 percent of the data is not stored in files. In most of the cases, the data is stored in a more structured way. The data storage software, in most of the cases, stores the data in relational databases or, speaking of a potentially new software, in NOSQL databases.

So when we need to acquire data for our data mining purposes, we need to read it from RDBMS. And in many cases, considering that the data is comes out from our Mahout analysis, we need to store it in structured tables so that it is possible for other software to read it for their displaying purposes.

Based on our experience with data mining, a good-structured environment for having the complete data mining frameworks should consist of an architecture as shown in the following screenshot:

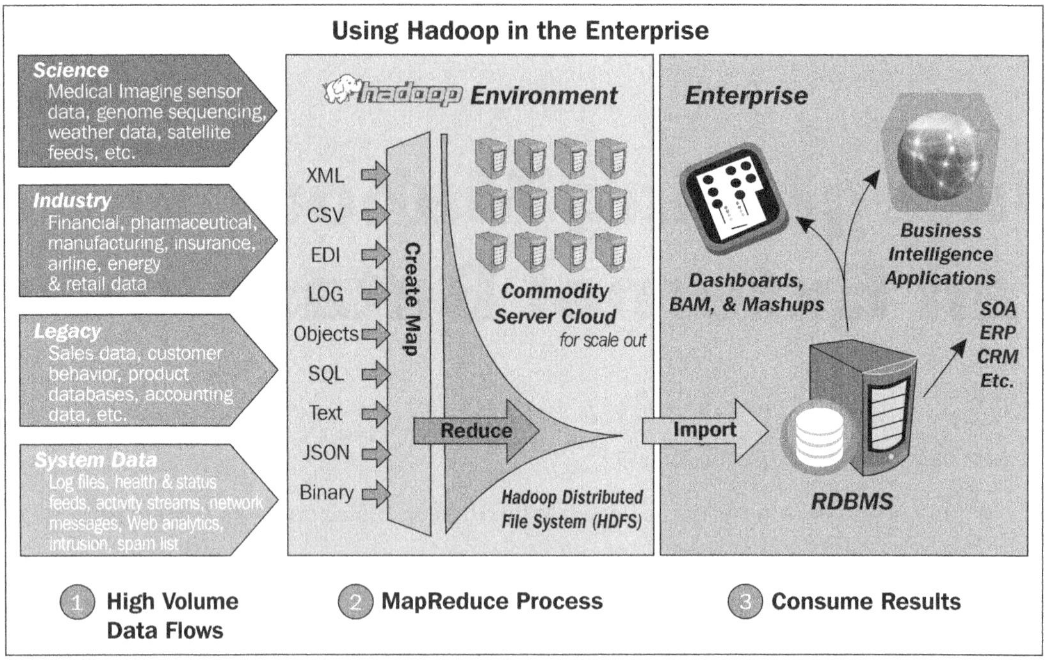

To arrange the import/export, we will use Sqoop. Sqoop is another Apache software foundation project devoted to the specific task of interfacing the Hadoop ecosystem with external datasources and RDBMS.

This tool is Java based and from the algorithm point of view, is MapReduce based. As you should have understood by now, reading data in parallel and using it in a distributed filesystem is different from a sequential access. This is because as we read a piece of data from RDBMS, the previously read pieces will be managed by other computational steps. So we do not need to finish retrieving all of the dataset before starting the computational phase as it happens during the sequential RDMS programming.

As for the other component of the Hadoop platform, it consists of a command-line utility and an API that can be used from the Hadoop code.

Let us now start with the first of our recipes, importing data into HDFS.

Importing an external datasource into HDFS

Obviously before proceeding, we need to create an RDBMS datasource that can be used for our test. We choose MySQL as the RDBMS system to install a test database that will be used both as a reading writing a storage with respect to HDFS. In this case, we made a test using a VirtualBox Ubuntu virtual machine with 3 GB of RAM and 1 CPU. The MySQL server version that we installed is displayed in the following screenshot:

```
mysql> SHOW VARIABLES LIKE "%version%";
+-------------------------+-------------------------+
| Variable_name           | Value                   |
+-------------------------+-------------------------+
| protocol_version        | 10                      |
| version                 | 5.1.66-0ubuntu0.10.04.3 |
| version_comment         | (Ubuntu)                |
| version_compile_machine | i486                    |
| version_compile_os      | debian-linux-gnu        |
+-------------------------+-------------------------+
5 rows in set (0.00 sec)
```

However, we have installed a test database on our machine; but in 90 percent of real-world Sqoop that we will use, RDBMS will be outside the machine where Sqoop is running.

Our procedure before starting the test will be the following:

- Installing a MySQL server
- Importing a test database into MySQL
- Installing and configuring Sqoop
- Formatting the HDFS

Getting ready

As we saw earlier, we need to install a working MySQL server and the client to connect and install a test database on it. After this step, we need to install and configure Sqoop for our first import.

To do this on our Ubuntu system, open up a terminal console and type in the following command from a non-root account:

```
sudo apt-get install mysql-server
```

During the installation procedure, the software will ask you to provide a password for your database root account, so provide one. We will use a sample database of statistics from the US baseball official championship for our test. The data is provided at `www.baseball-databank.org`. To download and install the database execute the following series of commands:

```
Wget http://www.baseball-databank.org/files/BDB-sql-2011-03-28.sql.zip
Unzip BDB-sql-2011-03-28.sql.zip
mysql -u root -p -e 'create schema bbdatabank;'
Mysql  -u  root -p  -s bbdatabank  < BDB-sql-2011-03-28.sql
```

When you return from the command-line option, you can use the following command to check whether everything worked:

```
hadoop-mahout@hadoop-mahout-laptop:~$ mysql -u root -p -s bbdatabank -e
'select distinct name from Teams limit 10;'
Enter password:
name
Boston Red Stockings
Chicago White Stockings
Cleveland Forest Citys
Fort Wayne Kekiongas
New York Mutuals
Philadelphia Athletics
Rockford Forest Citys
Troy Haymakers
Washington Olympics
Baltimore Canaries
```

Now that we have our database installed and ready to be used, we could start installing Sqoop. The installation procedure is pretty easy, but some prior setup is needed. This is because Sqoop uses JDBC drivers to attach itself to RDBMS. So we need to both download Sqoop and the `mysql jdbc` driver connector.

So to proceed, the reader should open up a terminal console and download Sqoop from `sqoop.apache.org`, and the MySQL JDBC driver JAR file from the MySQL website.

After resuming, we need to do the following:

1. Download Sqoop and the `mysql` JAR file.
2. Decompress Sqoop and copy the JAR into a folder.
3. Create a `SQOOP_HOME` environment variable.
4. Test whether everything works fine.

As Sqoop relies on Hadoop to work, we need to choose the correct version of Sqoop based on the previous Hadoop installation. In our case, we use the Sqoop 1.4.2 version that is currently supporting Hadoop 1.x, 0.20, 0.23, and 2.0. In any case, at `http://www.apache.org/dist/sqoop/1.4.2/`, you can see which version of Sqoop is compatible with Hadoop. The following screenshot shows the index of Version 1.4.2:

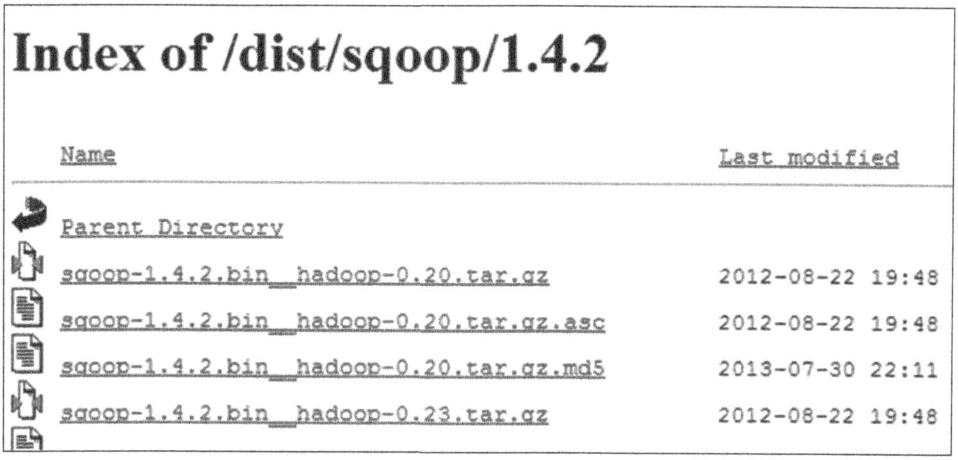

Do not forget to choose the correct Hadoop extension. In our case, as we have seen in *Chapter 1, Mahout is Not So Difficult!*, the version we downloaded is Hadoop 0.23.5. The binaries of Sqoop are available at different mirrors on the Sqoop Apache website. In this case, we use the command line to get the required version of Scoop:

```
wget http://www.apache.org/dist/Sqoop/1.4.2/sqoop-1.4.2.bin__hadoop-0.23.
tar.gz
```

Then we download the `mysql jdbc` driver connector using the following command:

```
wget http://dev.mysql.com/get/Downloads/Connector-J/mysql-connector-
java-5.1.22.tar.gz/from/http://cdn.mysql.com/
```

Then we extract Sqoop using the following command:

```
tar -xvzf sqoop-1.4.2.bin__hadoop-0.23.tar.gz
```

We extract the `mysql` JDBC driver connector using the following command:

```
tar -xvzf mysql-connector-java-5.1.22.tar.gz
```

Now it is time to configure and test Sqoop. As we did for Hadoop and Mahout, we will use the `.bashrc` file. So open up the `.bashrc` file with your preferred text editor and add the following lines at the end of the file:

```
export SQOOP_HOME=/home/hadoop-mahout/sqoop-1.4.2.bin__hadoop-0.23
export PATH=$PATH:$SQOOP_HOME/bin
```

Close the current terminal and open another terminal console. For testing your Sqoop installation, type the following command in it:

```
sqoop /help
```

The output should be as follows:

```
hadoop-mahout@hadoop-mahout-laptop:~$ sqoop help
Warning: /usr/lib/hbase does not exist! HBase imports will fail.
Please set $HBASE_HOME to the root of your HBase installation.
usage: sqoop COMMAND [ARGS]

Available commands:
  codegen            Generate code to interact with database records
  create-hive-table  Import a table definition into Hive
  eval               Evaluate a SQL statement and display the results
  export             Export an HDFS directory to a database table
  help               List available commands
  import             Import a table from a database to HDFS
  import-all-tables  Import tables from a database to HDFS
  job                Work with saved jobs
  list-databases     List available databases on a server
  list-tables        List available tables in a database
  merge              Merge results of incremental imports
  metastore          Run a standalone Sqoop metastore
  version            Display version information
```

See Sqoop's `help` command for information on a specific command. Now that we have established our environment, we are ready to use Sqoop.

How to do it...

As the reader can consider that HBASE is the Hadoop distributed database Sqoop expects to find it. To use Sqoop, HBase is not essential, but if you would like to better understand how HBase works, we suggest taking a look at *HBase Administration Cookbook, Yifeng Jiang, Packt Publishing*.

Don't be confused by the fact that Sqoop does not need to be installed in the same Hadoop node where the data should be imported. In this example, we have everything from RDBMS to Sqoop to Hadoop on one single machine; but in a real production environment, RDBMS is in another ecosystem that is only connected via the IP address to the machine where Sqoop is installed.

In a production environment, you probably need to assign a dedicated machine to Sqoop for making scheduled imports. Last but not least, after installing Sqoop, we need to add the `mysql` JAR file for working with the `mysql` databases that we created in the previous section. Follow these steps to do so:

1. Simply copy the `mysql-connector-java-5.1.22-bin.jar` file from the untarred archive to the `$SQOOP_HOME/lib` folder. Following our book's setup, we simply type the command:

   ```
   cp /home/hadoop-mahout/Downloads/mysql-connector-java-5.1.22/
   mysql-connector-java-5.1.22-bin.jar $SQOOP_HOME/lib
   ```

2. The preceding command is equivalent (considering our previous input) to the following command:

   ```
   cp /home/hadoop-mahout/Downloads/mysql-connector-java-5.1.22/
   mysql-connector-java-5.1.22-bin.jar /home/hadoop-mahout/sqoop-
   1.4.2.bin__hadoop-0.20/lib
   ```

Now it's time to test the import and understand how Sqoop/Hadoop and Mahout collaborate together.

To briefly recall the whole Hadoop infrastructure, Hadoop has a distributed filesystem that is shared between the nodes to read and write a sequence file and the text files. We saw in the previous chapter that when you use a MapReduce job, you can read/write files from HDFS.

Hadoop has its own database **HBase** for storing data and sharing it during MapReduce jobs, but in fact there is no equivalent to RDBMS in the Hadoop filesystem. An experienced reader should have asked themselves a question such as "So how can I move data, both files and the RDBMS data to HDFS?"

The answer is pretty easy in the case of files. Hadoop comes with a whole series of commands that mimic the basic commands present on the Linux terminal console.

For example, when you start with your first test on HDFS, a good practice is to format HDFS on the node you are using. The command to do this is pretty simple; simply open up a terminal window and type in the following command to format the node you are using:

```
hadoop namenode -format
```

In our case, we have a single node set up and the output will be the following:

```
13/01/15 11:08:22 INFO namenode.FSNamesystem: supergroup=supergroup
13/01/15 11:08:22 INFO namenode.FSNamesystem: isPermissionEnabled=true
13/01/15 11:08:23 INFO namenode.NameNode: Caching file names occurring
more than 10 times
13/01/15 11:08:23 INFO namenode.NNStorage: Storage directory /tmp/hadoop-
hadoop-mahout/dfs/name has been successfully formatted.
```

```
13/01/15 11:08:24 INFO namenode.FSImage: Saving image file /tmp/hadoop-hadoop-mahout/dfs/name/current/fsimage.ckpt_0000000000000000000 using no compression

13/01/15 11:08:24 INFO namenode.FSImage: Image file of size 128 saved in 0 seconds.

13/01/15 11:08:24 INFO namenode.NNStorageRetentionManager: Going to retain 1 images with txid >= 0

13/01/15 11:08:24 INFO util.ExitUtil: Exiting with status 0

13/01/15 11:08:24 INFO namenode.NameNode: SHUTDOWN_MSG:

/************************************************************

SHUTDOWN_MSG: Shutting down NameNode at hadoop-mahout-laptop/127.0.1.1

************************************************************/
```

> We would like to warn the reader that starting the utility from Hadoop 0.22 has been deprecated. The command line that should be used is the `hdfs` one. So for example, our formatting of HDFS should be done using the following format:
>
> **`hdfs namenode -format`**

Usage of all the commands provided for the HDFS utility is out side the scope of this chapter. We will point the reader who wants to learn more about the commands to the official Hadoop documentation. But we would like to clarify that when you use a sequence file or a text file to read/write the operation using a Hadoop MapReduce job; all these actions are saved into the HDFS.

Let us now start with our first import. Sqoop was designed to use JDBC for connecting to databases, so it is possible to transform the tables and queries into a different file format and put them in the HDFS. In this section, we will see how to import all of the `mysql` tables using a configuration file.

Before proceeding with the import of one single table or one single SQL query, let us first try to the import of all of the tables that are present into the `bbdatabank` MySQL database that we restored previously.

The console command to do this is the following:

```
sqoop import-all-tables --connect jdbc:mysql://localhost/bbdatabank
--user root -P --verbose
```

The most important parameters in the preceding command are as follows:

```
--connect jdbc:mysql://localhost/bbdatabank
```

The preceding command basically instructs Sqoop which driver should be used for the connection. The JAR with the driver should be in the classpath when invoking `sqoop`. That is why it is a good idea to put all the JAR files into the `$SQOOP_HOME/lib` folder that is silently added to the classpath every time one invokes the Sqoop script.

The value for the parameter connection is written in the JDBC connection string format. This implies that every database that supports a JDBC connection will be readable by Sqoop. However an experienced coder should know that every RDBMS system has its own particularities, so any new connection should be tested. To allow the other parameters, mimic the `mysql` command line, so we have:

- `--user`: It represents the `mysql` user who is trying to connect.
- `-P`: It is the password that is asked for at runtime. It is also possible even if it is not a good security practice to use the `--password` parameter and specify it from the command line.
- `--verbose`: It is used to enable full-logging mode so that we are allowed to see the outcome and in case of any issue, we are able to control the exception generated.

Instead of calling a long line parameter, it is possible to store everything in a file and then call Sqoop by only passing the path to the configuration file. So, for example, a file with the configuration for the last `sqoop` command should look like as follows:

```
#
# Options file for Sqoop
#

# Specifies the tool being invoked
import-all-tables

# Connect parameter and value
--connect
jdbc:mysql://localhost/bbdatabank

# Username parameter and value
--username
root
-P
--verbose
```

The call to pass this configuration file should be the following:

```
sqoop -options-file <path_to_file>
```

The final results of our import can be browsed in the HDFS filesystem with the following terminal command:

```
hadoop fs -ls
```

The preceding command is used to display the result of the following files:

```
Found 25 items
-rw-rw-rw-   1 hadoop-mahout hadoop     601404 2013-01-15 14:33 TEAMS
-rw-rw-rw-   1 hadoop-mahout hadoop     601404 2013-01-15 14:33
ALLSTARFULL
-rw-rw-rw-   1 hadoop-mahout hadoop     601404 2013-01-15 14:33
APPEARANCES
-rw-rw-rw-   1 hadoop-mahout hadoop     601404 2013-01-15 14:33
AWARDSMANAGERS
-rw-rw-rw-   1 hadoop-mahout hadoop     601404 2013-01-15 14:33
AWARDSPLAYERS
-rw-rw-rw-   1 hadoop-mahout hadoop     601404 2013-01-15 14:33
```

Only for this example, we will open the `TEAMS` file with the following command:

```
hadoop -fs tail TEAMS
```

The result should be the following:

```
,767,668,4.24,1,14,40,4310,1409,154,605,1268,144,135,0.980,"Chicago
Cubs","Wrigley Field",\N,108,108,"CHC","CHN","CHN"
2010,"NL","CIN","CIN","C",1,162,\N,91,71,"Y","N","N",
"N",790,5579,1515,293,30,188,522,1218,93,43,68,50,685,648,4.02,4,9,43,
4359,1404,158,524,1130,86,140,0.988,"Cincinnati Reds","Great American
Ball Park",\N,99,99,"CIN","CIN","CIN"
```

This format is the **comma separated values** (**CSV**) format.

How it works...

From the standard output; in the verbose mode, the import procedure is pretty simple. Every time you perform an import, all tasks or a single import, Sqoop connects to the database using the driver class that is in its classpath. This is the reason we put it in the `$SQOOP_HOME/lib` folder as this is where every JAR file is automatically loaded. Then based on the `import` parameter, Sqoop generates some mapping classes between the RDSM and the target destination. At the end, this mapper is used to transform the result into the final desired format.

There's more...

In this example, we used a very simplistic approach just to let the reader understand the importance of the Sqoop tool in a Hadoop environment. But a more high data analysis approach would be to import only the data necessary for the Mahout analysis.

Sqoop also offers the possibility to import data based on a SQL statement. To test everything, we will perform these two actions:

- Creating a Sqoop configuration file
- Running a Sqoop import using a free SQL statement

We use these techniques to leave the reader with the possibility to test different queries against the same database without having to retype everything. So open up a text editor and create the following connection property file for Sqoop:

```
#
# Options file for Sqoop
#

# Specifies the tool being invoked
import

# Connect parameter and value
--connect
jdbc:mysql://localhost/bbdatabank

# Username parameter and value
--username
root
-P
--verbose
```

Save the file as `sqoop.config` and place it in the `SQOOP_HOME` folder (in our case `/home/hadoop-mahout/sqoop-1.4.2.bin__hadoop-0.20`).

As you may have noticed, the most important change with respect to the previous configuration is that we specified the `import` command, so we do not import every table, but only a subset of the data contained. This is equal to launching a `sqoop import` command line. The MySQL statement to be run is shown in the following screenshot:

This statement returns all of the players in `BattingPost` that have teams in `SeriesPost`. So to put together the two parts that we have and import the results of the query as a CSV file into HDFS, we launch the following command:

```
sqoop  --options-file /home/hadoop-mahout/sqoop-1.4.2.bin__hadoop-0.20/
sqoop.config -query 'SELECT BattingPost.yearID, BattingPost.teamID,
BattingPost.lgID,  BattingPost.round, BattingPost.playerID FROM
BattingPost LEFT JOIN SeriesPost ON SeriesPost.yearID=BattingPost.
yearID AND SeriesPost.round=BattingPost.round AND  (teamIDwinner=teamID
OR teamIDloser=teamID) AND (lgIDwinner=lgID OR lgIDloser=lgID)  WHERE
SeriesPost.round IS NULL'
```

The output will be a series of plain CSV text files that are now stored in the HDFS filesystem and can be used by other MapReduce jobs.

We would like to refer the reader to some good documentation provided by Sqoop at `sqoop.apache.org`. We will point out a few other command-line parameters that can serve you during a real import. These parameters are as follows:

- `--as-sequencefile`
- `-m` and `--num-mappers`
- `--target-dir`

Considering them one by one, the `--as-sequencefile` parameter from the query forces the file to be saved using the Hadoop sequence file key/value format. In this case the key value, that for Hadoop computation must be unique is automatically generated while all the resultset is the value for that key.

Sqoop uses the parallelism provided by the MapReduce algorithm to import data from RDBMS. By default, if no parameter is specified, then four mappers are used to query RDBMS. But in the case of very large databases that contain hundreds of millions of records, you can increase the parallel mappers. Be aware of using this parameter indiscriminately because every mapper opens a dedicated RDMS connection. So, for example, if you put 100 as the parallel mapper, you increased the open connection number to your 100 units and this could potentially create some performance issues for other connected sessions.

So when you run a parallel task, the Sqoop mapper should identify a column that needs to be used for splitting the data to be imported. So, for example, if you decide to import a table that contains one million rows and four mappers are used to do this, Sqoop needs to uniquely identify how to assign the 250,000 records for each mapper. By default, Sqoop will identify the primary key column for doing this. However in a generic SQL statement, there could not be any primary key column so the `--split-by` parameter could be used to identify which column should be used for dividing the workload between the different mappers.

In the last parameter, we observed that HDFS mimics a Linux folder structure; so most of the time you need an import folder to be used. In this case, you could use the `- target-dir` parameter that lets you specify the folder inside HDFS where you need to put the result files that you import.

Exporting data from HDFS to RDBMS

As we stated in our introduction, we could divide an Hadoop/Mahout mining process into three main steps:

- Importing extracted data into the HDFS instance
- A computational task from Hadoop/Mahout
- Exporting the result to another RDMBS system where some third-party software will be in charge of displaying it

So now that we have seen the import part, we need to provide some examples of the export part. Following a command-line style, we will have to just call the Scoop main script using the `export` parameter.

We do not need any more configurations as everything we set up previously is valid also for exporting purposes.

How to do it...

Let us start with a basic example. Imagine that we have a CSV file in our HDFS that is placed in the `/export/` folder, and whose name is `export.csv`. We want to store this file in a MySQL table called `results`.

The command for doing this is the following:

```
sqoop export --connect jdbc:mysql://localhost/bbdatabank --user root -P
--verbose --export-dir /export/ --table results
```

As we can see, we have some optional parameters that can go hand in hand with just the `export` command, once it is set do the job. But as with the first import example, we need to give the reader some clarification.

How it works...

Since the destination is an RDBMS table, we will warn the reader that the destination table must exist in the target database. Sqoop is not able to create the destination table by itself. Without any other specification, Sqoop creates a set of `INSERT INTO sql` statements that will be performed on the target table. When running the Sqoop `export` command the mandatory parameters are as follows:

- `--export-dir`
- `--table`

If you have some prior experience with using SQL from Java and JDBC, you will for sure be aware of the potential problems that might arise when performing `insert` statements in a generic table. To summarize the potential issues, we have the following:

- Duplicate insertions or problems related to double insert of the same value
- A null value in required or not-null value fields

To handle this problem, Sqoop provides some more parameters that can be finetuned to avoid such problems. Let us examine them separately.

Returning to potential problems, let us see how we can manage duplicate `insert` statements. Sqoop, by default, creates only the `insert` statement so in case two of your source files contain the same record, an `insert` statement with a duplicate key will be created. So to avoid any potential runtime exception, you could use the `-- update-key` argument. This parameter lets you define the primary key column on your target table that can be used for doing updates instead of creating insertions.

To give you an example, we have the source CSV files with the rows' structure as follows:

```
Id, movie, score
1,1,0.1
2,1,10
```

So we create the table result with the `mysql` command as follows:

```
Create table results
(
Id int primary key not null
,movie int not null
,score float not null
)
```

If everything goes smoothly, you won't have any problems, but in case there are to with ID `1` then your export will generate a duplicate key exception. You have two possibilities. The first one is to use the `-update-key` argument and execute the following Sqoop command:

```
sqoop export --connect jdbc:mysql://localhost/bbdatabank --user root -P
--verbose --export-dir /export/ --table results --update-key id
```

The preceding command will force Sqoop, when doing the insert, to generate a SQL command like the following:

```
update result set movie=<movie_value>, score=<score_value> where id = ..
```

But this will not completely solve the problem. Even if you don't get an error, in the case of your first import or newly added ID with respect to previous one if the ID is not present into the destination table. So to correctly set up a workflow, you should first export the data to populate the table and then another one with the update-key to avoid the duplicated key exception.

Probably the most useful parameter in this context that can manage insert and update statements is the `--update-` mode coupled with `--update-key`. To clarify things, let us consider the following Sqoop `export` command:

```
sqoop export --connect jdbc:mysql://localhost/bbdatabank --user root -P
--verbose --export-dir /export/ --table results --update-key id -update-
mode allowinsert
```

In this case, by specifying the `allowinsert` mode, the import flow will follow this logic:

- Check whether the value for the update-key parameter exists on the target table
- If yes, create and update the command to update the information
- Otherwise create an `insert` statement

This will avoid any potential situation but remember that once you start to use the updated sentence only the last update is will have the final value.

When dealing with `insert` and `update`, the value of the field to be updated on a table needs to be carefully considered. If you allow, for example, a `string` field in the target destination table to accept null values, then you have to manage the null string in the corresponding source. The Sqoop `export` command provides a bunch of additional parameters to manage the input's delimiters and the null value; we refer the reader once again to the Sqoop website for the complete documentation. We cite only for reference two of the arguments that can be used:

- `--input-fields-terminated-by`: This argument if specified tells which character on the input file to be considered as field separator default is comma.
- `--input-lines-terminated-by`: This argument specifies which is the line separator. The default value is `\r`.

Considering the null value we have:

- `--input-null-string`: If this argument is specified, it instructs the export utility which string is to be considered as the null value. Note that by default, `null` is interpreted as `null string`.
- `--input-null-non-string`: If this argument is not specified (default), both empty `string` and `null` values will be considered null for the SQL statement.

Now that we have seen the two flux, both import and export, we could take a look at the Sqoop job and the Sqoop API.

Creating a Sqoop job to deal with RDBMS

Now that you have seen how the import/export utility named Sqoop works, we are ready to talk about creating a Sqoop job. From a developer's and even a maintenance point of view, once you correctly create your Sqoop statement, you need to invoke it from the command line. Sqoop jobs are particularly useful when you needs to update the final data destination from the input source that have changed. Typically, you need to set up a schedule job that runs through the night to extract all the new information that was stored in the source from the previous day. Once tested, the command line can be easily called by a cron schedule.

How to do it...

Sqoop offers a command-line parameter that allows us to create a configured job that can be invoked every time, without giving the command-line parameters that are meant to execute the import/export utility.

Moving from words to coding, let us create our first import Sqoop job:

1. As we saw, our first import was as follows:

```
sqoop import-all-tables --connect jdbc:mysql://localhost/
bbdatabank --user root -P --verbose
```

2. To create a job that does the same thing, we type the following command in our console:

```
sqoop job --create myimportjob  -- import-all-tables --connect
jdbc:mysql://localhost/bbdatabank --user root -P --verbose
```

How it works...

We saw a command that creates a job named `myimportjob`. The jobs are saved in a metastore repository that is a filesystem location, by default located in the `$SQOOP_HOME/.sqoop` directory.

There's more...

Once you create a job, it can be executed by giving the `exec` argument as shown in the following command that executes the `myimportjob` command:

```
sqoop job --exec myimportjob
```

To display the saved job, you can use the following command:

```
sqoop job --list
```

To display the configuration of the `myimport` job, the command will look like:

```
sqoop job --show myjob
```

At the end, to delete the saved job, use the following command:

```
sqoop job --delete myjob
```

So once you have created your job, you can manage it in this way. In case, you need to schedule a job execution by using the `cron` utility to be able to execute a scheduled job in the production environment.

We warn the reader that, apart from the command-line utility, one job is saved in the Sqoop repository by default. This storage does not save the passwords that are required when the job runs. So if you create a job that needs passwords to be stored, you will be asked for the password during job execution. Considering a scheduled job, you could be forcing Sqoop to store passwords by modifying a configuration file. This is not a secure practice as the Sqoop metastore is not the most secure one. But you can modify this setting by opening the `sqoop-site.xml` file; you just need to uncomment the following tag:

```
<property>
  <name>sqoop.metastore.client.record.password</name>
  <value>true</value>
  <description>If true, allow saved passwords in the metastore.
  </description>
</property>
```

Considering that Sqoop is basically some JARs interfaced by command-line utilities, it is possible to embed it in a Java application. We will see in the next section how to embed Sqoop into your Java code.

Importing data using Sqoop API

Sqoop provides a series of APIs that can be used to launch a Sqoop MapReduce import/export job from your Java code. As usual, we will use Maven on our NetBeans development environment to link the correct JARs.

Getting ready

Fire up NetBeans and create a new Maven project named `chapter 3`, as we did in the recipes in *Chapter 1, Mahout is Not So Difficult!*, and *Chapter 2, Using Sequence Files – When and Why?*. Then we link the Sqoop dependency using Maven, so right-click on the **Dependencies** folder and click on the **Add Dependency** item. On the form that appears, fill in the details as shown in the following screenshot:

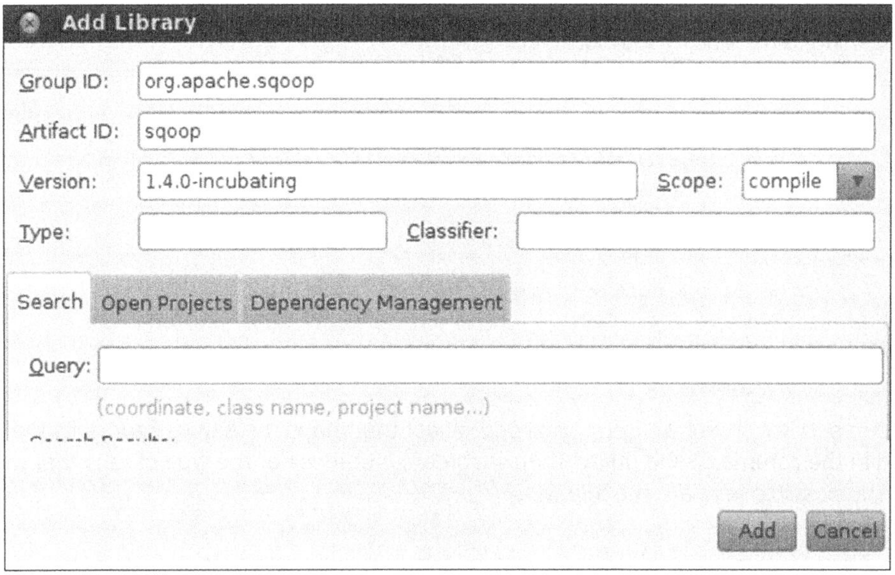

Then click on **Add** and you should see the JAR file in your **Dependencies** folder icon, as shown in the following screenshot:

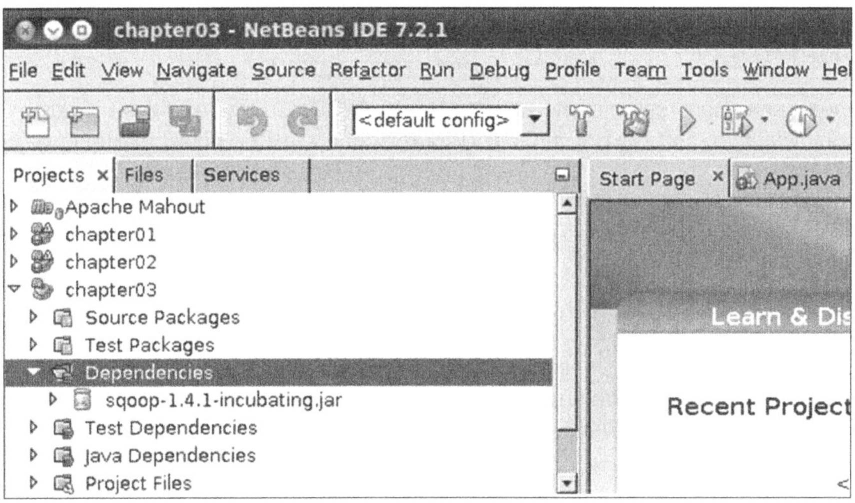

How to do it...

Now that we have configured our Maven project, it is now time to write some lines of code to see how to use Sqoop outside the command-line utility.

We will add our code to the default `App.java` class. So double-click on it and add the following code to the `main` method:

```
SqoopOptions o = new SqoopOptions();
o.setConnectString(null);
o.setExportDir("/tmp/piero");
String[] arguments = new String[10];
ImportAllTablesTool t = new ImportAllTablesTool();
int r;
r = Sqoop.runTool(arguments);
```

How it works...

As you can see, we create a `SqoopOptions` object that maps the same arguments that are involved in the command-line utility. Then we create instances of the type of jobs that we need to run. The possible jobs are the following:

- `ImportAllTablesTool`
- `ImportTool`
- `ExportTool`

The final step is to use the `runTool` method for every possible job's object. The result will be stored into an `int` type to allow the coder to understand if the job completion was successfully done.

We provided just a short recipe on how to use Sqoop API. To understand what is going on a simple but effective method, download the source code and see how it interacts with the command line.

If you open it up with a text editor, you should see the last line that invokes the `exec` command, which is as follows:

```
exec ${HADOOP_HOME}/bin/hadoop com.cloudera.sqoop.Sqoop "$@"
```

Thus, the entry point for every Sqoop command is the main class `Sqoop` inside the `com.cloudera.sqoop` package. We suggest willing readers take a look at the book's code to get a deeper understanding of what is going on behind the scenes.

4

Implementing the Naïve Bayes classifier in Mahout

In the previous chapters, we got familiar with Mahout and the way of using sequence file and connecting it to the external data sources. However, we did not go in much details on the kind of data mining algorithm that are available on the Mahout framework. Starting from this chapter, we are now entering the core of the Mahout framework and its available algorithms.

In this chapter, we will implement the Naïve Bayes classifier for creating clusters and aggregating unstructured information in a manageable way.

We will cover the following recipes in this chapter:

- Using the Mahout text classifier to demonstrate the basic use case
- Using the Naïve Bayes classifier from code
- Using Complementary Naïve Bayes from the command line
- Coding the Complementary Naïve Bayes classifier

Introduction

Bayes was a Presbyterian priest who died giving his "Tractatus Logicus" to the prints in 1795. The interesting fact is that we had to wait a whole century for the Boolean calculus before Bayes' work came to light in the scientific community.

The corpus of *Bayes*' study was conditional probability. Without entering too much into mathematical theory, we define conditional probability as the probability of an event that depends on the outcome of another event.

In this chapter, we are dealing with a particular type of algorithm, a classifier algorithm. Given a dataset, that is, a set of observations of many variables, a classifier is able to assign a new observation to a particular category. So, for example, consider the following table:

Outlook	**Temperature**	**Temperature**	**Humidity**	**Humidity**	**Windy**	**Play**
	Numeric	**Nominal**	**Numeric**	**Nominal**		
Overcast	83	Hot	86	High	FALSE	Yes
Overcast	64	Cool	65	Normal	TRUE	Yes
Overcast	72	Mild	90	High	TRUE	Yes
Overcast	81	Hot	75	Normal	FALSE	Yes
Rainy	70	Mild	96	High	FALSE	Yes
Rainy	68	Cool	80	Normal	FALSE	Yes
Rainy	65	Cool	70	Normal	TRUE	No
Rainy	75	Mild	80	Normal	FALSE	Yes
Rainy	71	Mild	91	High	TRUE	No
Sunny	85	Hot	85	High	FALSE	No
Sunny	80	Hot	90	High	TRUE	No
Sunny	72	Mild	95	High	FALSE	No
Sunny	69	Cool	70	Normal	FALSE	Yes
Sunny	75	Mild	70	Normal	TRUE	Yes

The table itself is composed of a set of 14 observations consisting of 7 different categories: temperature (numeric), temperature (nominal), humidity (numeric), and so on. The classifier takes some of the observations to train the algorithm and some as testing it, to create a decision for a new observation that is not contained in the original dataset.

There are many types of classifiers that can do this kind of job. The classifier algorithms are part of the supervised learning data-mining tasks that use training data to infer an outcome. The Naïve Bayes classifier uses the assumption that the fact, on observation, belongs to a particular category and is independent from belonging to any other category.

Other types of classifiers present in Mahout are the logistic regression, random forests, and boosting. Refer to the page `https://cwiki.apache.org/confluence/display/MAHOUT/Algorithms` for more information.

This page is updated with the algorithm type, actual integration in Mahout, and other useful information. Moving out of this context, we could describe the Naïve Bayes algorithm as a classification algorithm that uses the conditional probability to transform an initial set of weights into a weight matrix, whose entries (row by column) detail the probability that one weight is associated to the other weight. In this chapter's recipes, we will use the same algorithm provided by the Mahout example source code that uses the Naïve Bayes classifier to find the relation between works of a set of documents.

Our recipe can be easily extended to any kind of document or set of documents. We will only use the command line so that once the environment is set up, it will be easy for you to reproduce our recipe. Our dataset is divided into two parts: the training set and the testing set. The training set is used to instruct the algorithm on the relation it needs to find. The testing set is used to test the algorithm using some unrelated input. Let us now get a first-hand taste of how to use the Naïve Bayes classifier.

Using the Mahout text classifier to demonstrate the basic use case

The Mahout binaries contain ready-to-use scripts for using and understanding the classical Mahout dataset. We will use this dataset for testing or coding. Basically, the code is nothing more than following the Mahout ready-to-use script with the corrected parameter and the path settings done. This recipe will describe how to transform the raw text files into weight vectors that are needed by the Naïve Bayes algorithm to create the model.

The steps involved are the following:

- Converting the raw text file into a sequence file
- Creating vector files from the sequence files
- Creating our working vectors

Getting ready

The first step is to download the datasets. The dataset is freely available at the following link: `http://people.csail.mit.edu/jrennie/20Newsgroups/20news-bydate.tar.gz`. For classification purposes, other datasets can be found at the following URL: `http://sci2s.ugr.es/keel/category.php?cat=clas#sub2`.

The dataset contains a post of 20 newsgroups dumped in a text file for the purpose of machine learning. Anyway, we could have also used other documents for testing purposes, but we will suggest how to do this later in the recipe.

Before proceeding, in the command line, we need to set up the working folder where we decompress the original archive to have shorter commands when we need to insert the full path of the folder.

In our case, the working folder is `/mnt/new`; so, our working folder's command-line variables will be set using the following command:

```
export WORK_DIR=/mnt/new/
```

You can create a new folder and change the `WORK_DIR` bash variable accordingly.

> Do not forget that to have these examples running, you need to run the various commands with a user that has the `HADOOP_HOME` and `MAHOUT_HOME` variables in its path just as we set in *Chapter 1, Mahout is Not So Difficult!*.

To download the dataset, we only need to open up a terminal console and give the following command:

```
wget http://people.csail.mit.edu/jrennie/20Newsgroups/20news-bydate.tar.gz
```

Once your working dataset is downloaded, decompress it using the following command:

```
tar -xvzf 20news-bydate.tar.gz
```

You should see the folder structure as shown in the following screenshot:

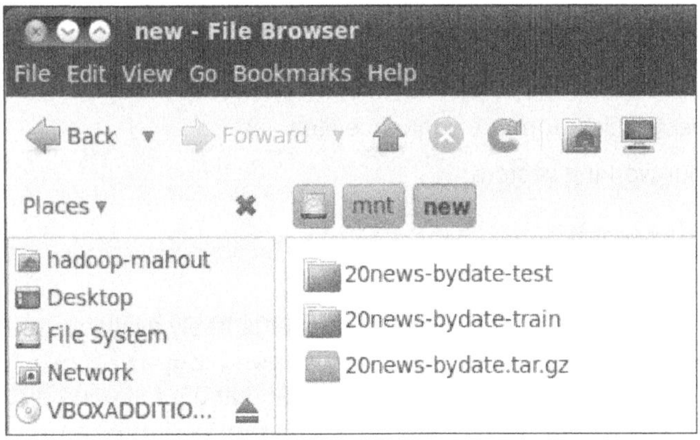

The second step is to sequence the whole input file to transform them into Hadoop sequence files. To do this, you need to transform the two folders into a single one. However, this is only a pedagogical passage, but if you have multiple files containing the input texts, you could parse them separately by invoking the command multiple times. Using the console command, we can group them together as a whole by giving the following command in sequence:

```
rm -rf ${WORK_DIR}/20news-all
 mkdir ${WORK_DIR}/20news-all
 cp -R ${WORK_DIR}/20news-bydate*/*/* ${WORK_DIR}/20news-all
```

Now, we should have our input folder, which is the `20news-all` folder, ready to be used:

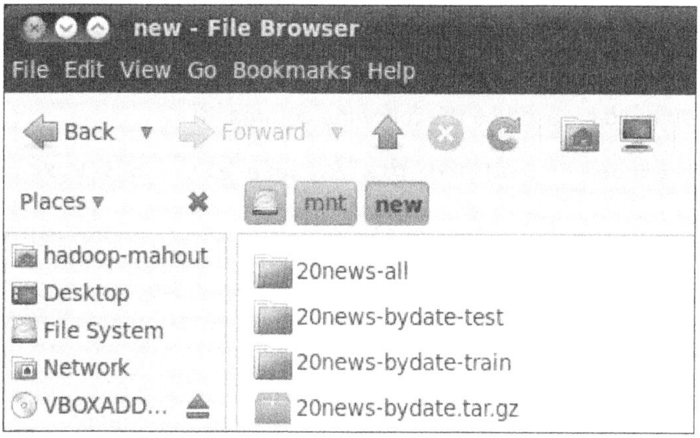

The following screenshot shows a bunch of files, all in the same folder:

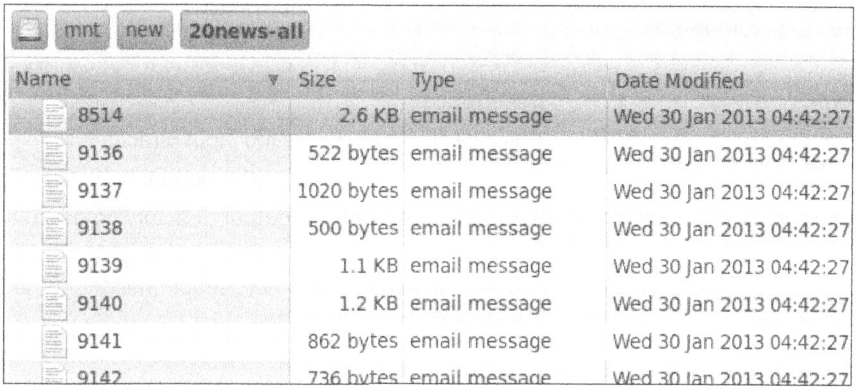

By looking at one single file, we should see the underlying structure that we will transform. The structure is as follows:

```
From: xxx
Subject: yyyyy
Organization: zzzz
X-Newsreader: rusnews v1.02
Lines: 50
jaeger@xxx (xxx) writes:
>In article xxx writes:
>>zzzz "How BCCI adapted the Koran rules of banking".  The
>>Times.  August 13, 1991.
>
> So, let's see. If some guy writes a piece with a title that implies
> something is the case then it must be so, is that it?
```

We obviously removed the e-mail address, but you can open this file to see its content. For any newsgroup of 20 news items that are present on the dataset, we have a number of files, each of them containing a single post to a newsgroup without categorization.

Following our initial tasks, we need to now transform all these files into Hadoop sequence files. To do this, you need to just type the following command:

```
./mahout seqdirectory  -i ${WORK_DIR}/20news-all  -o ${WORK_DIR}/20news-seq
```

This command brings every file contained in the `20news-all` folder and transforms them into a sequence file. As you can see, the number of corresponding sequence files is not one to one with the number of input files. In our case, the generated sequence files from the original 15417 text files are just one `chunck-0` file. It is also possible to declare the number of output files and the mappers involved in this data transformation. We invite the reader to test the different parameters and their uses by invoking the following command:

```
./mahout seqdirectory  --help
```

The following table describes the various options that can be used with the `seqdirectory` command:

Parameter	Description
`--input (-i) input`	This gives the path to the job input directory.
`--output (-o) output`	The directory pathname for the output.
`--overwrite (-ow)`	If present, overwrite the output directory before running the job.
`--method (-xm) method`	The execution method to use: sequential or `mapreduce`. The default is `mapreduce`.
`--chunkSize (-chunk) chunkSize`	The `chunkSize` values in megabyte. The default is 64 Mb.
`--fileFilterClass (-filter) fileFilterClass`	The name of the class to use for file parsing. The default is `org.apache.mahout.text.PrefixAdditionFilter`.
`--keyPrefix (-prefix) keyPrefix`	The prefix to be prepended to the key of the sequence file.
`--charset (-c) charset`	The name of the character encoding of the input files. The default is `UTF-8`.
`--overwrite (-ow)`	If present, overwrite the output directory before running the job.
`--help (-h)`	Prints the help menu to the command console.
`--tempDir tempDir`	If specified, tells Mahout to use this as a temporary folder.
`--startPhase startPhase`	Defines the first phase that needs to be run.
`--endPhase endPhase`	Defines the last phase that needs to be run.

To examine the outcome, you can use the Hadoop command-line option `fs`. So, for example, if you would like to see what is in the `chunck-0` file, you could type in the following command:

```
hadoop fs -text $WORK_DIR/20news-seq/chunck-0  | more
```

In our case, the result is as follows:

```
/67399    From:xxx
Subject: Re: Imake-TeX: looking for beta testers
Organization: CS Department, Dortmund University, Germany
Lines: 59
Distribution: world
NNTP-Posting-Host: tommy.informatik.uni-dortmund.de

In article <xxxxx>,
yyy writes:
|> As I announced at the X Technical Conference in January, I would
like
|> to
|> make Imake-TeX, the Imake support for using the TeX typesetting
system,
|> publically available. Currently Imake-TeX is in beta test here at
the
|> computer science department of Dortmund University, and I am
looking
|> for
|> some more beta testers, preferably with different TeX and Imake
|> installations.
```

The Hadoop command is pretty simple, and the syntax is as follows:

```
hadoop fs -text <input file>
```

In the preceding syntax, `<input file>` is the sequence file whose content you will see. Our sequence files have been created, and until now, there has been no analysis of the words and the text itself. The Naïve Bayes algorithm does not work directly with the words and the raw text, but with the weighted vector associated to the original document. So now, we need to transform the raw text into vectors of weights and frequency. To do this, we type in the following command:

```
./mahout seq2sparse  -i ${WORK_DIR}/20news-seq   -o ${WORK_DIR}/20news-
vectors  -lnorm -nv  -wt tfidf
```

The following command parameters are described briefly:

- The `-lnorm` parameter instructs the vector to use the `L_2` norm as a distance
- The `-nv` parameter is an optional parameter that outputs the vector as `namedVector`
- The `-wt` parameter instructs which weight function needs to be used

We end the data-preparation process with this step. Now, we have the weight vector files that are created and ready to be used by the Naïve Bayes algorithm. We will clear a little while this last step algorithm. This part is about tuning the algorithm for better performance of the Naïve Bayes classifier.

How to do it...

Now that we have generated the weight vectors, we need to give them to the training algorithm. But if we train the classifier against the whole set of data, we will not be able to test the accuracy of the classifier.

To avoid this, you need to divide the vector files into two sets called the 80-20 split. This is a good data-mining approach because if you have any algorithm that should be instructed on a dataset, you should divide the whole bunch of data into two sets: one for training and one for testing your algorithm.

A good dividing percentage is shown to be 80 percent and 20 percent, meaning that the training data should be 80 percent of the total while the testing ones should be the remaining 20 percent.

To split data, we use the following command:

```
./mahout split
-i ${WORK_DIR}/20news-vectors/tfidf-vectors
    --trainingOutput ${WORK_DIR}/20news-train-vectors
    --testOutput ${WORK_DIR}/20news-test-vectors
    --randomSelectionPct 40 --overwrite --sequenceFiles -xm sequential
```

As result of this command, we will have two new folders containing the training and testing vectors. Now, it is time to train our Naïves Bayes algorithm on the training set of vectors, and the command that is used is pretty easy:

```
./mahout trainnb
  -i ${WORK_DIR}/20news-train-vectors -el
  -o ${WORK_DIR}/model
  -li ${WORK_DIR}/labelindex
  -ow
```

Once finished, we have our training model ready to be tested against the remaining 20 percent of the initial input vectors. The final console command is as follows:

```
./mahout testnb
  -i ${WORK_DIR}/20news-test-vectors
  -m ${WORK_DIR}/model
  -l ${WORK_DIR}/labelindex\
  -ow -o ${WORK_DIR}/20news-testing
```

The following screenshot shows the output of the preceding command:

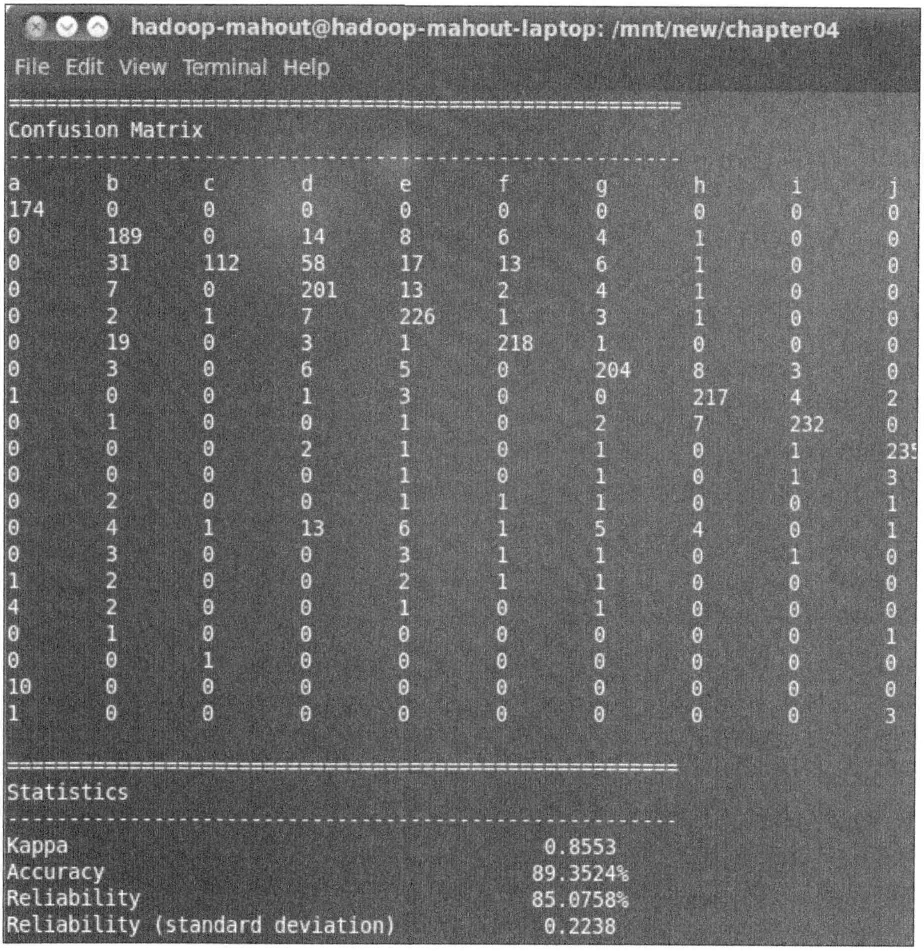

```
hadoop-mahout@hadoop-mahout-laptop: /mnt/new/chapter04
File Edit View Terminal Help
=======================================================
Confusion Matrix
-------------------------------------------------------
a       b       c       d       e       f       g       h       i       j
174     0       0       0       0       0       0       0       0       0
0       189     0       14      8       6       4       1       0       0
0       31      112     58      17      13      6       1       0       0
0       7       0       201     13      2       4       1       0       0
0       2       1       7       226     1       3       1       0       0
0       19      0       3       1       218     1       0       0       0
0       3       0       6       5       0       204     8       3       0
1       0       0       1       3       0       0       217     4       2
0       1       0       0       1       0       2       7       232     0
0       0       0       2       1       0       1       0       1       235
0       0       0       0       1       0       1       0       1       3
0       2       0       0       1       1       1       0       0       1
0       4       1       13      6       1       5       4       0       1
0       3       0       0       3       1       1       0       1       0
1       2       0       0       2       1       1       0       0       0
4       2       0       0       1       0       1       0       0       0
0       1       0       0       0       0       0       0       0       1
0       0       1       0       0       0       0       0       0       0
10      0       0       0       0       0       0       0       0       0
1       0       0       0       0       0       0       0       0       3

=======================================================
Statistics
-------------------------------------------------------
Kappa                                   0.8553
Accuracy                               89.3524%
Reliability                            85.0758%
Reliability (standard deviation)        0.2238
```

How it works...

We have given certain commands and we have seen the outcome, but you've done this without an understanding of why we did it and above all, why we chose certain parameters. The whole sequence could be meaningless, even for an experienced coder.

Let us now go a little deeper in each step of our algorithm. Apart from downloading the data, we can divide our Naïve Bayes algorithm into three main steps:

- Data preparation
- Data training
- Data testing

In general, these are the three procedures for mining data that should be followed. The data preparation steps involve all the operations that are needed to create the dataset in the format that is required for the data mining procedure. In this case, we know that the original format was a bunch of files containing text, and we transformed them into a sequence file format. The main purpose of this is to have a format that can be handled by the map reducing algorithm. This phase is a general one as the input format is not ready to be used as it is in most cases. Sometimes, we also need to merge some data if they are divided into different sources. Sometimes, we also need to use Sqoop for extracting data from different datasources.

Data training is the crucial part; from the original dataset, we extract the information that is relevant to our data mining tasks, and we bring some of them to train our model. In our case, we are trying to classify if a document can be inserted in a certain category based on the frequency of some terms in it. This will lead to a classifier that using another document can state if this document is under a previously found category. The output is a function that is able to determinate this association.

Next, we need to evaluate this function because it is possible that one good classification in the learning phase is not so good when using a different document. This three-phased approach is essential in all classification tasks. The main difference relies on the type of classifier to be used in the training and testing phase. In this case, we use Naïve Bayes, but other classifiers can be used as well. In the Mahout framework, the available classifiers are **Naïve Bayes**, **Decision Forest**, and **Logistic Regression**.

As we have seen, the data preparation consists basically of creating two series of files that will be used for training and testing purposes. The step to transform the raw text file into a Hadoop sequence format is pretty easy; so, we won't spend too long on it. But the next step is the most important one during data preparation. Let us recall it:

```
mahout seq2sparse  -i ${WORK_DIR}/20news-seq -o ${WORK_DIR}/20news-vectors  -lnorm -nv  -wt tfidf
```

This computational step basically grabs the whole text from the `chunck-0` sequence file and starts parsing it to extract information from the words contained in it. The input parameters tell the utility to work in the following ways:

- The `-i` parameter is used to declare the input folder where all the sequence files are stored
- The `-o` parameter is used to create the output folder where the vector containing the weights is stored
- The `-nv` parameter tells Mahout that the output format should be in the `namedVector` format
- The `-wt` parameter tells which frequency function to use for evaluating the weight of every term to a category
- The `-lnorm` parameter is a function used to normalize the weights using the `L_2` distance

- The `-ow:` parameter overwrites the previously generated output results
- The `-m:` parameter gives the minimum `log-likelihood` ratio

The whole purpose of this computation step is to transform the sequence files that contain the documents' raw text in the sequence files containing vectors that count the frequency of the term. Obviously, there are some different functions that count the frequency of a term within the whole set of documents. So, in Mahout, the possible values for the `wt` parameter are `tf` and `tfidf`. The `Tf` value is the simpler one and counts the frequency of the term. This means that the frequency of the W_i term inside the set of documents is the ratio between the total occurrence of the word over the total number of words. The second one considers the sum of every term frequency using a logarithmic function like this one:

$$W_i = TF_i \log\left(\frac{N}{DF_i}\right)$$

In the preceding formula, W_i is the TF-IDF weight of the word indexed by *i*. *N* is the total number of documents. DF_i is the frequency of the *i* word in all the documents.

In this preprocessing phase, we notice that we index the whole corpus of documents so that we are sure that even if we divide or split in the next phase, the documents are not affected. We compute a word frequency; this means that the word was contained in the training or testing set.

So, the reader should grasp the fact that changing this parameter can affect the final weight vectors; so, based on the same text, we could have very different outcomes.

The `lnorm` value basically means that while the weight can be a number ranging from 0 to an upper positive integer, they are normalized to 1 as the maximum possible weight for a word inside the frequency range. The following screenshot shows the output of the output folder:

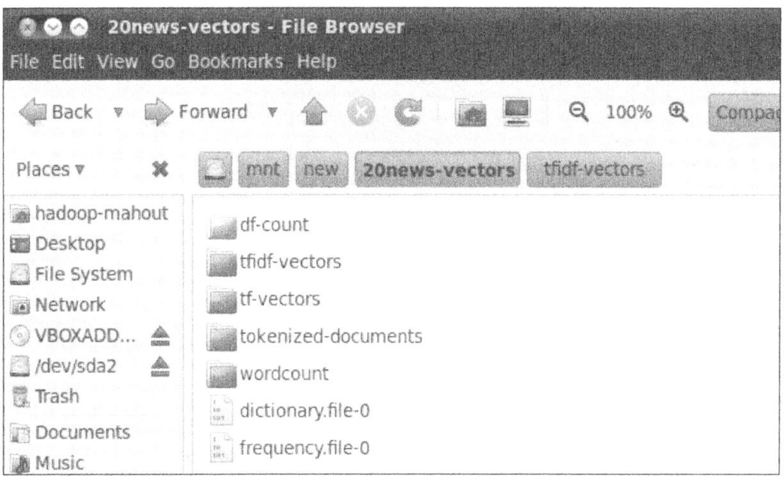

Various folders are created for storing the word count, frequency, and so on. Basically, this is because the Naïve Bayes classifier works by removing all periods and punctuation marks from the text. Then, from every text, it extracts the categories and the words.

The final vector file can be seen in the `tfidf-vectors` folder, and for dumping vector files to normal text ones, you can use the `vectordump` command as follows:

```
mahout vectordump  -i   ${WORK_DIR}/20news-vectors/tfidf-vectors/
part-r-00000 -o
${WORK_DIR}/20news-vectors/tfidf-vectors/part-r-00000dump
```

The dictionary files and word files are sequence files containing the association within the unique key/word created by the MapReduce algorithm using the command:

```
hadoop fs -text  $WORK_DIR/20news-vectors/dictionary.file-0  | more
one can see for example
adrenal_gland    12912
adrenaline       12913
adrenaline.com   12914
```

The splitting of the dataset into training and testing is done by using the `split` command-line option of Mahout. The interesting parameter in this case is that `randomSelectionPct` equals 40. It uses a random selection to evaluate which point belongs to the training or the testing dataset.

Now comes the interesting part. We are ready to train using the Naïve Bayes algorithm. The output of this algorithm is the `model` folder that contains the model in the form of a binary file. This file represents the Naïve Bayes model that holds the weight Matrix, the feature and label sums, and the weight normalizer vectors generated so far.

Now that we have the model, we test it on the training set. The outcome is directly shown on the command line in terms of a confusion matrix. The following screenshot shows the format in which we can see our result.

Finally, we test our classifier on the test vector generated by the split instruction. The output in this case is a confusion matrix. Its format is as shown in the following screenshot:

```
Summary
-------------------------------------------------------
Correctly Classified Instances          :       6753       89.8483%
Incorrectly Classified Instances        :        763       10.1517%
Total Classified Instances              :       7516

=======================================================
Confusion Matrix
-------------------------------------------------------
a       b       c       d       e       f       g       h       i       j
292     0       0       0       0       0       0       0       2       0
0       345     6       19      6       11      8       1       0       1
0       23      267     69      17      17      8       0       0       0
0       8       7       330     20      4       13      0       0       0
e
0       6       2       8       348     1       10      1       0       0
0       21      1       4       0       360     2       1       0       0
```

We are now going to provide details on how this matrix should be interpreted. As you can see, we have the total classified instances that tell us how many sentences have been analyzed. Above this, we have the correctly/incorrectly classified instances. In our case, this means that on a test set of weighted vectors, we have nearly 90 percent of the corrected classified sentences against an error of 9 percent.

But if we go through the matrix row by row, we can see at the end that we have different newsgroups. So, `a` is equal to `alt.atheism` and `b` is equal to `comp.graphics`.

So, a first look at the detailed confusion matrix tells us that we did the best in classification against the `rec.sport.hockey` newsgroup, with a value of 418 that is the highest we have. If we take a look at the corresponding row, we understand that of these 418 classified sentences, we have 403/412; so, 97 percent of all of the sentences were found in the `rec.sport.hockey` newsgroup. But if we take a look at the `comp.os.ms-windows.miscwe` newsgroup, we can see overall performance is low. The sentences are not so centered around the same new newsgroup; so, it means that we find and classify the sentences in `ms-windows` in another newsgroup, and so we do not have a good classification.

This is reasonable as sports terms like "hockey" are really limited to the hockey world, while sentences about Microsoft could be found both on Microsoft specific newsgroups and in other newsgroups.

We encourage you to give another run to the testing phase on the training phase to see the output of the confusion matrix by giving the following command:

```
./bin/mahout testnb
  -i ${WORK_DIR}/20news-train-vectors
  -m ${WORK_DIR}/model
  -l ${WORK_DIR}/labelindex
  -ow -o ${WORK_DIR}/20news-testing
```

As you can see, the input folder is the same for the training phase, and in this case, we have the following confusion matrix:

```
-------------------------------------------------------
Correctly Classified Instances          :      11210       99.2562%
Incorrectly Classified Instances        :         84        0.7438%
Total Classified Instances              :      11294

=======================================================
Confusion Matrix
-------------------------------------------------------
a       b       c       d       e       f       g       h       i       j
469     0       0       0       0       0       0       0       0       0
0       527     0       3       0       3       0       0       0       0
0       1       567     18      0       3       0       0       0       0
0       0       0       570     0       0       1       0       0       0
e
0       0       0       1       595     0       2       0       0       0
0       2       1       0       1       615     1       0       0       0
0       1       0       1       0       0       594     0       0       0
```

In this case, we can see it using the same set both as the training and testing phase. The first consequence is that we have a rise in the correctly classified sentences by an order of 10 percent, which is even bigger if you remember that in terms of weighted vectors with respect to the testing phase, we have a size that is four times greater. But probably the most important thing is that the best classification has now moved from the hockey newsgroup to the `sci.electronics` newsgroup.

There's more

We use exactly the same procedure used by the Mahout examples contained in the binaries folder that we downloaded. But you should now be aware that starting all process need only to change the input files from the initial folder. So, for the willing reader, we suggest you download another raw text file and perform all the steps in another type of file to see the changes that we have compared to the initial input text.

We would suggest that non-native English readers also look at the differences that we have by changing the initial input set with one not written in English. Since the whole text is transformed using only weight vectors, the outcome does not depend on the difference between languages but only on the probability of finding certain word couples.

As a final step, using the same input texts, you could try to change the way the algorithm normalizes and counts the words to create the vector sparse weights. This could be easily done by changing, for example, the `-wt tfidf` parameter into the command line Mahout `seq2sparce`. So, for example, an alternative run of the `seq2sparce` Mahout could be the following one:

```
mahout seq2sparse  -i ${WORK_DIR}/20news-seq -o ${WORK_DIR}/20news-vectors  -lnorm -nv  -wt tfidf
```

Finally, we not only choose to run the Naïve Bayes classifier for classifying words in a text document but also the algorithm that uses vectors of weights so that, for example, it would be easy to create your own vector weights.

Using the Naïve Bayes classifier from code

Now, we have used Mahout with the command-line option for the Naïve Bayes classification. In this recipe, we will code the same classifier that we used in the previous recipe, but we will call and use it directly from the Java code instead of the command line. We will see how to tune parameters and how to extend the possible configuration parameter. We will also see how to use the Naïve Bayes classifier from the code, and we will show you the possibility of changing some parameters that cannot be modified using the command line. Coding a classifier using the MapReduce framework could be a difficult task, but it would be better if you could use the already coded classifier to fine-tune your data-mining tasks.

Getting ready

To be ready for the coding part, we have to create a new project on NetBeans and link the correct POM files for the dependency libraries that we are going to use. So, using the Netbeans Maven functionality, create a new Maven project called `chapter04`. Now, you should have something similar to the following screenshot:

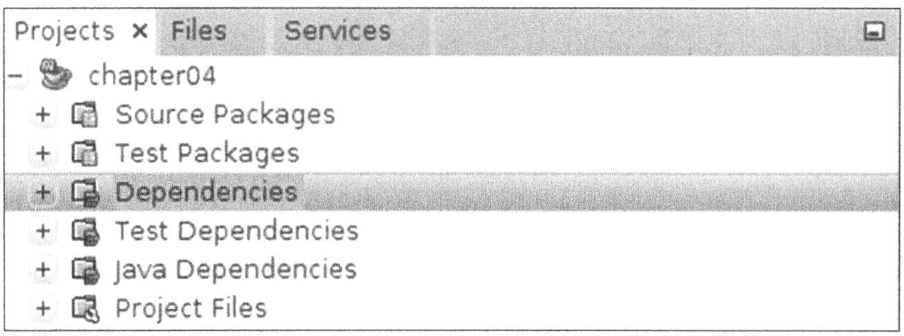

Now, it is time to add the dependencies needed to invoke the Naïve Bayes classifier. To do this, right-click on the **Dependencies** folder and choose the **Add Dependency item** option from the pop-up menu. The following screenshot shows the form where you type the `mahout` word in the **Search** text so that the system will display the local Mahout compiled source. The JARs required are `mahout-core` and `mahout-math`.

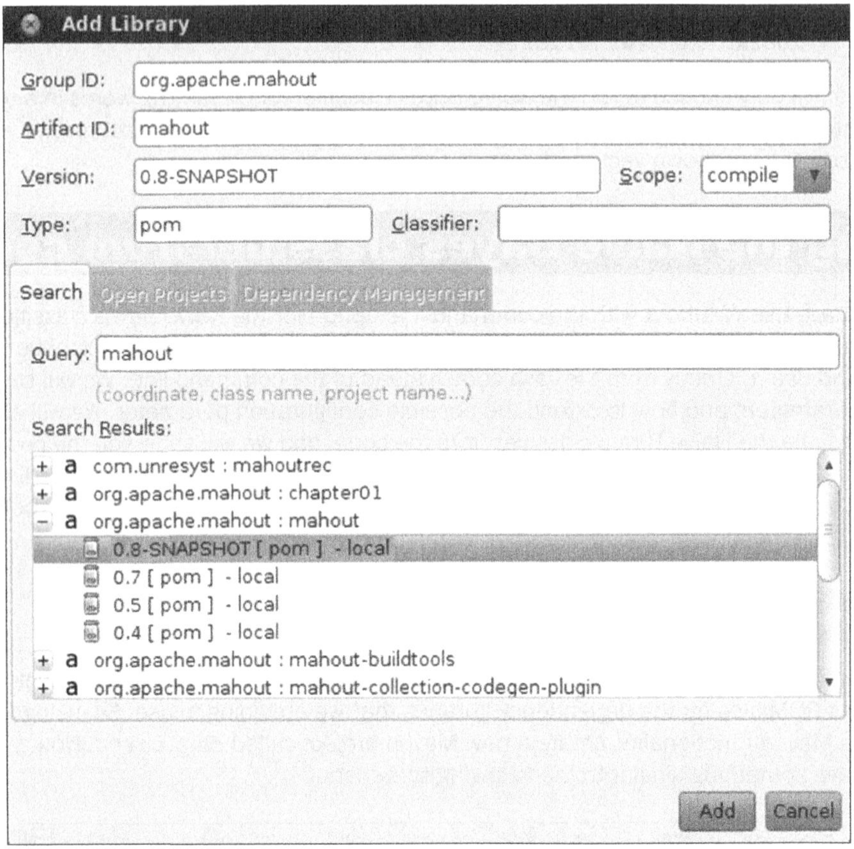

How to do it...

Now, we have everything that we need to code our example. Carry out the following steps in order to achieve this:

1. Open up the `app.java` default file. First, we need to set the parameters to be used:

```
final BayesParameters params = new BayesParameters();
params.setGramSize( 1 );
params.set( "verbose", "true" );
params.set( "classifierType", "bayes" );
params.set( "defaultCat", "OTHER" );
```

```
params.set( "encoding", "UTF-8" );
params.set( "alpha_i", "1.0" );
params.set( "dataSource", "hdfs" );
params.set( "basePath", "/tmp/output" );
```

2. Then, we need to train the classifier by providing the input and output folders for the input to be used and for the output of the model, respectively:

```
  try {
      Path input = new Path( "/tmp/input" );
      TrainClassifier.trainNaiveBayes( input, "/tmp/output",
params );
```

3. Next, we need to use the Bayes algorithm to evaluate the classifier as follows:

```
      Algorithm algorithm = new BayesAlgorithm();
      Datastore datastore =
      new InMemoryBayesDatastore( params );
      ClassifierContext classifier =
      new ClassifierContext( algorithm, datastore );
      classifier.initialize();

      final BufferedReader reader =
      new BufferedReader( new FileReader( args[ 0 ] ) );
      String entry = reader.readLine();

      while( entry != null ) {
          List< String > document = new NGrams( entry,
          Integer.parseInt( params.get( "gramSize" ) ) )
                              .generateNGramsWithoutLabel();

          ClassifierResult result =
          classifier.classifyDocument(
          document.toArray( new String[ document.size() ]
           ),
          params.get( "defaultCat" ) );

          entry = reader.readLine();
      }
  } catch( final IOException ex ) {
   ex.printStackTrace();
  } catch( final InvalidDatastoreException ex ) {
   ex.printStackTrace();
  }
```

Simple, isn't it? Once compiled, check the input files and observe the output of the code that is provided. We are now ready to go into the details to understand the differences between the Mahout classifiers and to underline the possibilities offered by them.

How it works...

As we can see, we have the following actions:

- Initializing the parameters for the trainer
- Reading the input files
- Training the classifier using the parameters and the input files
- Output the results

First of all, we initialize the parameters' objects that store every available input parameter for the classifier. We should notice the following parameters:

```
params.set( "classifierType", "bayes" );
```

Until now, we have used the Naïve Bayes classifier. Once we initialize the parameters, we are ready to move to the core part. A `TrainClassifier .trainNaiveBayes` static method is invoked by passing the parameters and the input path to the weight vector files.

This phase builds the binary model file that is saved into the output folder and defines itself into the `params` object using the following code:

```
params.set( "basePath", "/tmp/output" );
```

So, we now have our model saved and stored.

> Try creating two different classifiers to be trained on the same input vector to have a model ready to be tested on a different set of data. This idea is also a good one in the development phase before going into production to evaluate which is the best algorithm to be used for training purposes.

As a final step, we need to read the input file and generate `NGrams` and use this according to the classifier used. This can be done using the following code:

```
        final BufferedReader reader = new BufferedReader( new
FileReader( args[ 0 ] ) );
        String entry = reader.readLine();

        while( entry != null ) {
            List< String > document = new NGrams( entry,
                            Integer.parseInt( params.get( "gramSize" ) )
)
                            .generateNGramsWithoutLabel();

            ClassifierResult result = classifier.classifyDocument(
```

```
                                document.toArray( new String[ document.
size() ] ),
                                params.get( "defaultCat" ) );

            entry = reader.readLine();
```

We need to provide a few details on how the Naïve Bayes classifier works. In a sentence, a group of words is called an **n-grams**. A single word is a 1-gram; but, for example, *Barack Obama*, even if composed of two 1-grams, is normally associated, so it is counted as a 1-gram.

So, in this case, the minimum gram size is set to `1` in the parameters with the following code:

```
params.setGramSize( 1 );
```

However, you can change this minimum size for the grams so as to avoid considering single words but counting the frequency of at least a couple of words combined instead. So, setting `setGramSize` to `1` means that "Obama" as well as "Barack" is counted as one while with `2`, the occurrence "Barack Obama" will be see as one in frequency count.

Now, we can test against a different data set by re-using Mahout's `testnn` command-line option by giving the generated model and the input corpus document provided for testing. This will display the confusion matrix that will allow us to evaluate better how the training took place.

There's more

Text classification is probably one of the most interesting tasks in a classification algorithm. This is because teaching a machine to make sense of a document the way we humans do is never easy.

A lot of settings eventuate to create a good classifier. Let us review them briefly:

- The language of the documents
- The size of the documents
- The way we create vectors
- The way we divide and create the training and testing sets

Only to give some hits, if we have a document with many sentences written in a different language, the classification task is not so easy. The size of the documents is another important task; obviously, the more you have the better it is, but beware. We do not have a cluster large enough to test this, but as pointed out by the Mahout project site, the Naïve Bayes algorithm and the Complementary Naïve Bayes algorithm can handle millions to hundreds of millions of documents.

As we mentioned earlier, the vectors can be created using different ways to evaluate the word count and the granularity. For the willing reader, we point out that there are other techniques that can be used for counting words or to decide the best frequency to be used for counting occurrences. We encourage you to take a look at the source code of Mahout to see how it is possible to extend the analyzer class to add some of these evaluation methods.

When evaluating a classifier, we also recommend you to give multiple runs of the algorithm using the code we provided. These multiple runs give the trainer an algorithm to have different outcomes so that it would be possible to evaluate better which parameter combination is the best one for the input dataset.

Using Complementary Naïve Bayes from the command line

We are now ready to use the Complementary Naïve Bayes Mahout classifier from the command line.

Getting ready

We are ready with the input because we will use the same input that we used for the Naïve Bayes classifier. So, this recipe will be prepared for the same way that we prepared for the Naïve Bayes classifier. So, in the `${WORK_DIR}/20news-train-vectors` folder, you should have the training vectors with the weight coded as a key/value pair that is ready to be used.

How to do it...

Now, we can enter the following command from a terminal console:

```
./mahout trainnb
    -i ${WORK_DIR}/20news-train-vectors -el
    -o ${WORK_DIR}/model
    -li ${WORK_DIR}/labelindex
    -ow cbayes
```

The output will be a model created as a binary file in the `model` subfolder. To test the Complementary Naïve Bayes classifier, we give the following command:

```
./bin/mahout testnb
    -i ${WORK_DIR}/20news-train-vectors
    -m ${WORK_DIR}/model
    -l ${WORK_DIR}/labelindex
    -ow -o ${WORK_DIR}/20news-testing
    cbayes
```

How it works...

The Complementary Naïve Bayes classifier is linked to the Naïve Bayes classifier. Basically, the main difference between the two is how they evaluate the final weight of the classifier. In the Complementary Naïve Bayes case, the weight is calculated using the following formula:

Weight = Log [(Sigma_j - W-N-Tf-Idf + alpha_i) / (Sigma_jSigma_k - Sigma_k + N)]

So you could easily change the type of algorithm from Naïve Bayes to Complementary Naïve Bayes by only changing a parameter.

See also

- You can refer to the *Tackling the Poor Assumptions of Naïve Bayes Text Classifiers* paper for an evaluation of the differences between the two classifiers. It is available at `http://people.csail.mit.edu/jrennie/papers/icml03-nb.pdf`.

Coding the Complementary Naïve Bayes classifier

Now that we have seen how the Complementary Naïve Bayes classifier can be invoked from the command line, we are ready to use it from our Java code.

Getting ready

Create a new Maven project and link it to your local Mahout-compiled Maven project as we did in *Chapter 1, Mahout is Not So Difficult!*. In this case, since we have already created the `chapter04` Mahout project, we will simply add to it a new Java class. If you're referring to this recipe directly, refer to the previous *Getting Ready* section on how to set up the project.

So, fire up NetBeans, right-click on `chapter04`, and choose **New Java Class**. Complete the form as shown in the following screenshot, and click on **Finish**.

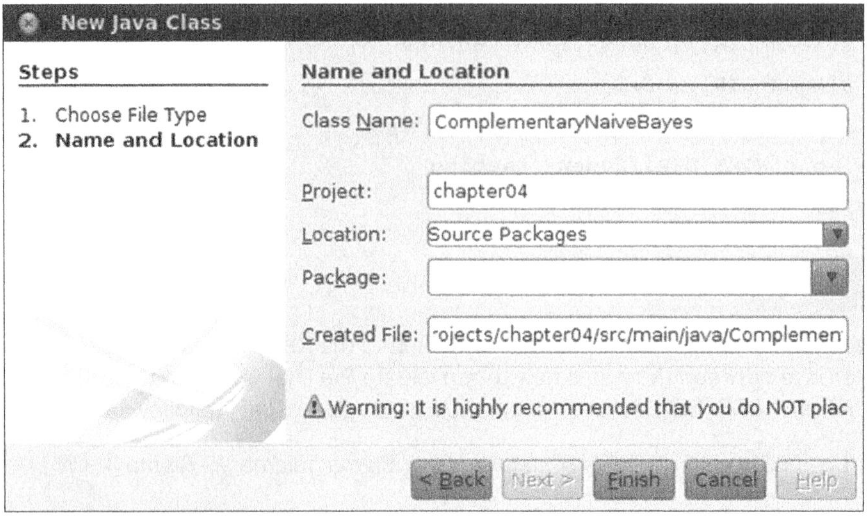

How to do it...

Now that our class is ready to use, you could type in the same code that we used in the previous recipe. We refer you to the book code. We only need one little change in the code; we need to change the `params.set( "classifierType", "bayes" );` line to the following line:

```
params.set( "classifierType", "cbayes" );
```

This will change the trainer by telling it to use the `cbayes` weight formula to calculate the weights.

How it works...

As we have seen, the same parameters are used from the command line. In fact, we only recoded the same behavior of the command-line utility.

Take a look at the Mahout source code to understand how the trainer classifier changes between the Naïve Bayes case and the Complementary Naïve Bayes case. The purpose is only to show that applying different classifiers to the same input is easier to code and could help in fine-tuning the data-mining tasks.

> For a more general introduction on the Complementary Naïve Bayes classifier in Mahout, refer to the Mahout website, `https://cwiki.apache.org/confluence/display/MAHOUT/Bayesian`.

We only point out these little changes to show that you could use the existing Naïve Bayes classifier and change it according to the way you would like.

The main difference between Naïve Bayes and Complementary Naïve Bayes is the way in which the two algorithms calculate the weight of words. So basically, the only change from an algorithmic perspective is that of a function. However, you could adapt the function to what you would like to test.

5

Stock Market Forecasting with Mahout

The recipes we will cover in this chapter are as follows:

- Preparing data for logistic regression
- Predicting GOOG movements using logistic regression
- Using adaptive logistic regression in Java code
- Using logistic regression on large-scale datasets
- Using Random Forests to forecast market movements

Introduction

In this chapter, we will use another type of classification algorithm to find movements in the stock market using logistic regression and other classification algorithms.

Before beginning with the recipes, we warn the reader that these recipes will not make you rich. We are not responsible for any use you put these recipes to or anything you use this algorithm for. All of the recipes that we will see in this chapter are only examples meant to enhance your knowledge. But as usual, many of the data mining processes are focused on finding out if it is possible to understand if the market goes up or down.

Preparing data for logistic regression

One of the first data mining tasks that was developed late in the 90s concerned the stock market. This is basically because of the following two facts:

- Huge amounts of data
- Unsupervised algorithms seem to work better for forecasting stock market movements

In this chapter, we will use classification algorithms to classify future market movements. As for what we did in *Chapter 04, Implementing the Naïve Bayes classifier in Mahout*, we use a three-step algorithm based on Mahout.

The first step is the preparation of the dataset. Next, we move on to training a model based on a classification algorithm and then test this model against some other data.

We will detail our intentions by first looking at a simple logistic regression analysis.

Getting ready

We chose GOOG, the stock market acronym for Google Inc, but any other stock title could be used.

For our purposes, we will use all historical prices of the GOOG stock title available at the Google Finance site, `finance.google.com`. Once we have the dataset downloaded, the actions that we will take are as follows:

- Removing the first column from the file to be left with just numerical data
- Adding an extra column that will be used for our analysis

As we did in other recipes, we need to do some arrangement before having the final dataset, which are as follows:

1. Download the original raw data from the Internet.
2. Transform it by adding some extra columns.
3. Save it in a Mahout manageable format.

As usual, let's first download the dataset and take a look at it. To get it, open up a console and type in the following command:

```
wget http://ichart.finance.yahoo.com/table.csv?s=GOOG&d=10&e=29&f=2013&g=d&a=7&b=19&c=2004&ignore=.csv
```

As you can see, you need to change the parameters `d`, `e`, and `f` to get the current day. Otherwise, open up a browser and go to `http://finance.yahoo.com/q/hp?s=GOOG+Historical+Prices`.

The dataset is provided on the Google Finance website and is free to use. It contains daily observations of the Google stock market index. You can take a look at the format by visiting `https://www.google.com/finance/historical?q=NASDAQ%3AGOOG`.

Start your system, open up a terminal bash shell, and type in the following commands:

```
mkdir /tmp/logistic
export WORK=/tmp/logistic
mkdir $WORK /train
mkdir $WORK /test
mkdir $LOGISTIC_HOME/model
```

So, we have our folder structure ready to be used, as shown in the following screenshot:

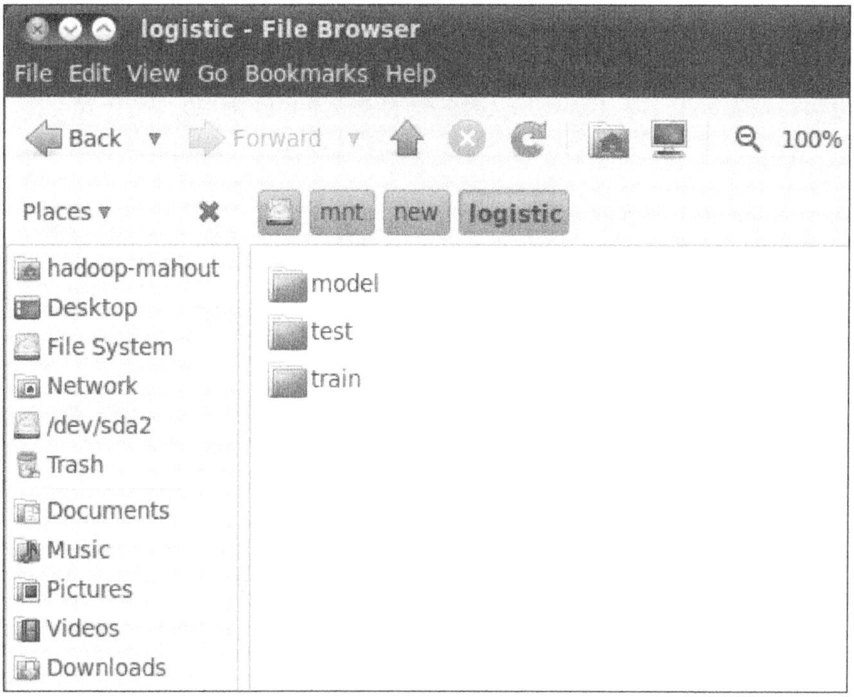

We now need to download our training dataset. The commands to do this are as follows:

```
cd $WORK_DIR/train
wget --output-document=google.csvhttp://ichart.finance.yahoo.com/table.
csv?s=GOOG
```

You should then have a file named `google.csv` in the `$WORD_DIR/train` folder.

Once downloaded, we can have a look at the content of the file with a text editor. The output should be similar to the one shown in the following screenshot:

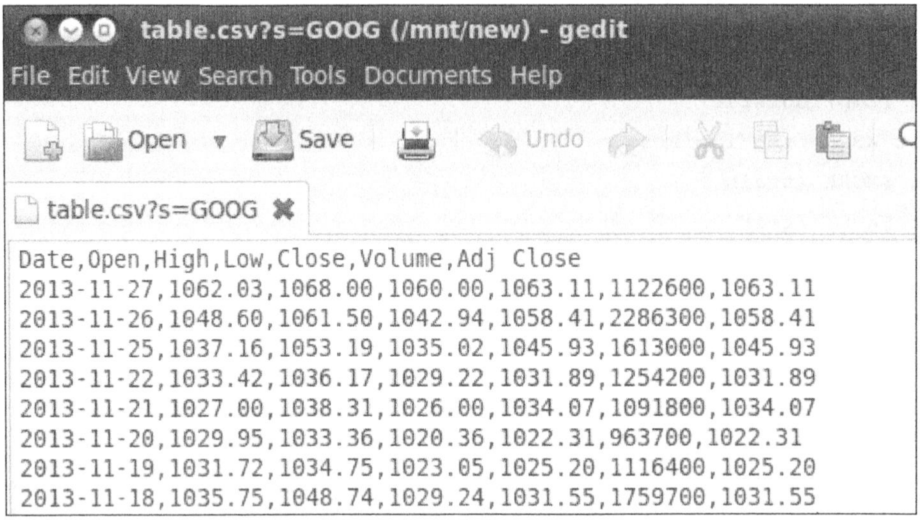

The structure of the file is explained in the following table:

Column	Description
`Date`	The day of recorded observation in the format `yyyy-mm-dd`
`Open`	The opening USD value of the stock
`High`	The maximum USD value of the stock during the whole day
`Low`	The minimum USD value of the stock during the whole day
`Close`	The closing USD value of the stock
`Volume`	The USD amount of trading transaction
`Adj`	The closing USD adjusted value of the stock

Before proceeding, as the dates are difficult to treat with respect to the logistic regression algorithm, we remove them using the following command:

```
cut -d , -f 2-7 google.csv  > training.csv
```

This produces a record file as shown in the following screenshot:

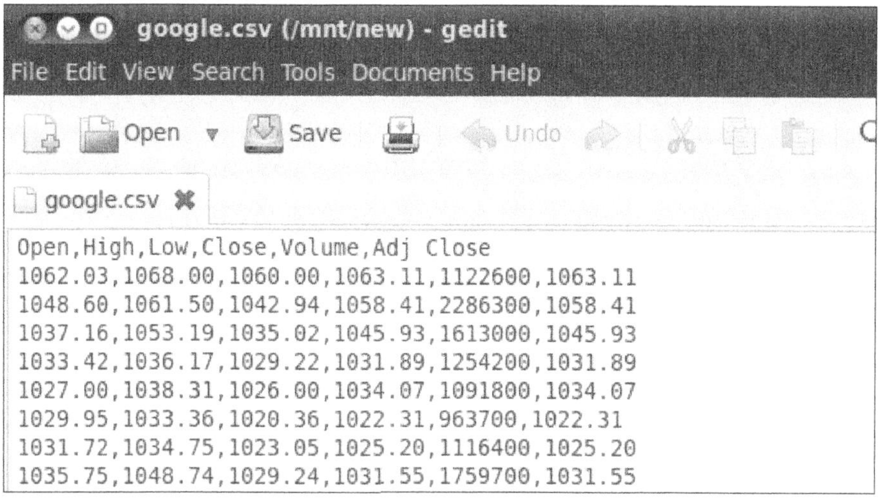

As a final step, we need to create an extra column that defines the action to be taken using simply this algorithm.

How to do it...

If the closing price of the previous day is lower than that of the current day, update the last column to `SELL` or to `BUY`.

To do this, we create a simple parse that can also be used for the next recipe:

```
    public static void main(String[] args) throws
FileNotFoundException, IOException {
        CSVReader reader = new CSVReader(new FileReader("$WORK_DIR/
train/train.csv"));

        String [] nextLine;
        String [] previousLine;
        String [] headernew = new String [reader.readNext().length +
1];

        CSVWriter writer = new CSVWriter(new FileWriter("$WORK_DIR/
train/final.csv"), ',');

        nextLine = reader.readNext();

        for (int i = 0; i < nextLine.length;i++)
        {
```

```
            headernew[i] = nextLine[i];
        }

        headernew[headernew.length-1] = "action";
        writer.writeNext(headernew);

        previousLine = reader.readNext();

        while ((nextLine = reader.readNext()) != null) {
            // nextLine[] is an array of values from the line
            System.out.println(nextLine[0] + nextLine[1] + "etc...");
            headernew = new String [nextLine.length + 1];

            for (int i = 0; i < headernew.length-1;i++)
            {
                headernew[i] = nextLine[i];
            }

            if (
                    Double.parseDouble(previousLine[4]) < Double.
parseDouble(nextLine[4])
                )
            {
                    headernew[headernew.length] = "SELL";
            } else {
                headernew[headernew.length] = "BUY";
            }

            writer.writeNext(headernew);

            previousLine = nextLine;


        }

        reader.close();
        writer.close();

    }
```

How it works...

Basically, we create a simple procedure that creates a new file called `final.csv` in the `$WORK_DIR/train` folder. Before starting, we need to create a new header that contains every column of the previous one and adds a last column named `action`. Then, for every line of the original CSV file, we store it on an array of strings called `newline` that has one more field than the original one. We also stored the previous line. We calculate the value of the last column by using `SELL` if the close price of this line is greater than the previous line; otherwise, we use `BUY`. Finally, we write this new line in a new CSV file.

This way of assigning the `SELL`/`BUY` operation is very common when dealing with stock market operations, despite the simplicity of the rule.

We code it in Java so that we can reuse it, but you are also free to use any other strategy for file parsing.

Sqoop can also be used to perform the same tasks by first creating the dataset table and then using query statements to export the required data, as we have seen in *Chapter 3, Integrating Mahout with an External Datasource*.

We are now ready to code our recipe.

Predicting GOOG movements using logistic regression

Now, we have everything ready for our analysis. The purpose of this recipe is to try and forecast what is the next action (`BUY` versus `SELL`) that we need to perform while giving an input. The assumption is that the `BUY` action depends on a combination of the other dependent inputs, plus some coefficients.

Getting ready

We use the whole previous recipe to create the correct input file. To ensure that everything is working correctly, type into a console the following command in the `$WORK_DIR/train` folder:

```
hadoop-mahout@hadoop-mahout-laptop:/$ cat  final.csv | more
```

The output should be the following:

```
Date,Open,High,Low,Close,Volume,Adj Close
2013-02-14,779.73,788.74,777.77,787.82,1735300,787.82, BUY
2013-02-13,780.13,785.35,779.97,782.86,1198200,782.86, SELL
2013-02-12,781.75,787.90,779.37,780.70,1859000,780.70, SELL
```

How to do it...

The recipe for training our logistic regression classifier is no more difficult than the previous recipes. Open up a command prompt and type in the following command:

```
mahout trainlogistic
--input $WORK_DIR/training/final.csv
--output $WORK_DIR/model/model
--target Action
--predictors Open Close High
--types word
--features 20
--passes 100
--rate 50
--categories 2
```

The output is likely be similar to the following:

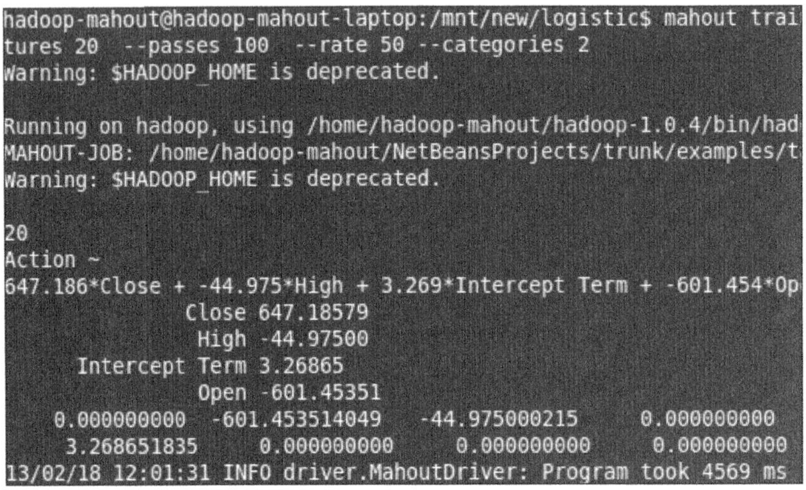

By searching for the model created, you should find it in the `$WORD_DIR/model` folder as shown in the following screenshot:

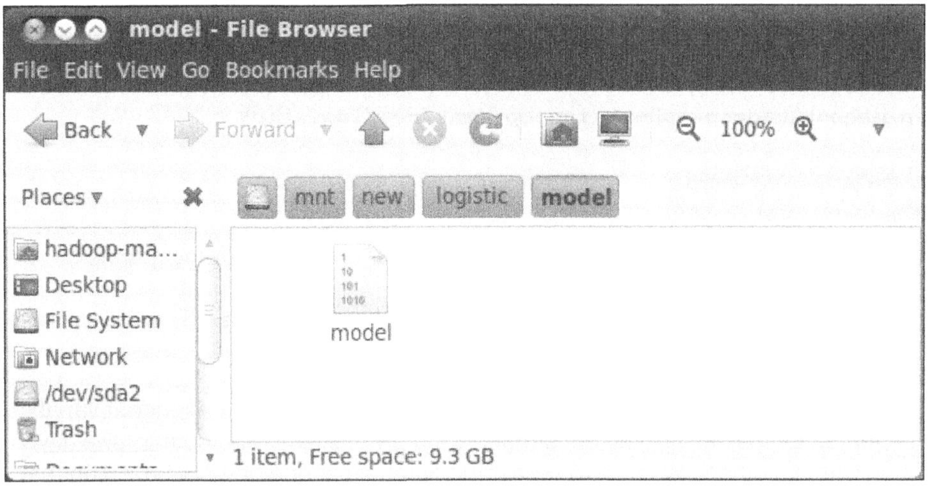

Now, to test the model, we can reuse the same input set (even if we have an exact classification). We would only like to show the command needed to perform this.

The command for the testing phase is as follows:

```
mahout runLogistic
--input $WORK_DIR/training/enter.csv
--model $WORK_DIR/model/model
--auc
--confusion
```

The standard output is the following one:

```
hadoop-mahout@hadoop-mahout-laptop:/mnt/new/logistic$ mahout runlogistic
--input $WORK_DIR/train/enter.csv --model $WORK_DIR/model/model


Running on hadoop, using /home/hadoop-mahout/hadoop-1.0.4/bin/hadoop and
HADOOP_CONF_DIR=
MAHOUT-JOB: /home/hadoop-mahout/NetBeansProjects/trunk/examples/target/
mahout-examples-0.8-SNAPSHOT-job.jar
```

```
AUC = 0.87
confusion: [[864.0, 176.0], [165.0, 933.0]]
entropy: [[NaN, NaN], [-37.8, -6.8]]
13/02/18 12:32:48 INFO driver.MahoutDriver: Program took 380 ms (Minutes: 0.006333333333333333)
hadoop-mahout@hadoop-mahout-laptop:/mnt/new/logistic$
```

How it works...

Basically, our algorithm starting from the set of data works in the following manner:

- Training the file using a logistic regression from the command line
- Applying the generated model against another set of data

So, we have a number of observations that contain independent and dependent variables. The **independent** variables are the ones that are simply observed and do not have any correlation with the others. We try to forecast the outcome of one of them based on the previous observations.

The variables range between the following types:

- Numerical
- Categorical
- Textual

The numerical variables contain numerical values, the categorical variables contain a subset of predefined choices, and the textual/word variables contain generic text.

To evaluate the probability of the dependent variable, we use the logistic function that is a very well-known and studied function in mathematics. Let us consider the observations as a set composed by *n* distinct vectors such as the following:

$$x_1, \ldots, x_k$$

One of these variables is the one to be forecasted. We will try to describe the next value of the selected variables by stating that it can be seen as a combination of the previous one:

$$x_j = \sum_{i-1}^{k-1} a_i x_i$$

The logistic regression tries to find the coefficient a_i.

To do this, we use a logistic function to fit the data, which you can see in the following diagram:

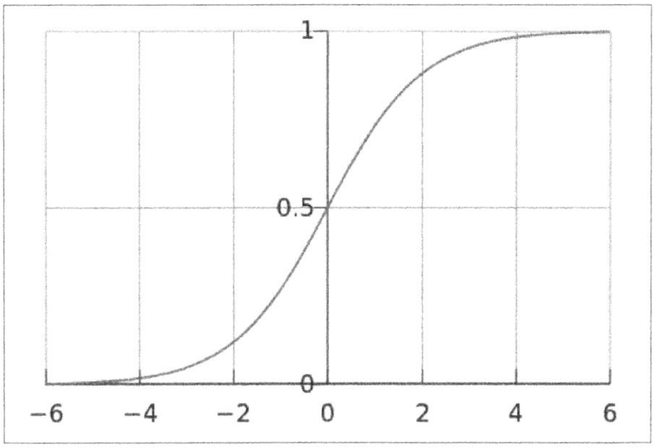

Logistic regression is not a parallelized algorithm so it runs in a sequential mode, but it is very efficient in terms of memory usage, so you could train it against huge datasets without encountering too many performance issues. On the other hand, we have the possibility of an increased CPU consumption, so the reader should be aware of this as well.

First of all let us point out that this algorithm, even with a small amount of data and being sequential, is very fast. Even if the algorithm is a sequential one, the amount of memory used does not grow linearly with the size of the dataset.

Basically, the algorithm tries to classify one column of a CSV based on the other columns of the same.

To train the classifier from the command line, we use the train logistic option of the `mahout` command. The main command options are shown in the following table:

Command	Meaning
`--input`	Tells the training algorithm to find the original CSV
`--output`	Declares the target folder to place the model in once created
`--target`	Specifies the target column of the CSV file that will be classified
`--categories`	Specifies how many different values of the target variable we could have
`--predictors`	Specifies the names of the columns on the CSV input to be used for the evaluation of the target variable
`--types`	Declares the type of the predictor variables
`--passes`	Declares the number of times the algorithm should reuse the input dataset
`--rate`	Sets the initial learning rate
`--features`	Sets the size of the internal vector to be used

So, using our recipe, we trained the logistic regression against our CSV using the following parameters:

- `$WORK_DIR/train/google.csv` as input
- `$WORK_DIR/model/` as the output model
- `Action` as the target variable
- The type of the action variable is a word
- The `predictors` columns are the `Open`, `Close`, and `High` columns, each being of the numeric type

The outcome is a binary file containing the model. Obviously, when using the logistic algorithm, great attention should be given to choosing the right predictors for the target variable. In our case, as the target variable has been created based on the closing price, it is highly correlated. But from datasets, where the target variable is not so well defined, many tries should be used to identify the best predictors for a target variable. The target variable (in our case, a word variable) consists only of two possible outcomes (`BUY` or `SELL`).

The numbers that are output are from the logistic function with values between 0 and 1 that tell us mathematically how the various dependent variables are combined to fit the target variable. So, in our case, we used `Open Close High` as the predictor for `Action`.

To evaluate our train model, we used the same training set and, as the output, we got the following:

```
AUC = 0.87
confusion: [[864.0, 176.0], [165.0, 933.0]]
```

The first parameter is the acronym for **Area Under the Curve**. As the area under the logistic can be expressed as a probability, this parameter is the probability of the model that classifies the data correctly. The `AUC` parameter tells us the number of true positives, so the higher the value between 0 and 1, the fewer false positives we have.

So the values could range from 0, which is a wrong model, to 1, which is a perfect model. In our case, `0.87` told us that the model's probability fails in the classification of the remaining 13 percent of the cases. This value is higher but not high enough for a good model.

Besides, we have the `confusion` matrix that tells that the model performs well in 864 out of 1040 test cases (864 + 176).

The confusion matrix

As with every classifier training or testing, the more you try, the more you could improve your results. In our case, we could also add the minimum stock market USD price to see if the model could perform better.

We give it a second run with the following terminal command:

```
mahout trainlogistic
--input $WORK_DIR/training/enter.csv
--output $WORK_DIR/model/model
--target Action
--predictors Open Close High
--types word
--features 20i
--passes 100
--rate 50
--categories 2
```

Followed by the subsequent command:

```
mahout runLogistic
--input $WORK_DIR/training/enter.csv
--model $WORK_DIR/model/model
--auc
--confusion
```

The output of the confusion matrix will be as follows:

```
AUC = 0.87
confusion: [[866.0, 172.0], [163.0, 937.0]]
```

In this case, we get better performance even if it is not as good as expected. But in the case of millions of records, this little improvement could be a valuable one.

Using adaptive logistic regression in Java code

So far, we have seen that Mahout's logistic regression algorithm does not use the Hadoop MapReduce computational power, so it is easy to embed it into a portion of the Java code. Let us now recode the previous example using NetBeans and Maven.

In this recipe, we will use a more sophisticated version of the logistic regression algorithm—the adaptive logistic regression algorithm—that chooses the best outcome of the logistic algorithm to decide about classification.

Getting ready

To get ready, simply open up a terminal window and type in the following command:

```
mvn archetype:create -DarchetypeGroupId=org.apache.maven.archetypes
-DgroupId=com.packtpub.mahoutcookbook -DartifactId=chapter05
```

Then, open up your project with NetBeans and add the reference to the Mahout Maven local project as we did in the previous chapters.

Now that everything is ready, let's code!

How to do it...

The code to simulate the training phase is as follows:

```
        String inputFile = "/mnt/new/logistic/train/google.csv";
        String outputFile = "/mnt/new/logistic/model/modelfromcode";

        AdaptiveLogisticModelParameters lmp = new
AdaptiveLogisticModelParameters();
        int passes = 50;
        boolean showperf;
        int skipperfnum = 99;
        AdaptiveLogisticRegression model;

        CsvRecordFactory csv = lmp.getCsvRecordFactory();
        model = lmp.createAdaptiveLogisticRegression();
        State<Wrapper, CrossFoldLearner> best;
        CrossFoldLearner learner = null;

        for (int pass = 0; pass < passes; pass++) {
                BufferedReader in = open(inputFile);

                // read variable names
                csv.firstLine(in.readLine());

                String line = in.readLine();
                int lineCount = 2;
                while (line != null) {
                  // for each new line, get target and predictors
                  Vector input = new RandomAccessSparseVector(lmp.
getNumFeatures());
                  int targetValue = csv.processLine(line, input);
```

```
                // update model
                model.train(targetValue, input);
                k++;

                line = in.readLine();
                lineCount++;
              }
              in.close();
            }

          best = model.getBest();
          if (best != null) {
            learner = best.getPayload().getLearner();
          }

          OutputStream modelOutput = new
FileOutputStream(outputFile);
          try {
            lmp.saveTo(modelOutput);
          } finally {
            modelOutput.close();
          }
```

The output should be less descriptive than the command line. What we did was basically only rewrite the command-line parameter used in the previous recipe in the Java code. This code is the Java translation of the code used by the command-line utility when calling the Mahout `trainlogistic` analysis.

We will briefly comment on the code so that it can be reused as needed.

How it works...

The most important part to focus on is the train method called from the `AdaptativeLogistic` object:

```
model.train(targetValue, input);
```

The training phase is inserted inside a `for` loop because of the passing rate that is defined previously.

Every loop consists of the following actions:

- Opening and reading, line by line, the content of the CVS input file defined previously
- Creating a vector containing the target and predictors for each line
- Training every vector

At the end (outside the loop), we will have found the best model resulting from the training phase. After this, the model is saved into a file.

The code to choose the best logistic regression model is pretty easy. It is as follows:

```
best = model.getBest();
if (best != null) {
  learner = best.getPayload().getLearner();
}
```

Here, `learner` is an object of type `CrossFoldLearner`. After this, we store the file with an `outputstream` object. As the final step, we save our `learner` object to a file using the following command:

```
OutputStream modelOutput = new
FileOutputStream(outputFile);
try {
  lmp.saveTo(modelOutput);
} finally {
  modelOutput.close();
}
```

In this case, we did not give any further information on the model created.

Using logistic regression on large-scale datasets

Thus far, we have seen how logistic regression works in a sequential mode. In this recipe, we will see how to make the logistic regression algorithm work using the Hadoop MapReduce implementation. Because the official Mahout implementation does not support the Hadoop implementation of the logistic regression algorithm at the moment, we will move to the GitHub site where the code implements this feature.

Getting ready

To get ready, we need to download the code and the example dataset from GitHub. Perform the following steps to do so:

1. Go to `https://github.com/WinVector/Logistic/tree/master`.
2. Open up a terminal and create a working environment by typing in the following commands:

   `export WORK_DIR=/mnt/hadoop-logistic`

   `mkdir $WORK_DIR`

   `cd $WORK_DIR`

3. Let us download a JAR file with the full source code, compiled and ready to be run from the command line using the `wget` command:

```
wget github-windows://openRepo/https://github.com/WinVector/Logist
ic?branch=master&filepath=WinVectorLogistic.Hadoop0.20.2.jar
```

4. Finally, we'll download two small datasets for our testing purposes:

```
wget http://www.win-vector.com/dfiles/WinVectorLogisticRegression/
uciCarTrain.tsv
```

```
wget http://www.win-vector.com/dfiles/WinVectorLogisticRegression/
uciCarTest.tsv
```

5. We'll see the following structure inside our `$WORK_DIR` folder:

We download two datasets: one for the training phase and the other for the testing phase. For a full description of the dataset, refer to the UCI machine learning site, `http://archive.ics.uci.edu/ml/machine-learning-databases/car/`.

Recall that we are going to use the whole set of columns of the tab-delimited files to forecast the rate of a car.

How to do it...

Now, we need to simply link the correct JAR files and run the software with the correct parameters.

So open up a terminal window and type in the following command:

```
hadoop jar WinVectorLogistic.Hadoop0.20.2.jar logistictrain uciCarTrain.
tsv "rating ~ buying + maintenance + doors + persons + lug_boot"
```

The result of the computation will be displayed as follows:

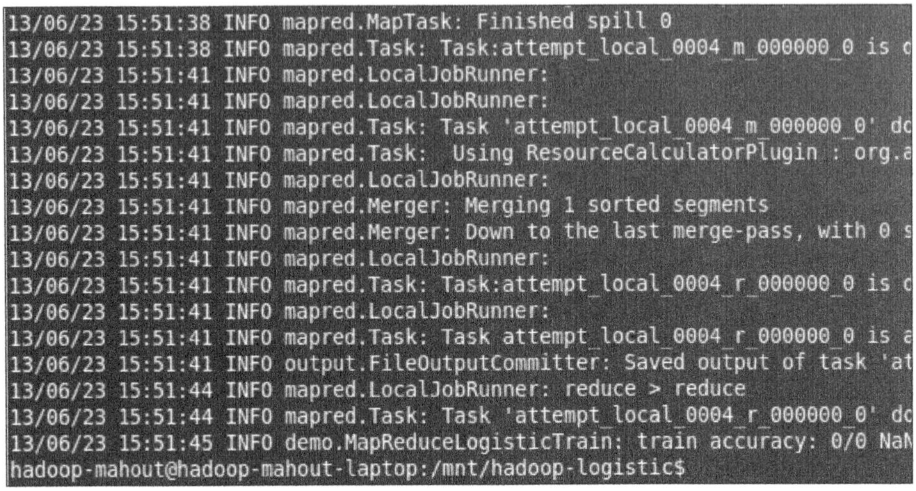

The results should be in a file with the `.ser` extension in the same folder we have all the files, as shown in the following screenshot:

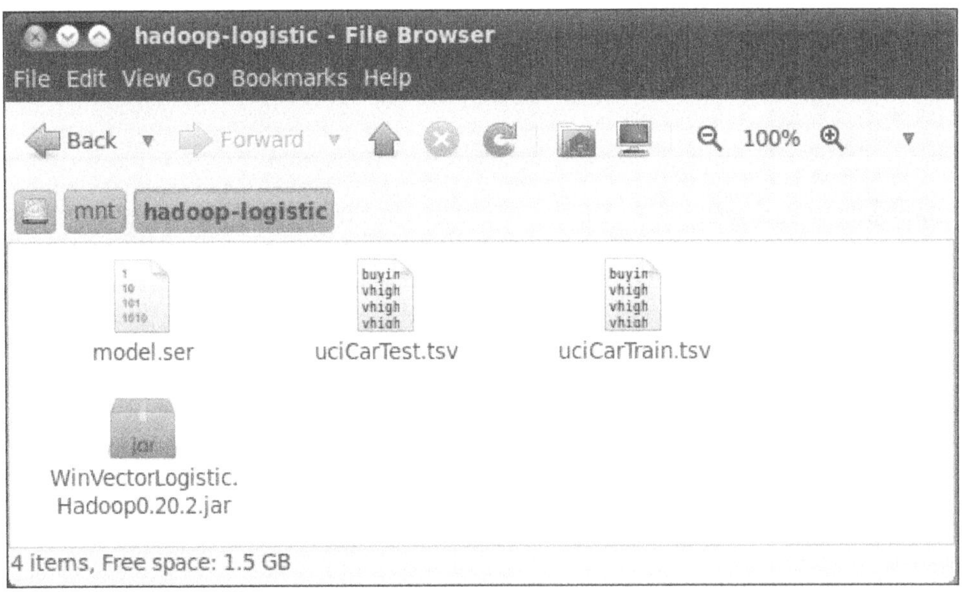

Now, we need to run our model over the testing set of values. The command is pretty easy; just type the following command in the same command window:

```
hadoop jar WinVectorLogistic.Hadoop0.20.2.jar logisticscore model.ser
uciCarTest.tsv scoredDir
```

The result on the console will be as follows:

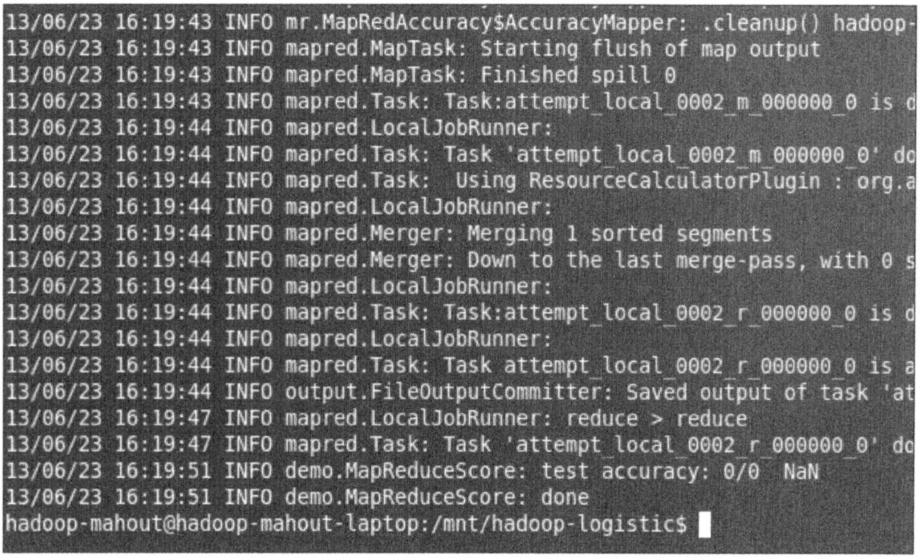

At the filesystem level, we see that the results are stored in a sequence file in the `scoreDir` folder:

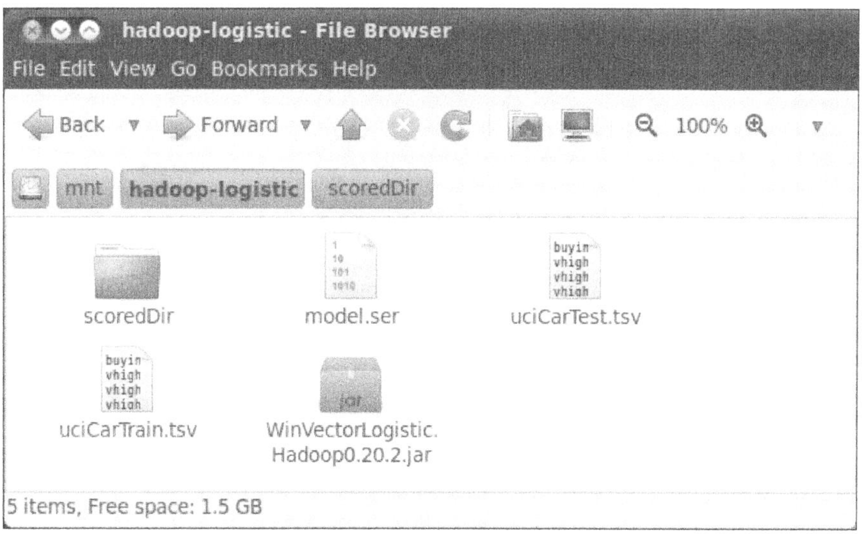

Using the following command, one can see the final result of our computation:

```
hadoop dfs -text scoreDir/part-r-00000
```

The final result is as follows:

```
File.Offset   predict.rating      predict.rating.score   buying
maintenance  doors    persons    lug_    boot    safety    rating
0       0.9999999999999392   6.091299561082107E-14   vhigh   vhigh      2
2   small    low    FALSE
1       0.9999999824028766   1.759712345446162E-8   vhigh   vhigh      2
2   small    high    TRUE
```

How it works...

As we have seen, we have a two-step procedure that, in this case, performs the following actions:

1. Creates a model file with the `.ser` extension.
2. Creates the final rating file using the Hadoop sequence file format.

In the first case, this implementation uses the `hadoop jar` command to execute the `logistictrain` class inside the `WinVectorLogistic.Hadoop0.20.2.jar` file for the logistic phase. The other mandatory parameters are as follows:

- `uciCarTrain.tsv` (the source file)
- `rating ~ buying + maintenance + doors + persons + lug_boot + safety` (the way we train the logistic)
- `model.ser` (the file model name)

So basically, we try to identify the rating based on the assumption that the rating depends on the columns buying, maintenance, doors, person, lug_boot, and safety:

buying	maintenance	doors	persons
vhigh	vhigh	2	2
vhigh	vhigh	2	2
vhigh	vhigh	2	2
vhigh	vhigh	2	2
vhigh	vhigh	2	2
vhigh	vhigh	2	4
vhigh	vhigh	2	4
vhigh	vhigh	2	4
vhigh	vhigh	2	4

The whole set of columns is buying, maintenance, doors, persons, lug_boot, safety, and rating. If we take a look at the source code in the GitHub repository, we can see that the logistictrain class is written in a way that respects the Hadoop specification for implementing the MapReduce job (see https://github.com/WinVector/Logistic/blob/master/src/com/winvector/logistic/LogisticTrain.java).

The MapReduce job is performed by readying a portion of the same data file, transforming them into sequence files and then evaluating every portion of data to obtain a set of scores that are evaluated to find the best one. Next, the reducer aggregates all of the data into the model.ser file.

We point out that this implementation has been done to allow scaling to Hadoop, so the job that is running can be changed to define the mapper and the reducers.

See also

The whole implementation has been coded by *John Mount*, who also maintains a blog about data mining and the implementation of the logistic regression using Hadoop. We strongly suggest that you follow his blog, which is available at http://www.win-vector.com/blog/.

Using Random Forest to forecast market movements

This recipe will act on the same dataset we have used so far. The difference is that we are going to use a different type of algorithm called **Random Forest**.

This kind of algorithm is very efficient in classifying forecasts on a huge set of predictors. We will use it to forecast Google's market movement, but a potentially better algorithm is the one that forecasts the movement of the NASDAQ based on all of the stock market titles that compose the NASDAQ basket. So, if for every tile we have five attributes (`Open`, `Close`, `High`, `Low`, and `Volume`), we could have hundreds of numerical predictors to forecast only a single moment.

This recipe has been built out of the information provided by *Jennifer Smith* on GitHub.

Getting ready

To get started with this example, create a new Maven project with the following command:

```
mvn archetype:create -DarchetypeGroupId=org.apache.maven.archetypes
-DgroupId=com.packtpub.mahoutcookbook -DartifactId=chapter05b
```

We need to add the references to your local Mahout Maven project as well.

How to do it...

The basic steps for this algorithm are as follows:

1. Read a CSV value file to convert it into an array of strings.
2. Divide the resulting array into the training and testing data using a 90 percent approach, meaning that the training set is 90 percent of the whole dataset.
3. Run the `runIteration` method with a defined number of trees to create a descriptor object.

To run this example, we need to add the following code into the `main` method of the `App.java` class automatically generated by Maven:

```
String trainingSetFile = "/mnt/new/logistic/train/google.csv";

int numberOfTrees = 100;
boolean useThresholding = true;

System.out.println("Building " + numberOfTrees + " trees.");
String[] trainDataValues = fileAsStringArray(trainingSetFile, 42000,
useThresholding);
```

```
String[] testDataValues = new String[]{};

String descriptor = buildDescriptor(trainDataValues[0].split(",").
length - 1);

// take 90 percent to be the test data
String[] part1 = new String[trainDataValues.length / 10 * 9];
String[] part2 = new String[trainDataValues.length / 10];

System.arraycopy(trainDataValues, 0, part1, 0, part1.length);
System.arraycopy(trainDataValues, part1.length, part2, 0, part2.
length);

trainDataValues = part1;
testDataValues = part2;

long startTime = System.currentTimeMillis();
runIteration(numberOfTrees, trainDataValues, testDataValues,
descriptor);
long endTime = System.currentTimeMillis();
double duration = new BigDecimal(endTime - startTime).divide(new
BigDecimal("1000")).doubleValue();
System.out.println(numberOfTrees + " took " + duration + " seconds");
```

How it works...

The main method to focus on is `runIteration` where the whole calculation takes place. The code is as follows:

```
System.out.println("numberOfTrees = " + numberOfTrees);
Data data = loadData(trainDataValues, descriptor);
Random rng = RandomUtils.getRandom();

DecisionForest forest = buildForest(numberOfTrees, data);
saveTree(numberOfTrees, forest);

Data test = DataLoader.loadData(data.getDataset(), testDataValues);

try {
   FileWriter fileWriter = new FileWriter("attempts/out-" + System.
currentTimeMillis() + ".txt");
   PrintWriter out = new PrintWriter(fileWriter);

   int numberCorrect = 0;
   int numberOfValues = 0;
```

```
    for (int i = 0; i < test.size(); i++) {
        Instance oneSample = test.get(i);
        double actualIndex = oneSample.get(0);
        int actualLabel = data.getDataset().valueOf(0, String.
valueOf((int) actualIndex));

        double classify = forest.classify(test.getDataset(), rng,
oneSample);
        int label = data.getDataset().valueOf(0, String.valueOf((int)
classify));

        System.out.println("label = " + label + " actual = " +
actualLabel);
        if (label == actualLabel) {
            numberCorrect++;
        }
        numberOfValues++;
        out.println(label + ", " + actualLabel);
    }
    double percentageCorrect = numberCorrect * 100.0 / numberOfValues;
    System.out.println("Number of trees: " + numberOfTrees + " ->
Number correct: " + numberCorrect + " of " + numberOfValues + " (" +
percentageCorrect + ")");

    out.close();
} catch (Exception e) {
    e.printStackTrace();
    System.err.println("Error: " + e.getMessage());
}
```

As you can see, the calculation part is done by the `DecisionForest` object that uses the number of trees defined in the parameters used to call the function and the `data` object containing the `Data` vectors as result of the input CSV file parsing. After building the `forest` object, we have the possibility to use it to invoke the `classify` method to perform the classification tasks.

See also

Random Forests are great tools for classifying variables based on hundreds of predictors. They are very useful when dealing with a lot of independent variables.

We refer you to the paper *Forecasting Stock Index Movement: A Comparison of Support Vector Machines and Random Forest*, freely available at `http://papers.ssrn.com/sol3/papers.cfm?abstract_id=876544`, for some possible applications of this to stock market forecasting.

6

Canopy Clustering in Mahout

The recipes we will look over in this chapter are as follows:

- Command-line-based Canopy clustering
- Command-line-based Canopy clustering with parameters
- Using Canopy clustering from the Java code
- Coding your own clustering distance evaluation

Introduction

Canopy clustering is a fast and powerful algorithm that can be used to cluster the groups' sparse information grouped in some *n*-dimensional arrays. This chapter is dedicated to various recipes for using such clustering techniques.

Command-line-based Canopy clustering

Basically speaking, the problem of clustering can be seen as the best way to group information together. So, the classification problems are a major field of application of clustering techniques. When we deal with classification tasks, we mean in most of the cases with multidimensional observation. Let us imagine this simple scenario: You have the navigation log of a very large website. For every connection, you could have lots of information as follows:

- IP address
- Browser used
- Number of times a page has been displayed
- Number of links on the page

Obviously, this log file could contain billions of lines and hundreds of different observations. When we classify this information, we do not look for a single instance of the information to be classified, but for the classification of many of them together.

So, for example, we could ask ourselves what are the first five countries, by rank, that surf our website coupled with the browser to extract the first five couples (country and browser).

As the Mahout framework deals with a very big dataset, obviously, the first coded algorithms were the clustering ones. The clustering algorithms implemented in Mahout up to Version 0.8 are:

- Canopy clustering
- K-means clustering
- Hierarchical clustering

And for the other clustering algorithms, we refer you, as usual, to the official Mahout page (`https://cwiki.apache.org/confluence/display/MAHOUT/Algorithms`).

The difference between the types of algorithms used depends on the way the clusters are built, so the way you decide two different multidimensional vectors are similar. In this chapter, we will show you the Canopy clustering algorithm to introduce you to the argument. The Canopy clustering algorithm bases its name on the fact that during the algorithm some canopies are generated. We will go into more detail about the whole process, but the core idea of this algorithm is to build some grouping sets during the computational phase, and then evaluate them.

The simplest way to use the Canopy clustering algorithm is by using the command-line option available to us. Canopy clustering can be used both as a sequential and a parallelized algorithm.

Getting ready

As with the recipes in the previous chapters, we need to create our environment and add some test data to be used. Start your system, open up a terminal bash shell, and type in the following commands:

```
mkdir /tmp/canopy
export WORK_DIR=/tmp/canopy
```

Now, we will use the dataset whose description can be found at the following link: `http://archive.ics.uci.edu/ml/datasets/Synthetic+Control+Chart+Time+Series`.

The dataset is composed of 600 rows and 60 columns, where every row represents a time-series observation. By plotting the first three rows, we have the following chart that will represent the artificially generated time series:

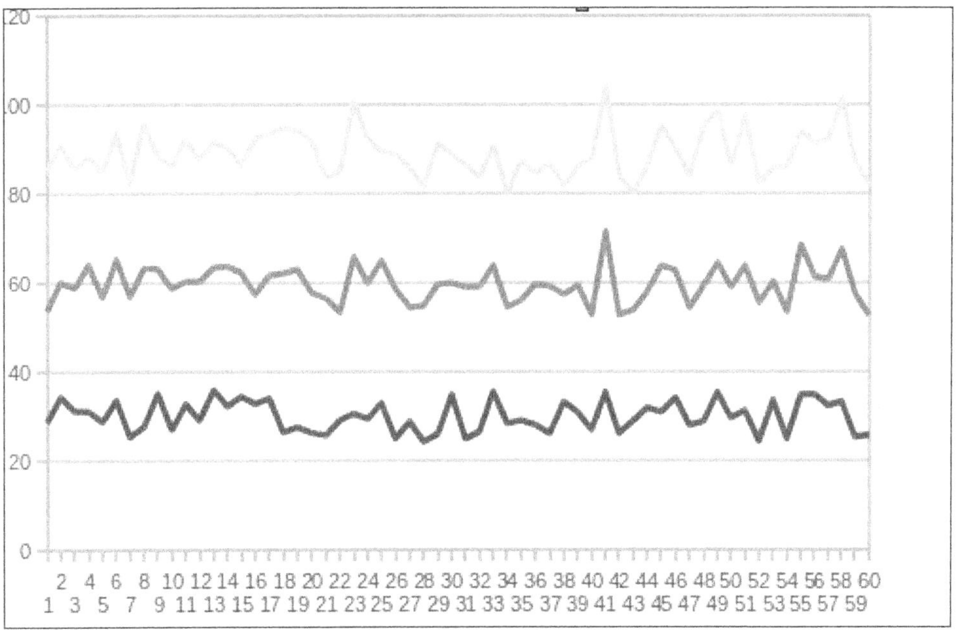

In order to download it, we type in the following command:

```
cd $WORK_DIR
wget http://archive.ics.uci.edu/ml/databases/synthetic_control/synthetic_control.data
```

Once downloaded, the content of the file should look like the following screenshot:

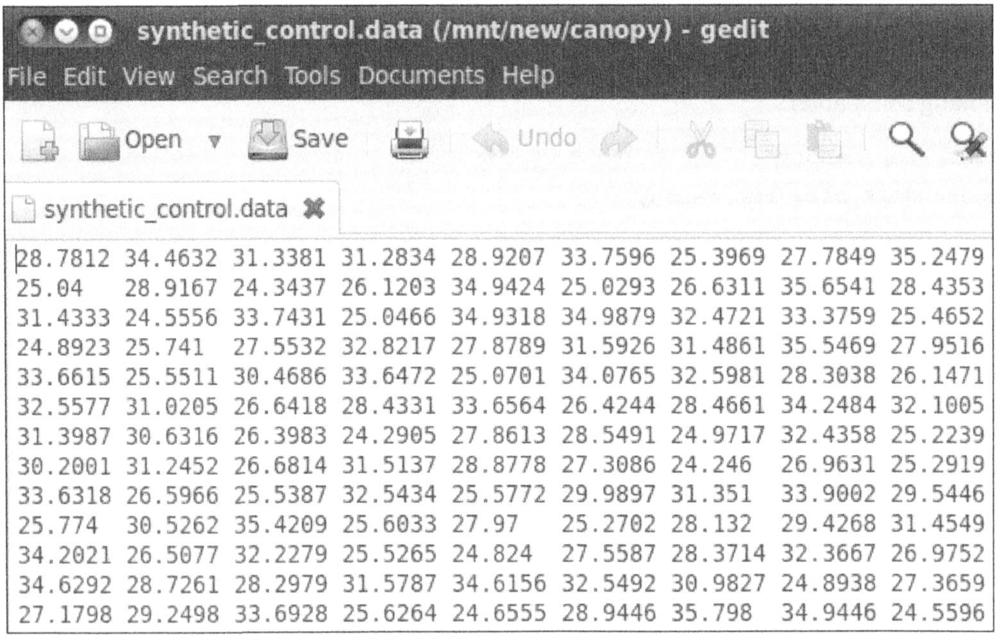

The Canopy cluster functionality works with the sequence vector file, which needs to be generated starting from the file we downloaded.

How to do it...

The Canopy clustering implementation coded with Mahout is composed of several different steps. The principal ones are the following:

1. Convert the source data into vector sequential files containing a value composed of a vector of numbers for every key.
2. For every set of this *n*-dimensional numeric data point, a mapper creates Canopy centers, which are centers of aggregation for the input point set.
3. The reducer groups together the created Canopy centers to create the final centers.
4. The initial data points are grouped together on the aggregated clusters.

In order to realize our analysis, we need to carry out some actions, in particular:

1. Create an `HDFS` test folder.
2. Put the file containing our dataset into it.
3. Transform the original dataset in the sequence file using the Mahout Canopy cluster command-line utility.

Considering that the Canopy works with the HDFS filesystem and the basic Canopy cluster uses a predefined working folder, we need to type the following commands in the terminal:

```
cd $WORK_DIR
hadoop fs -mkdir testdata
```

The `hadoop fs -ls` command gives the following output:

```
drwxr-xr-x   - hadoop-mahout hadoop-mahout      4096 2013-03-14 14:23 /
mnt/new/canopy/testdata
-rw-r--r--   1 hadoop-mahout hadoop-mahout    288374 1999-06-14 22:41 /
mnt/new/canopy/synthetic_control.data
```

Then, we need to move the file out into the created folder with the HDFS filesystem, to store the `synthetic_control.data` file in the `testdata` HDFS folder:

```
hadoop fs -put ${WORK_DIR}/synthetic_control.data testdata
```

To launch a Canopy cluster analysis on the test data, you simply need to type in the following command:

```
mahout org.apache.mahout.clustering.syntheticcontrol.canopy.Job
```

After a while, the output should be the following:

```
        1.0: [31.022, 28.140, 26.730, 26.570, 29.561, 26.966, 28.049, 25.67
 31.947, 35.491, 30.730, 25.820, 24.651, 25.528, 31.343, 29.005, 31.825, 26
 16.660, 15.021, 9.891, 9.216, 11.550, 8.877, 18.220, 9.477, 10.342, 16.430
        1.0: [29.625, 25.503, 31.598, 31.466, 33.549, 28.294, 28.924, 30.69
 29.153, 24.125, 25.376, 15.918, 22.231, 18.264, 24.582, 18.679, 26.370, 24
37, 15.079, 17.333, 26.747, 18.880, 21.332, 23.692, 22.310, 19.136, 15.285,
        1.0: [27.414, 25.397, 26.460, 31.978, 26.125, 27.463, 30.489, 34.92
 29.121, 26.424, 33.452, 33.623, 29.457, 35.025, 26.607, 34.442, 34.847, 28
3, 18.317, 15.323, 19.106, 11.455, 16.888, 18.269, 11.583, 14.118, 20.229,
        1.0: [35.899, 26.672, 34.191, 35.827, 25.101, 24.856, 25.814, 30.63
 22.703, 17.698, 16.281, 18.186, 24.016, 24.553, 21.452, 15.836, 21.311, 20
22, 19.671, 26.299, 21.879, 16.002, 15.288, 16.946, 17.534, 16.846, 16.546,
        1.0: [24.538, 24.280, 28.281, 27.132, 26.662, 32.110, 32.810, 30.48
 9.600, 12.675, 16.575, 19.760, 13.349, 18.137, 7.993, 16.751, 16.341, 15.3
.402, 19.628, 19.644, 11.524, 15.419, 12.670, 13.116, 8.235, 12.042, 19.310
        1.0: [34.335, 30.938, 31.953, 31.146, 24.519, 24.393, 27.696, 29.87
 26.581, 34.825, 34.026, 8.823, 12.634, 12.694, 6.279, 13.644, 16.651, 18.0
96, 11.028, 10.608, 15.190, 9.076, 17.909, 9.846, 15.013, 13.913, 11.743, 1
13/03/14 14:30:10 INFO clustering.ClusterDumper: Wrote 6 clusters
13/03/14 14:30:10 INFO driver.MahoutDriver: Program took 28816 ms (Minutes:
hadoop-mahout@hadoop-mahout-laptop:/mnt/new/canopy/original$
```

The displayed numbers are the result of our computation, representing the series that Mahout considers clusters. So, our analysis created six clusters that were displayed in the standard output.

It is also possible to call some other parameter, but this will be covered in the next recipes. Let us see at a high level how it works.

How it works...

In this recipe, we have used a default Java class file provided with the Mahout code that carries out the Canopy clustering on the synthetic control data.

The key concept for creating the cluster is to first have a rough division algorithm, by taking a set of the *n*-dimensional vectors, and divide them using a first distance. Then, on the second stage, use a more accurate distance to find which cluster the points should appertain to. The original algorithm was first coded without using a MapReduce framework. The only difference between the sequential and MapReduce implementation is the fact that we have different parallel processes that create the cluster, and then in the final stage, the data is aggregated to produce the final results.

In this case, everything is done using a simple Java class coded inside the Mahout distribution. The whole class does the full job as described previously, and it can be used for performing the Canopy clustering analysis. In this, we do not need to provide anything considering that the first entry in the `Job` class contains the following code:

```
if (args.length > 0) {
  log.info("Running with only user-supplied arguments");
  ToolRunner.run(new Configuration(), new Job(), args);
} else {
  log.info("Running with default arguments");
  Path output = new Path("output");
  HadoopUtil.delete(new Configuration(), output);
  run(new Path("testdata"), output, new
    EuclideanDistanceMeasure(), 80, 55);
}
```

So, automatically, in case we do not provide any arguments, the ETL of the `synthetic_control.data` file transforms into a `sequencefile`.

If we take the analysis to a deeper level, we focus on the following line, which contains the basic parameter to run a generic Canopy cluster analysis:

```
run(new Path("testdata"), output, new EuclideanDistanceMeasure(),
  80, 55);
```

As we stated before, the Canopy clustering is done using a distance measure between the different points that are *n*-dimensional vectors. A first rough, but very fast, estimation is done using the number `80` as a threshold value, and a second one using the same distance but with a threshold value of `55`. The two thresholds are meant to be the limit. So, if we have two multidimensional arrays, we use `T1` as the limit to consider the two arrays as part of the first generated cluster. `T2` has the same meaning but in the second generated cluster.

The measure to evaluate how near a point is to a cluster is, in this case, the `EuclideanDistance`. Only for the sake of clarity, considering two *n*-valued vectors *x = (x_1,..x_n)* and *y = (y_1,...,y_n)*, the Euclidean distance is calculated using the following formula:

$$D(x,y) = \sqrt{\sum_{i=1}^{n}(x_i - y_i)^2}$$

But, as usual, other possible ways of calculating the distance between two *n*-dimensional arrays can be used or created. We will see in the next recipes how to create your own measure distance.

Command-line-based Canopy clustering with parameters

In the previous recipe, we used the code directly to execute a predefined Canopy clustering on a predefined dataset. In this chapter we will do the same thing, but in this case, we will use some command-line parameters so as to allow you to understand better how to prepare a Canopy clustering analysis.

Getting ready

In this case, a predefined ETL transform needs to be done first because the input for Canopy clustering is a sequence file that has a key/value pair as follows:

- **Key**: A unique identifier, for example, an automatic generated auto-incremental counter
- **Value**: An *n*-sized vector of numeric value

So, before continuing, we need to transform our dataset into a sequence vector file, where every line becomes a 600-coordinate sparse vector.

Moving ahead from the recipes of *Chapter 2, Using Sequence Files – When and Why?*, we code the following transformation class, which is present in the book's source code at `www.packtpub.com/support`:

```
/**
 *
 * @author hadoop-mahout
 */
public class CreateVectorsFile {
    public static void main(String[] args) throws IOException
    {
        Configuration conf = new Configuration();
        FileSystem fs = FileSystem.get(conf);

        String input = "/mnt/new/canopy/original/synthetic_control.
data";
        String output = "/mnt/new/canopy/sequencefile/synthetic_
control.seq";


        BufferedReader reader = new BufferedReader(new
FileReader(input));
        SequenceFile.Writer writer = new SequenceFile.Writer( fs,
conf,new Path(output), LongWritable.class, VectorWritable.class);


        String line;
        long counter = 0;
        while ((line = reader.readLine()) != null) {

            String[] c;
            c = line.split(" ");
            double[] d = new double[c.length];
            for (int i = 0; i < 61; i++) {

                try
                {
                    d[i] =  Double.parseDouble(c[i]);
                }catch(Exception ex)
                {
                    d[i] = 0;
                }

            }

            Vector vec = new RandomAccessSparseVector(c.length);
```

```
            vec.assign(d);


            VectorWritable writable = new VectorWritable();
            writable.set(vec);
            writer.append(new LongWritable(counter++), writable);
        }
    writer.close();

}
```

As you can see, we only read the original file line by line and create `SparseVector`, where each entry is the value grabbed from the file. Considering that a vector file is a sequence file, the key is the line number (that is unique), and the value is the vector containing the values. We also add a try-catch block to avoid any incorrect input on the vector. We warn you that, in this case, we considered the following hypothesis.

Considering that not all the lines have the same amount of entries—some have 66 and some 60—we cut off all the length of the vector to 60. A more sophisticated approach would have been to force the length of the vectors to 66 (in this file, this is the maximum value), and manage the vectors that are not of the same length. There is a considerable amount of reference material available online on how to evaluate the missing entry point. In case you would like to try this second option, you could go on and choose a randomly generated value between the minimum/maximum values of all the vectors. It is not difficult to code something like this in Java. But this is out of the scope of the book.

Remember that for the Canopy cluster analysis, having differently-sized vectors can compromise the running of the algorithm. This practically means that if, for example, in the synthetic control file you have a line with a different number of points (not 60), and this could create problems.

As usual the `synthetic_control.data` file does not need to be significantly re-managed, but in case your input file contains lines with text characters, you'd need to assign a numeric value to each text value. How to do this is out of the scope of this recipe. You could try your hand at working with different datasets. On completion of our running code, we have the `synthetic_control.seq` file created in the `$WORK_DIR/sequencefile` location.

Now, we can do our Canopy cluster analysis.

How to do it...

To create our analysis, we need to do the following:

1. Call the Mahout Canopy command line.
2. Use the `clusterdump` command-line option to display the clusters.

The process is described in detail as follows:

1. Now that we have everything ready, we can simply call Mahout with the Canopy option. Execute the following line in the terminal/command prompt:

   ```
   mahout canopy -i $WORK_DIR/sequencefile/synthetic_control.seq -o
   $WORK_DIR/output/canopy.output -t1 80 -t2 55
   ```

2. The final lines of the output should be as follows:

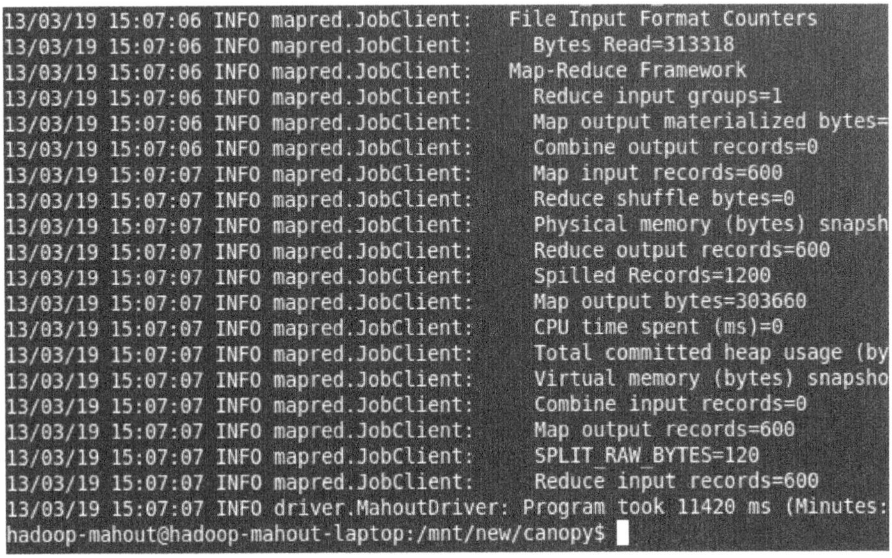

3. The output of the Canopy cluster analysis is a file model that is present in the `output` folder. To see the content, use the `seqdumper` utility by typing the following command:

   ```
   mahout clusterdump -i $WORK_DIR/output/canopy.output/clusters-0-
   final/  -o $WORK_DIR/output/clusteranalyze.txt
   ```

4. You should get the `clusteranalyze` file, whose first line should look like the following one:

   ```
   C-0{n=116 c=[0:28.781, 1:34.463, 2:31.338, 3:31.283, 4:28.921,
   5:33.760, 6:25.397, 7:27.785, 8:35.248, 9:27.116, 10:32.872,
   11:29.217, 12:36.025, 13:32.337, 15:34.525, 16:32.872, 17:34.117,
   18:26.524, 19:27.662, 20:26.369  60:34.932] r=[3.463]}
   ```

How it works...

The previous output can be interpreted as follows:

- `C-0` is name of the cluster
- `N= 116` is the number of the points aggregated into the cluster

- `C=[..]` are the 166 points related to the cluster and the first one refers to the center of the cluster
- `r` is the radius of the cluster, that is, the maximal Euclidean distance between the farthest point and the center of the cluster

As we stated before, not only the Canopy but the cluster analysis is based on the idea that all the vectors can be thought of as a point, and so a cluster is a sphere that contains a subset of points grouped into a cluster.

The Canopy command comes with a set of options; the most important of which are as follows:

- `-i`: Input vector's directory
- `-o`: Output working directory
- `-dm`: Distance measure
- `-t1`: T1 threshold
- `-t2`: T2 threshold
- `-ow`: Overwrite output directory if present

By default, `-dm` is the Java class name that needs to be used for evaluating the distance. If no class is specified, `org.apache.mahout.common.distance.SquaredEuclideanDistanceMeasure` is used.

This is the standard Euclidean distance in an *n*-dimensional space. This Java class object implements the `DistanceMeasure` interface. Mahout comes with other implementations that can be used; for example, `CosineDistanceMeasure`. So, in this case, using the command line of the recipe, one can call the following command:

```
mahout canopy -i $WORK_DIR/sequencefile/synthetic_control.seq -o $WORK_
DIR/output/canopy.output -t1 80 -t2 55 -ow -dm org.apache.mahout.common.
distance.CosineDistanceMeasure
```

The `-ow` option tells you every time to overwrite the resulting model.

Probably, two of the most important parameters for the Canopy analysis are `t1` and `t2`. These give the threshold value for the distance, to discriminate in the first and second step of the algorithm. These parameters are mandatory and so need to be provided. We need to point out that these thresholds do not depend on the dimension of the data, provided on the metrics involved to evaluate the cluster. However, the better they are tuned, the better the output will be. Unfortunately, when mining huge datasets, it is difficult to repeat the canopy algorithm many times to fine-tune the best threshold values, we will give you some suggestions for choosing the possible corrected values.

If it is possible, a first very rough estimation can be to set the two parameters equally. The `t2` parameter sets the number of the final cluster, so the smaller values of `t2` yield larger numbers of cluster and vice versa.

We invite you to try different values on the same dataset to evaluate the final number of clusters generated.

Using Canopy clustering from the Java code

The Mahout command-line option is nothing more than a low-level interface to the Java classes used, so it is not difficult to embed them into a Java code.

Getting ready

We need to set up the Maven project as usual, so fire up NetBeans, and create a new Maven project from the archetype using the following settings:

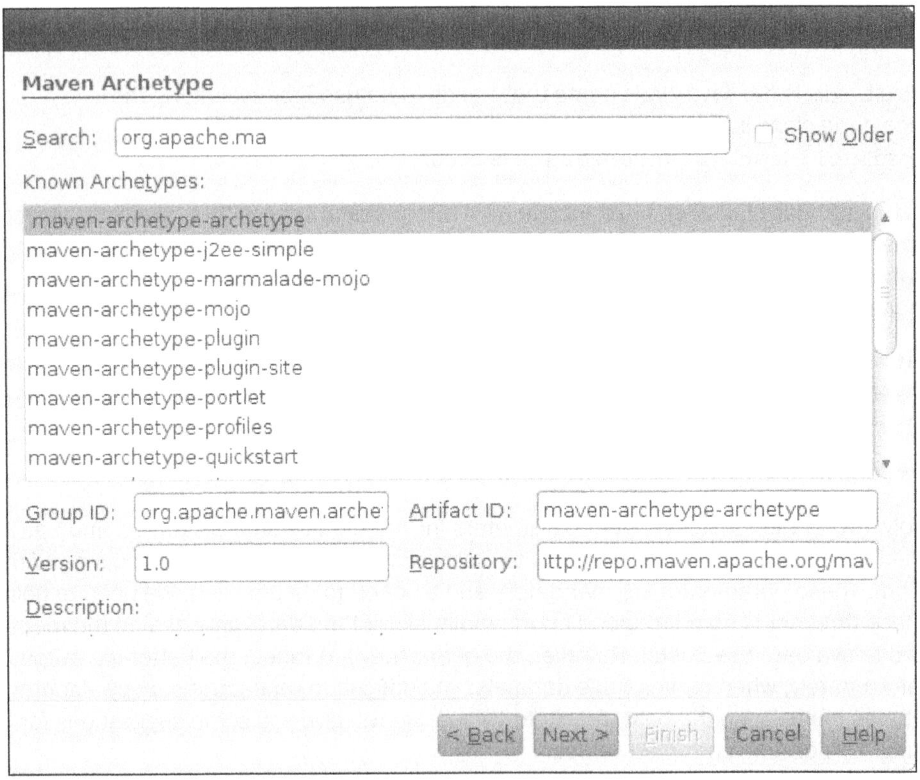

Then, choose the project name, as shown in the following screenshot:

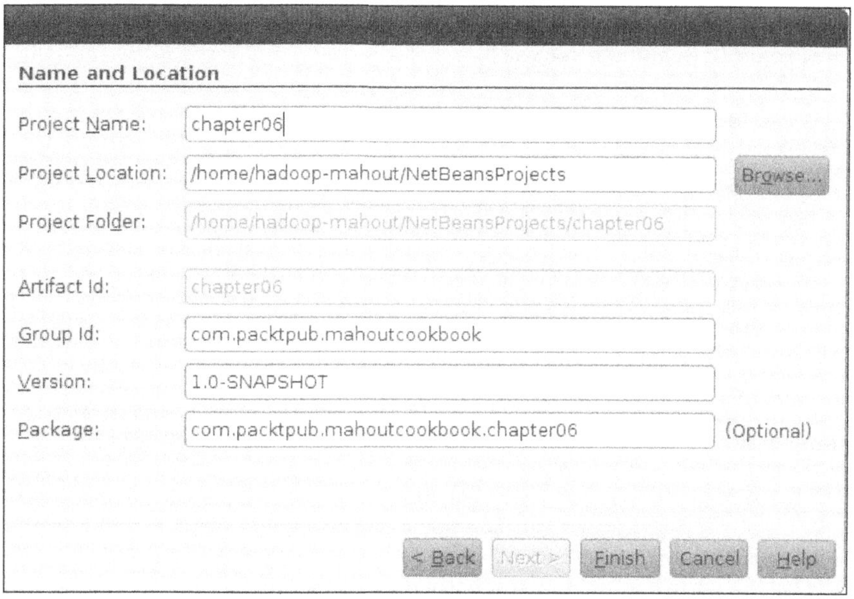

Finally, add the dependency to our local Mahout Maven project, as we did in the previous recipes.

How to do it...

Now, we are ready to code the example of the previous recipe in the Java language.

1. The code is pretty easy and only needs to be added to the main method of the `App.java` file created automatically by NetBeans. The code is as follows:

```
import org.apache.mahout.clustering.canopy.CanopyDriver;
import org.apache.hadoop.fs.Path;
import org.apache.mahout.common.distance.EuclideanDistanceMeasure;

public class App
{
    public static void main( String[] args ) throws Exception
    {
        //setting all parameters
        String inputFileName = new String("/mnt/new/canopy/
sequencefile/synthetic_control.seq");
        String outputFileName = new String("/mnt/new/canopy/
output/output.model");
```

```
        Path inputPath = new Path(inputFileName);
        Path outputPath = new Path(outputFileName);
        EuclideanDistanceMeasure measure = new
EuclideanDistanceMeasure();

        double t1;
        double t2;
        double clusterClassificationThreshold;

        t1 = 50;
        t2 = 80;
        clusterClassificationThreshold = 3;
        boolean runSequential = true;

        CanopyDriver.run(inputPath , outputPath,measure,t1,t2,runS
equential,clusterClassificationThreshold,runSequential);

    }
}
```

2. On running this program, the result will be as follows:

```
13/03/19 15:07:06 INFO mapred.JobClient:   File Input Format Counters
13/03/19 15:07:06 INFO mapred.JobClient:     Bytes Read=313318
13/03/19 15:07:06 INFO mapred.JobClient:   Map-Reduce Framework
13/03/19 15:07:06 INFO mapred.JobClient:     Reduce input groups=1
13/03/19 15:07:06 INFO mapred.JobClient:     Map output materialized bytes=
13/03/19 15:07:06 INFO mapred.JobClient:     Combine output records=0
13/03/19 15:07:07 INFO mapred.JobClient:     Map input records=600
13/03/19 15:07:07 INFO mapred.JobClient:     Reduce shuffle bytes=0
13/03/19 15:07:07 INFO mapred.JobClient:     Physical memory (bytes) snapsh
13/03/19 15:07:07 INFO mapred.JobClient:     Reduce output records=600
13/03/19 15:07:07 INFO mapred.JobClient:     Spilled Records=1200
13/03/19 15:07:07 INFO mapred.JobClient:     Map output bytes=303660
13/03/19 15:07:07 INFO mapred.JobClient:     CPU time spent (ms)=0
13/03/19 15:07:07 INFO mapred.JobClient:     Total committed heap usage (by
13/03/19 15:07:07 INFO mapred.JobClient:     Virtual memory (bytes) snapsho
13/03/19 15:07:07 INFO mapred.JobClient:     Combine input records=0
13/03/19 15:07:07 INFO mapred.JobClient:     Map output records=600
13/03/19 15:07:07 INFO mapred.JobClient:     SPLIT_RAW_BYTES=120
13/03/19 15:07:07 INFO mapred.JobClient:     Reduce input records=600
13/03/19 15:07:07 INFO driver.MahoutDriver: Program took 11420 ms (Minutes:
hadoop-mahout@hadoop-mahout-laptop:/mnt/new/canopy$
```

How it works...

Basically, all the clustering algorithms work the same way. The main invocation is done by the following line:

```
CanopyDriver.run(inputPath ,
  outputPath,measure,t1,t2,runSequential,clusterClassificationThresh
  old,runSequential);
```

In this case, we use the Canopy implementation of the interface cluster that always has a `run` method. The implementation in this case is done using the following parameters:

- `inputPath`
- `outputPath`
- `measure`
- `t1`
- `t2`
- `runSequential`
- `clusterClassificationThreshold`

They are the same parameters used from the command-line utility except for `runSequential`, which is a flag for forcing to use sequential or parallelized implementation of an algorithm.

You should have noticed, however, that both the input and the output paths are passed using the Hadoop path object; this implies that you cannot use the algorithm by directly using the normal filesystem. So, beware when using the Canopy analysis in a production environment.

Apart from the `t1` and `t2` values for the two-stage threshold, we point out that you need to pass a measure for evaluating the distance between the *n*-dimensional vector points.

In our case, we explicitly declare to use the standard Euclidean distance. But, as for the command line, it is possible to use other types of distances.

Mahout, by default, comes with the following distance' measures to evaluate the clusters ready to be used; we'll cover these in the next section.

Coding your own cluster distance evaluation

In this recipe we will implement our own `DistanceClass` for the Canopy algorithm, as we stated, apart from the threshold values.

Getting ready

We only need to add a new class to our Maven project. To do this, simply right-click on the project icon, choose **New Java Class**, and complete the form as follows:

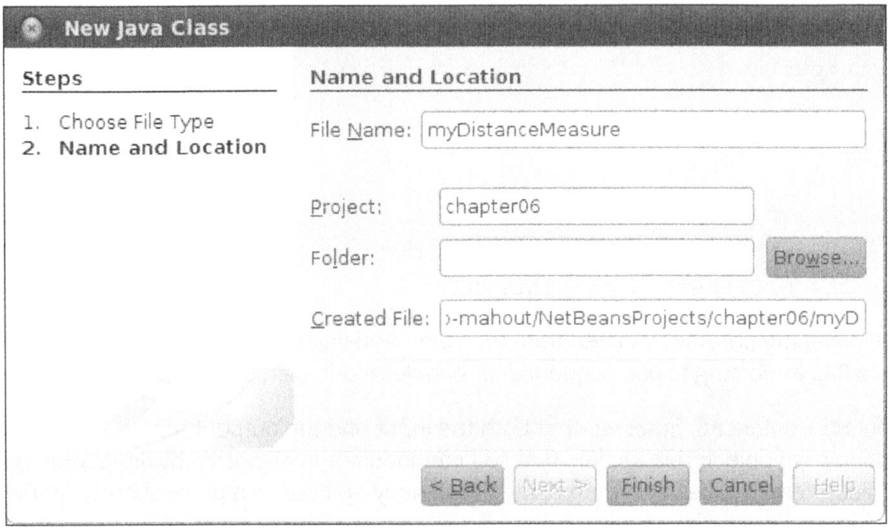

Then, click on **Finish**.

How to do it...

1. We only need to implement the `DistanceMeasure` interface contained in the `org.apache.mahout.common.distance` package. The code to do this is as follows:

```
import java.util.Collection;
import java.util.Collections;

import org.apache.hadoop.conf.Configuration;
import org.apache.mahout.common.distance.DistanceMeasure;
import org.apache.mahout.common.parameters.Parameter;
import org.apache.mahout.math.Vector;

public class myDistance implements DistanceMeasure {
```

```
  @Override
  public void configure(Configuration job) {
  // nothing to do
  }

  @Override
  public Collection<Parameter<?>> getParameters() {
    return Collections.emptyList();
  }

  @Override
  public void createParameters(String prefix, Configuration
jobConf) {
  // nothing to do
  }

  @Override
  public double distance(Vector v1, Vector v2) {
    return 3;
  }

  @Override
  public double distance(double centroidLengthSquare, Vector
centroid, Vector v) {
    return centroidLengthSquare - 3 * v.dot(centroid) +
v.getLengthSquared();
  }
}
```

2. Now, you can change the previous recipe's `App.java` file by replacing the following line:

```
EuclideanDistanceMeasure measure = new
  EuclideanDistanceMeasure();
```

Replace the preceding line with the following:

```
myDistance measure = new myDistance();
```

How it works...

As we stated in the previous section, we have implemented the `DistanceMeasure` interface. The methods to focus on are:

- `distance(Vector v1, Vector v2)`
- `distance(double centroidLengthSquare, Vector centroid, Vector v)`

In our case, we create a very simple implementation by always returning the number three in one case, and in the other by returning three times the square distance instead of the square distance.

This is only an example, but we challenge the willing reader to take a look at the implementation done with the classic Euclidean distance to understand how Mahout implements this mathematical concept.

See also

- *Chapter 5, Stock Market Forecasting with Mahout*

7
Spectral Clustering in Mahout

This chapter is devoted to illustrating the spectral clustering technique for a big dataset. The recipes that we will cover in this chapter are as follows:

- Using EigenCuts from the command line
- Using basic EigenCuts from Java code
- Creating a similarity matrix from raw data
- Using spectral clustering with image segmentation

Introduction

This chapter is continuation of *Chapter 6, Canopy Clustering in Mahout*. The argument still remains related to the same clustering techniques. We are interested in showing you some other ways we can build clusters from billions of pieces of information and many different observed behavioral patterns. We will consider in this recipe the spectral clustering algorithm. In this algorithm, we will use the spectral division of a graph to show how to build clusters. The spectral clustering technique has been demonstrated to be very powerful in terms of ease in which to implement and for the concepts involved.

Using EigenCuts from the command line

In graph theory, it is possible to associate a similarity matrix with every graph; that is, a set of nodes called **vertices** connected by links called edges.

Just to give an example, one could consider the following graph:

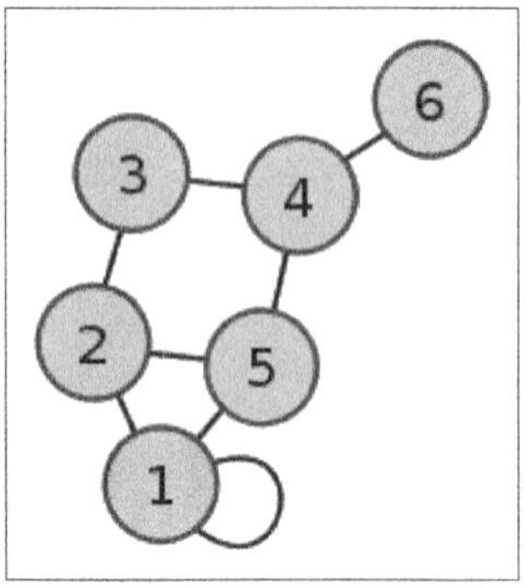

Consisting of vertices from 1 to 6 and 8 edges, one can easily associate this graph with the following matrix called the adjacency matrix:

$$\begin{pmatrix} 1 & 1 & 0 & 0 & 1 & 0 \\ 1 & 0 & 1 & 0 & 1 & 0 \\ 0 & 1 & 0 & 1 & 0 & 0 \\ 0 & 0 & 1 & 0 & 1 & 1 \\ 1 & 1 & 0 & 1 & 0 & 0 \\ 0 & 0 & 0 & 1 & 0 & 0 \end{pmatrix}$$

Here the entry for the row `i`, representing the node `i` and the column/node `j`, is `1` if the two nodes are connected or otherwise it is `0`.

Note that node `1` is self-connected, so its value is `1` while the other nodes are not self-connected, so their values are `0`.

Clustering analyses are particularly useful for analysis graphs, which are the natural representation for social networks and user connection. **Mahout** has a series of clustering algorithms to perform dimension reduction. Spectral clustering can be used with or without Mahout. In this recipe, we will illustrate how to use the EigenCuts algorithm from the command line.

Getting ready

Considering the fact that spectral clustering works with matrices, we need to create one from scratch. We also need to transform this matrix into a CSV file which is suitable to be read by the command-line input. So before proceeding, let us set up our working environment.

To do this, let us first create the input and output folders. So open up a command-line terminal and type in the following command:

```
export WORK_DIR=/mnt/spectral
mkdir $WOKR_DIR/input
mkdir $WOKR_DIR/output
```

This will create the folder with the usual structure that we used in the previous recipes. Now we need to create a similarity matrix to place in the `$WORK_DIR/input` folder that will be analyzed by the Mahout EigenCuts algorithm. We will code the example in Java to help you in case of future integrations.

In the terminal console, we will type in the following Maven command:

```
mvn archetype:create -DarchetypeGroupId=org.apache.maven.archetypes
-DgroupId=com.packtpub.mahoutcookbook -DartifactId=chapter07
```

This will create the usual `Maven` folder project.

Now fire up NetBeans and add a new class into the newly created chapter folder. This can be done by using the following action command:

Right-click on the **project** icon and choose **New Java class** and enter the data as shown in the following screenshot:

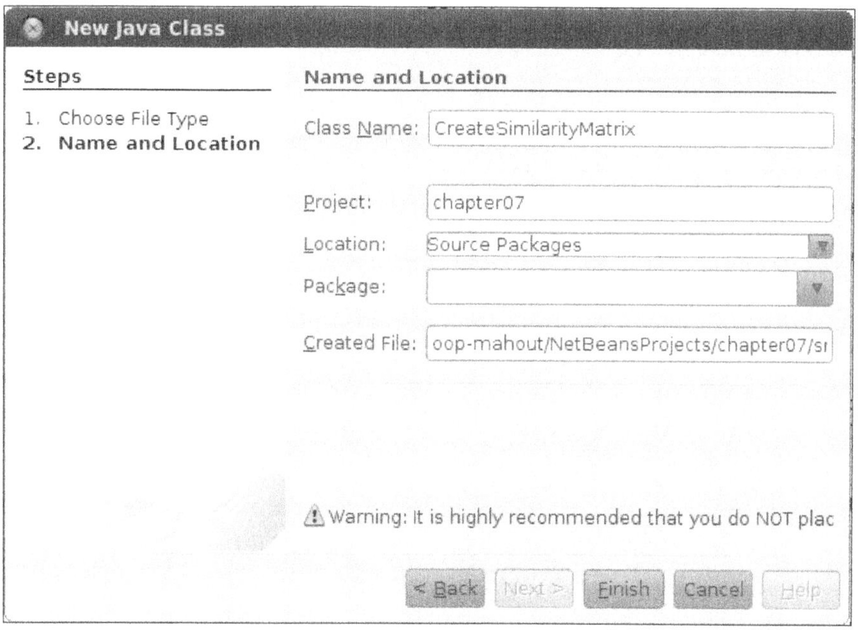

Once we have created the new class, `CreateSimilarityMatrix`, let us move to the code.

The code for the class is pretty easy. The need is basically to create a CSV file that will be used as input. The actions required are as follows:

- Populate a square matrix with random numbers ranging from 0 to 1
- Save the matrix into a CSV file

The code can be seen as follows:

```
double[][] smatrix = new double[1000][1000];
String filePath = new String("/mnt/spectral/input/matrix.csv");
//populating the matrix by rows and columns
for (int i=0; i < 1000; i++)
{
  for (int j=0; j < 1000; j++)
  {
    smatrix[i][j] = Math.random();
  }

}
//saving as a csv
FileWriter fw = new FileWriter(filePath);

for (int i=0; i < 1000; i++)
{
  for (int j=0; j < 1000; j++)
  {

    fw.write( Integer.toString(i) + "," + Integer.toString(j) + "," +
Double.toString(smatrix[i][j])  );
  }
   fw.flush();
}
fw.close();
```

By pressing *F6*, the Java class should create a file called `matrix.csv` in the `$WORK_DIR/output` folder. If we open it up, we should see the following format:

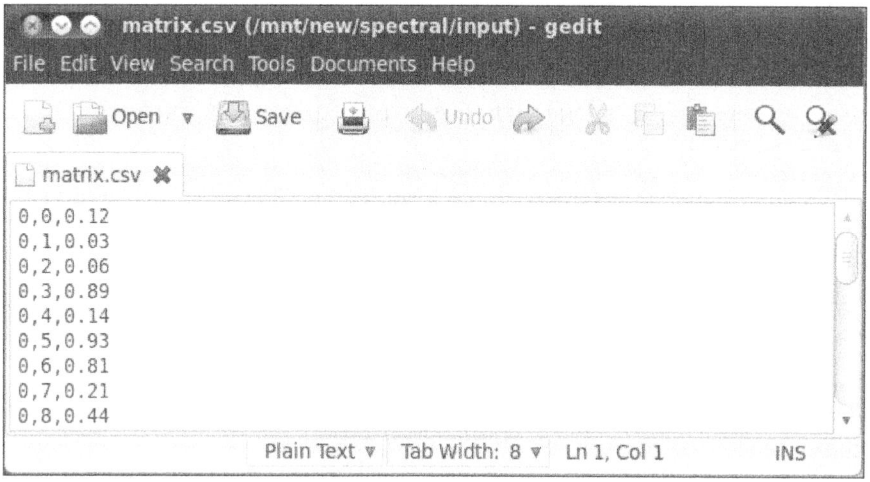

Before proceeding further, some clarifications are due.

As you may have noticed, the line format for the CSV file to be used by the spectral algorithm is as follows:

```
node_i, node_j, similarity value
```

Here, `node_i` is the row of the similarity matrix starting from zero. The `node_j` column is the column of the matrix starting from zero. The final value is the value of the `i`, `j` entry.

This format is mandatory. In our case, we tested a matrix representing a graph of 1000 vertices, so the expected CSV file should have 1,000,000 = (1000 x 1000) lines.

As you can see, when dealing with graphs, the matrix to be manipulated grows with the square of the number of the vertices.

As a last word, we create a matrix using random values, but in real applications, the creation of the similarity matrix is a very important task that would need some complex data transformation.

How to do it...

Now we are ready for the interesting part. Basically, now that we have our input file, we simply need to launch the correct command line. So open up a terminal window and type in the following command:

```
bin/mahout eigencuts -i $WOKR_DIR/input/matrix.csv -o $WORK_DIR/output/
output -b 2 -d 1000
```

The result will be the cluster description as we have seen in *Chapter 6, Canopy Clustering in Mahout*.

Using EigenCuts from Java code

Now that we have had some advice on how to use the command-line interface for EigenCuts, it is now time to move on to the Java code. Basically, we will recode the same example in a 100 percent Java implementation.

Getting ready

We have just created the `Maven` project file, so the only thing to do is to create the new class. So fire up NetBeans, and on the **project** icon, perform the following steps:

1. Right-click on **New** | **Java Class**.
2. Complete the form as shown in the following screenshot:

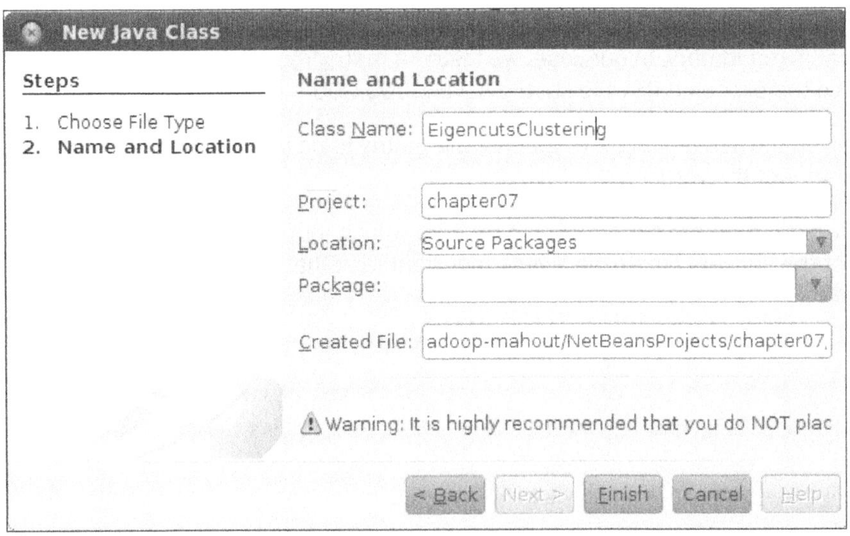

3. Click on **Finish**.

Then you need to refer to the libraries of the Mahout framework as dependencies. To do this, you need to do the following actions on the **dependencies** icon:

1. Right-click on **Add dependency**.
2. Complete the form as shown in the following screenshot:

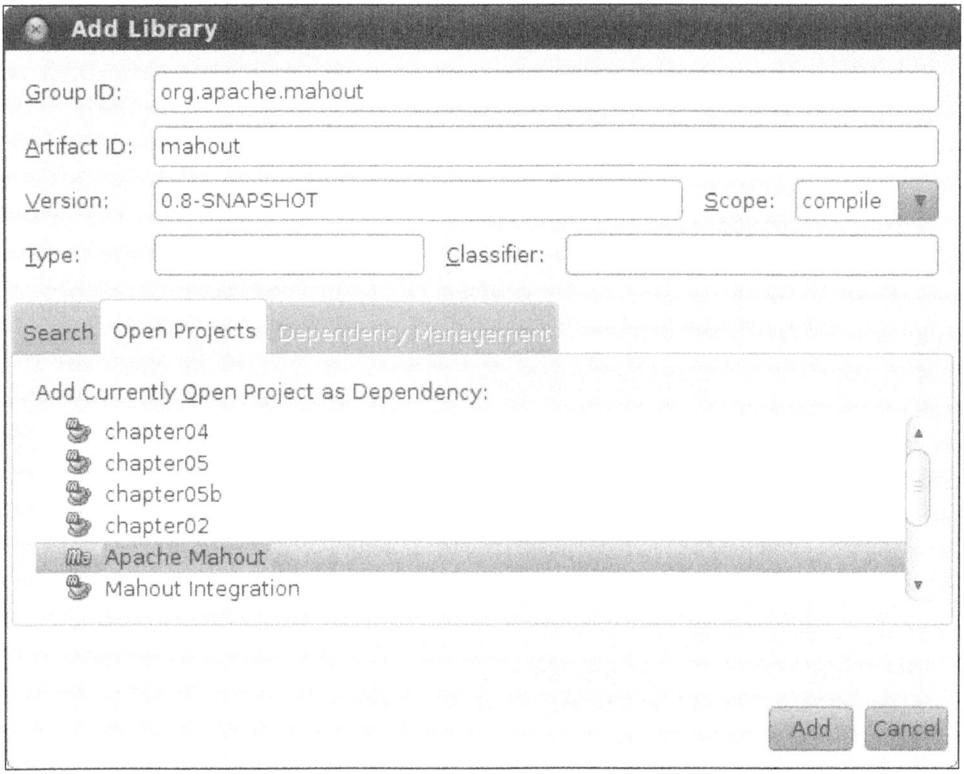

3. Click on **Add**.

We are now ready to insert some code in the `main` method.

How to do it...

First of all, we need to create the set of parameters to be used. So, inside the `main` method of the `EigencutsClustering` class, insert the following code for the parameter to be used:

```
String inputSimilarityMatrixFilePath;
String  outputFilePath;
inputSimilarityMatrixFilePath = "/mnt/new/spectral/input/matrix.csv";
outputFilePath = "/mnt/new/spectral/outputn/output";
```

```
Path input = new Path(inputSimilarityMatrixFilePath);
Path output = new Path(outputFilePath);
```

Then we start with calculations. The first one is the following code:

```
DistributedRowMatrix A = AffinityMatrixInputJob.runJob(input,
outputCalc, dimensions);
Vector D = MatrixDiagonalizeJob.runJob(A.getRowPath(), dimensions);
long numCuts;
do {
  // first three steps are the same as spectral k-means:
  // 1) calculate D from A
  // 2) calculate L = D^-0.5 * A * D^-0.5
  // 3) calculate eigenvectors of L
  DistributedRowMatrix L =
    VectorMatrixMultiplicationJob.runJob(A.getRowPath(), D,
      new Path(outputCalc, "laplacian-" + (System.nanoTime() &
0xFF)));
  L.setConf(new Configuration(conf));
  // eigendecomposition (step 3)
  int overshoot = (int) ((double) eigenrank * OVERSHOOT_MULTIPLIER);
  LanczosState state = new LanczosState(L, eigenrank,
    DistributedLanczosSolver.getInitialVector(L));
  DistributedRowMatrix U = performEigenDecomposition(conf, L, state,
eigenrank, overshoot, outputCalc);
  U.setConf(new Configuration(conf));
  List<Double> eigenValues = Lists.newArrayList();
  for (int i = 0; i < eigenrank; i++) {
  eigenValues.set(i, state.getSingularValue(i));
  }
  // here's where things get interesting: steps 4, 5, and 6 are unique
  // to this algorithm, and depending on the final output, steps 1-3
  // may be repeated as well
  // helper method, since apparently List and Vector objects don't
play nicely
  Vector evs = listToVector(eigenValues);
  // calculate sensitivities (step 4 and step 5)
  Path sensitivities = new Path(outputCalc, "sensitivities-" +
(System.nanoTime() & 0xFF));
  EigencutsSensitivityJob.runJob(evs, D, U.getRowPath(), halflife,
tau, median(D), epsilon, sensitivities);
  // perform the cuts (step 6)
  input = new Path(outputTmp, "nextAff-" + (System.nanoTime() &
0xFF));
```

```
    numCuts = EigencutsAffinityCutsJob.runjob(A.getRowPath(),
  sensitivities, input, conf);
    // how many cuts were made?
    if (numCuts > 0) {
    // recalculate A
    A = new DistributedRowMatrix(input,
                  new Path(outputTmp,
   Long.toString(System.nanoTime())), dimensions, dimensions);
     A.setConf(new Configuration());
    }
  } while (numCuts > 0);
```

Once launched, you should see the correct completion of the task with the output creation.

How it works...

Using our code, we are now able to understand how the EigenCuts algorithm works.

The EigenCuts algorithm belongs to the big family of unsupervised learning algorithms. As we have discussed before, Eigenvalues work with graphical representations where every vertex is an *n*-dimensional data point. The edges in this case represent the strength of the relations between the nodes. In this case, the graph is undirected, meaning that the relation between the nodes `x` and `y` is the same as between the nodes `y` and `x`.

To some readers familiar with the graph theory, we point out that in mathematical terms for a generic graph, the matrix that we called the affinity of similarity matrix has the same meaning as the adjacency matrix, so we will use these terms synonymously.

The first step is to create a new matrix from the initial one. The trace matrix, that is, the diagonal matrix where all the elements are 0 except the ones on the diagonal, is calculated with the following formula:

$$d_{jj} = \sum_{i-1}^{n} A_{ij}$$

The DistributedRowMatrix (called *M*) is the matrix calculated with the following formula:

$$M = A^{-1}D$$

Here, A^{-1} is the inverse matrix of *A*. With these two matrices now, it is possible to create the Laplacian matrix *L* that is given by the following definition:

$$L = \frac{1}{\sqrt{D}} A \sqrt{D}$$

As a final step, we calculate the Eigenvectors of *L*. By definition, an Eigenvector *X* is a vector for the Laplacian matrix *L* and its corresponding Eigenvalue λ is a real value, shown as follows:

$$LX = \lambda X$$

As a final step from the original matrix *A*, the edges, that is, the entries into the matrix *A*, are removed if they are above the sensitivity or above a threshold.

Then we repeat the step for the new matrix *A*. The whole loop is iterated until no more deletions have to be done.

So to resume, as we can see, the EigenCuts algorithm performs this way:

1. Calculate *D* from *A*.
2. Calculate *L = D^-0.5 * A * D^-0.5*.
3. Calculate the Eigenvectors of *L*.
4. Calculate sensitivities.
5. Perform the cuts.

Steps 2 to 5 are performed iteratively until a threshold condition is reached. What we have done here is only implement the EigenCuts algorithm as described in its original paper; that is, the Mahout implementation. However, as you can see, we did not have any way of seeing the output in this way except by creating the new iterated matrix *A*.

Creating a similarity matrix from raw data

The main problem before using the EigenCuts algorithm is to create the similarity matrix from raw data. This can be a little bit difficult when dealing with the *n*-dimensional data point.

In this recipe, we will detail how to obtain a similarity matrix based on raw data.

Getting ready

Before proceeding, we need to first prepare our environment. We will create a single solution with Java to be able to generate the affinity initial matrix in one single solution.

The two steps involved are as follows:

- Create the folder environment
- Download the dataset

So, open up a terminal console and type in the following set of commands:

```
export WORK_DIR=/mnt/cancer
mkdir $WOKR_DIR/input
mkdir $WOKR_DIR/output
cd $WOKR_DIR/input
wget http://archive.ics.uci.edu/ml/machine-learning-databases/breast-
cancer-wisconsin/wdbc.data
```

This will download a file called `wdbc.data` into the `/mnt/cancer/input` folder. This is one of the most used datasets in a data mining task and it is freely available from the link of the machine learning repository available at the URL `http://archive.ics.uci.edu/ml/datasets/Breast+Cancer`.

For a whole description of the dataset, you could take a look at the rich website of the machine learning repository maintained at the URL `http://archive.ics.uci.edu/ml/`.

The dataset is a CSV file that contains 569 rows (every row is a medical observation on one patient) and every observation contains the following attributes:

- ID number
- Diagnosis (M = malignant, B = benign)
- Ten real-valued features are computed for each cell nucleus:
  - Radius (mean of distances from center to points on the perimeter)
  - Texture (standard deviation of gray-scale values)
  - Perimeter
  - Area
  - Smoothness (local variation in radius lengths)
  - Compactness (*perimeter^2 / area - 1.0*)
  - Concavity (severity of concave portions of the contour)
  - Concave points (number of concave portions of the contour)
  - Symmetry
  - Fractal dimension

The features are computed from a digitized image of a fine needle aspirate (FNA) of a breast mass. They describe the characteristics of the cell nuclei present in the image.

So we have a 32-dimensional dataset that needs to be transformed into a 569 x 569 square affinity matrix.

How to do it...

Now based on our `input` folder, we will create a class that outputs the similarity matrix. The steps involved in creating and coding the class are as follows:

- Create the class
- Read the original file to create a new CSV file, all filled with numeric values
- Code the affinity matrix
- Save the affinity matrix into a sequence file

The steps involved are as follows:

1. You can start creating the environment by firing up NetBeans by right-clicking on the **project** folder and adding a new Java class called `CreateSimilarityMatrix`. The screen should look as follows:

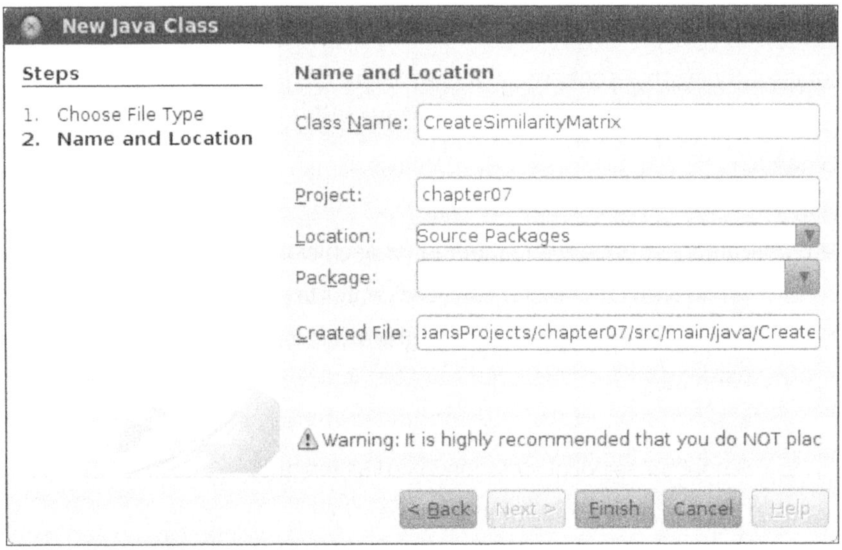

2. Now enter the following properties for the class:

```
String inputcsvFile = "/mnt/cancer/wdbc.data";
String outputcsvFile = "/mnt/cancer/cancernumerical.csv";
BufferedReader br = null;
BufferedWriter wr = null;
String line = "";
String cvsSplitBy = ",";
```

3. Now enter the `main` method and add the following code:

```
ETL2Numeric();
createMatrix();
SaveSimilarityMatrix();
```

4. Next, we only need to write the following code into every method that we add:

```
private void ETL2Numeric() {
  try {
    br = new BufferedReader(new FileReader(inputcsvFile));
    wr = new BufferedWriter(new FileWriter(outputcsvFile));
    while ((line = br.readLine()) != null) {
      String[] observation = line.split(cvsSplitBy);
      String[] observation2write = observation;
      observation2write[1] = "m".equals(observation[1].
toLowerCase()) ? "1": "0";
      wr.write(line + "\r\n");
    }
  } catch (Exception e) {
    e.printStackTrace();
  } finally {
    if (br != null) {
      try {
        br.close();
      } catch (IOException e) {
        e.printStackTrace();
      }
    }
  }
  System.out.println("Done");
}
And
private void createMatrix() {
  try {
    br = new BufferedReader(new FileReader(inputcsvFile));
    int k = 0;
    while ((line = br.readLine()) != null) {
      String[] observation = line.split(cvsSplitBy);
      for (int j= 0; j < observation.length; j++)
      {
        matrix[k][j] =
 Double.parseDouble(observation[j]);
      }
      k++;
    }
```

```
        for (int i = 0; i < matrix.length; i++)
        {
          double d = 0;
          int start  = i+1;
          for (int j = i+1; j < matrix.length-1; j++)
          {
            d = MeanErrorDistance(matrix[i],matrix[j]);
          }
          if (d < 0.1)
          {
            AffinityMatrix[i][start] = d;
            AffinityMatrix[start][i] = d;
          }
        }

      } catch (Exception e) {
        e.printStackTrace();
      } finally {
        if (br != null) {
          try {
          br.close();
          } catch (IOException e) {
            e.printStackTrace();
          }
          }
      }
      System.out.println("Done");
    }
```

5. At the end of the code, we add the following code in the `SaveSimilarityMatrix` method:

```
private void SaveSimilarityMatrix() throws IOException {
  Path path = new Path("/mnt/cancer/output/cancersequenced");
  org.apache.hadoop.fs.RawLocalFileSystem fs = new org.apache.
hadoop.fs.RawLocalFileSystem();
  SequenceFile.Writer writer = new SequenceFile.Writer(fs, conf,
path, IntWritable.class, DoubleWritable.class);
  for (int i = 0; i < AffinityMatrix.length;i++)
    for (int j = 0; j < AffinityMatrix[i].length;j++)
    writer.append( new IntWritable(i), new
DoubleWritable(AffinityMatrix[i][j]));
  System.out.println("Done");
}
```

How it works...

As we mentioned before, we need to transform every node of our graph that is an observation into a vertex and more importantly, to create a way to represent the distance between two nodes (observation).

This is done in three steps:

1. Transform every non-numerical attribute into a numerical one.
2. Define a distance between two observations and activate a threshold value to define how near the two observations are.
3. Save the matrix created in a sequence file.

So in our algorithm, the first part is pretty easy being that the only non-numerical attribute is `m/b` represented on the first CSV column whenever the observation confirms a malignant or benign tumor mass in the breast. So the first loop roughly transforms the original CSV file into a new one where all the observations are made of a numerical attribute. So for example, the first observation that consists of a single row like the following:

```
842302,M,17.99,10.38,122.8,1001,0.1184,0.2776,0.3001,0.1471,…
```

The preceding row is transformed into the following:

```
842302,1,17.99,10.38,122.8,1001,0.1184,0.2776,0.3001,0.1471,..
```

Next, there is the most interesting one. We need to define what the weight of the edge that connects two nodes is, that is, two observations.

To do this, we adopt a rough yet very efficient approach. Apart from the `m/b` tag, we compute the Euclidean distance between the two remaining lists of 30 values. We will warn you that this distance is the worst one to be used but we have shown it only to allow you to understand what is going on behind the scenes.

So for example, the first two new rows are:

```
842302,1,17.99,10.38,122.8,1001,0.1184,0.2776,0.3001,0.1471,…
842517,1,20.57,17.77,132.9,1326,0.08474,0.07864,0.0869
```

The Euclidean distance that we remember is defined as follows:

$$d(x,y)=\sqrt{(x_1-y_1)^2+(x_2-y_2)^2+\ldots+(x_n-y_n)^2}$$

So in our case, the distance for the first two observations is:

$$d(x,y)=\sqrt{(1-1)^2+(17.99-20.57)^2+\ldots}$$

The method devoted to this is the `MeanErrorDistance` method. It takes two arrays of double values representing the observations and returns the distance:

```
private double MeanErrorDistance(double[] d, double[] d0) {
    double med = 0;
    double sum = 0;
    for (int i = 1; i < d.length; i++)
    {
        sum += (d[i]-d0[i])* (d[i]-d0[i]);
    }
    med = Math.sqrt(sum);
    return med;
}
```

As you may have noticed, we have two assumptions on the method:

- The first one is that the computation starts from index 1, ignoring the first column of the observation, that is, recordID.
- The second one is that the mean error distance is zero if we have the array `d` equal to `d0`, so the two observations have the same outcome.

Another important thing to point out is that as the similarity matrix is symmetrical, so is the entry:

$$A_{ij} = A_{ji}$$

In the code, every time we found that we needed to enter the non-zero distance, we added it in two different indexes because the matrix is symmetric:

```
AffinityMatrix[i][start] = d;
AffinityMatrix[start][i] = d;
```

Note that the loop does not spam the whole set every time because the `AffinityMatrix` object is a symmetric matrix. So for example, if we consider the two first observations, we give value to the entry row 1 and column 2 as well as row 2 and column 1 of the `AffinityMatrix` object.

At the end, we need to save our result to a sequence file so that our affinity matrix could be used by another application (in our case, a slight change of the previous recipe).

Considering that we have a whole matrix Java object called `AffinityMatrix`, we can save the first entry with the index of the Java array matrix to a sequence file by assigning and then the value of the entry as done by the piece of code.

```
private void SaveSimilarityMatrix() throws IOException {
  Path path = new Path("/mnt/cancer/output/cancersequenced");
```

```
  org.apache.hadoop.fs.RawLocalFileSystem fs = new org.apache.hadoop.
fs.RawLocalFileSystem();
  SequenceFile.Writer writer = new SequenceFile.Writer(fs, conf, path,
IntWritable.class, DoubleWritable.class);
  for (int i = 0; i < AffinityMatrix.length;i++)
    for (int j = 0; j < AffinityMatrix[i].length;j++)
    writer.append( new IntWritable(i), new
DoubleWritable(AffinityMatrix[i][j]));
  System.out.println("Done");
}
```

From the point of the EigenCuts algorithm, it would be better to save the affinity matrix using the `DistributedRowMatrix` method, that is, the standard method used by the Mahout implementation of the algorithm. Unfortunately, the constructor of the `DistributedRowMatrix` method uses a path to a sequence file:

```
public DistributedRowMatrix(Path inputPath, Path outputTmpPath, int
numRows, int numCols, boolean keepTempFiles)
```

So from our point of view, it is better to directly create a sequence file that can be used as the input.

Using spectral clustering with image segmentation

In this recipe, we propose a well-known example of using spectral clustering techniques in image segmentation. The problem can be described by stating that each image can have subjects that can be arranged in clusters. A practical application can be given in a large photo to identify the group of subjects that can be clustered together.

So, we will start from a picture and transform it into a similarity matrix that is the input for the EigenCuts algorithm.

The output will be the matrix that can be used to determinate the clusters. The problem could look like a difficult one. However, these techniques have been applied fruitfully in detecting breast cancer or ovarian cancer using a mammogram image taken using SAR techniques. For the willing reader, take a look at this link to a medical oriented paper that will describe these techniques in a real-world scenario: (`http://www.ncbi.nlm.nih.gov/pubmed/17015928`).

Getting ready

In this recipe, we are not interested in the algorithm that we described in the previous recipes, but we are interested in the way we create a similarity matrix from an image. The advantage of grouping images is clear when we need to classify images in a cluster.

We also need to point out that medical images are created using a high-resolution vector format. Also, in most of the cases, even though the file format that is used to capture this image is a propriety one like the DICOM format, it is not so easy to read the images. As an example, we have a DICOM image downloaded from the USA National Biomedical Image Archive, as shown in the following screenshot:

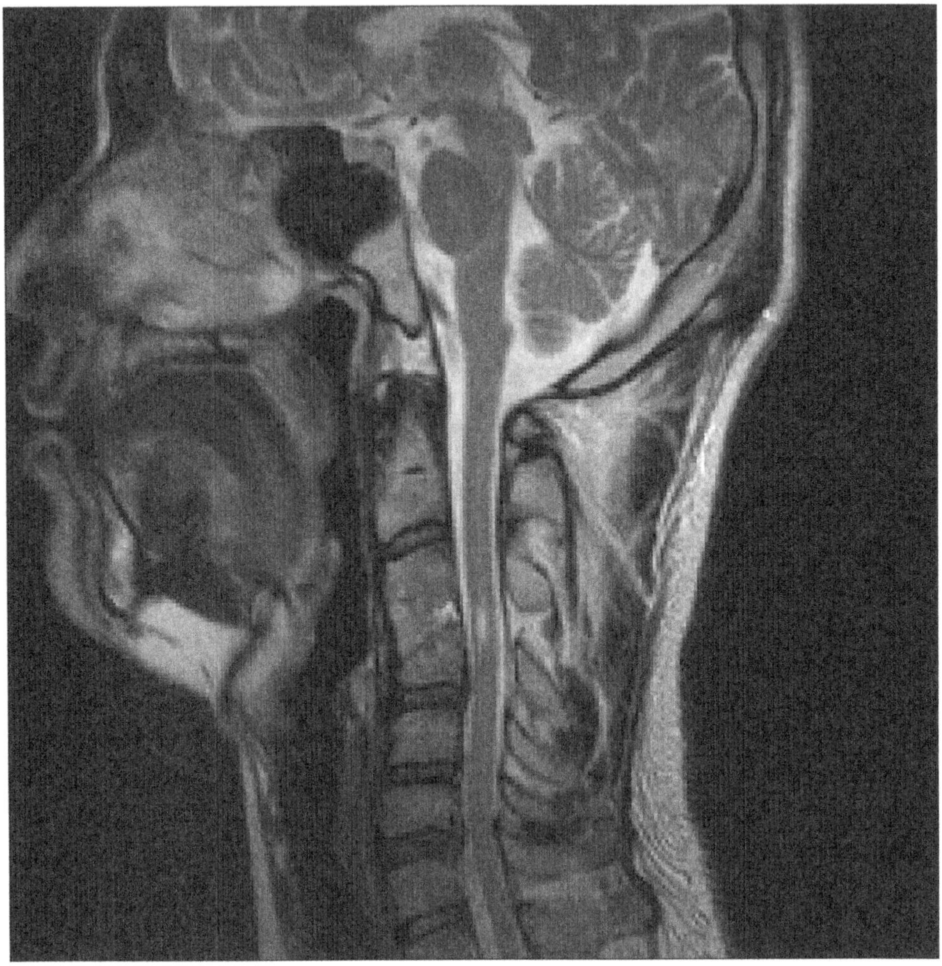

Parsing a DICOM file to create an affinity matrix is out of the scope of this recipe. So, we will use an image in PNG format. Do not forget that if you are thinking of using the same techniques for a real production environment, it is better to use a DICOM to BMP converter, because they do not lose important information during the conversion and they can be called using many parameters to optimize the output format.

To get started, as usual we create our working environment by typing the following sequence of commands in a terminal console:

```
export WORK_DIR=/mnt/tac
mkdir $WORK_DIR
cd $WORK_DIR
```

Now it is time to download our test image by giving the following command:

```
wget  http://www.intechopen.com/source/html/19695/media/image2.png
```

You should now have an image downloaded into the `$WORK_DIR` folder.

Now create a Java class called `ImageSegmentation` as we did in the previous recipes.

How to do it...

Now that we have created the class called `ImageSegmentation` in the *Getting ready* section, we only need to add three methods that will perform the following steps:

- Converting the image into a similarity matrix
- Computing the EigenCuts algorithm
- Converting the final matrix into an image

For every step, we need to code the corresponding method inside the `main` class. To do this, we will code every preceding step into the following methods:

```
ConvertImageIntoSimilarityMatrix
ComputingEigencuts
ConvertingSimilarityMatrixToImage
```

The steps involved are as follows:

1. Let us start with the `ConvertImageIntoMatrix` method, whose code is pretty easy:

```
public static void ConvertImageIntoSimilarityMatrix()
{
  File inputFile = new File("/mnt/tac/image2.png");
  BufferedImage bufferedImage = ImageIO.read(inputFile);
  int w = bufferedImage.getWidth();
  int h = bufferedImage.getHeight(null);
  double[][] A = new double[w][h];
  for (int i = 0; i <w; i++)
  {
    for (int j=0; j < h ; j++)
    {
```

```
            A[i][j] = A[j][i] = org.apache.mahout.common.distance.
ManhattanDistanceMeasure.distance(, bufferedImage.getRGB(j,i));
        }
      }
    }
```

2. Then we need to perform the inverse operation and output the image:

```
public static void ConvertSimilarityMatrixToImage(string
inputFile))
{
  File inputFile = new File("/mnt/tac/image-out.png");
  BufferedImage bufferedImage = ImageIO.write(outputFile);
  for (int i = 0; i <w; i++)
  {
    for (int j=0; j < h ; j++)
    {
bufferedImage.setRGB(j,i));
    }
  }
}
```

3. Once the algorithm ends up in the `$WORK_DIR` folder, there should be an additional image like the following screenshot:

How it works

The difficult part of this algorithm is that we need to transform every pixel of one single image into an *n*-dimensional-vector array composed by numbers.

An image pixel consists of x and y coordinates that correspond to the position of the pixels, and the color is represented by a 4-byte (32 bits) integer:

```
00000000 00000000 00000000 11111111
```

Here, the first group of bytes represents: alpha, red, green, and blue respectively. So from this data, we can calculate the mean for every entry. So every pixel can be associated to a numerical array. Now, to evaluate the distance between two pixels, we only need to use the distance between two numerical arrays associated with two different pixels. The piece of code devoted to this is the following:

```
int[][] A = new int[w][h];
for (int i = 0; i <w; i++)
{
  for (int j=0; j < h ; j++)
  {
    A[i][j] = A[j][i] = org.apache.mahout.common.distance.
ManhattanDistanceMeasure.distance(bufferedImage.getRGB(i,j),
bufferedImage.getRGB(j,i));
  }
}
```

As we can see, we basically assume the Manhattan distance as the main distance for evaluating how far two pixels are from each other. As we are evaluating the distance between two arrays of integer numbers, it is not so difficult to test this by using different distance measures.

Once we have done our EigenCuts analysis, we can move on to transforming the final matrix into an image. The method basically uses the `ImageBuffered` object to output the final image using its `setRGB` method.

8
K-means Clustering

Following up from the previous chapter's recipes, we will consider a way to use the K-means clustering algorithm.

The recipes that we will cook in this chapter are:

- Using K-mean clustering from Java code
- Clustering traffic accidents using K-means
- K-means clustering using MapReduce
- Using K-means clustering from the command line

Introduction

The K-means algorithm is one of the oldest and well-established algorithms for clustering purposes. The first version is dated 1957, but the modern implementation of it has been in place since 1982. The algorithm has proved to be very efficient for classification purposes. The fields of application for the K-means algorithm are medicine, agriculture, and finance. Mahout's implementation also benefits from the possibility offered by the MapReduce framework, so users can use the algorithm with a very large dataset. However, the algorithm requires a prior input parameter such as the number of clusters, and a wrong initial choice of this parameter can greatly affect the performance of the algorithm in terms of classification and running time. It is also possible to evaluate some of the initial parameters using the Canopy clustering procedure. We will not see these sophisticated methods, but we will give the reader some hints on the initial parameters.

Using K-means clustering from Java code

In this fast example, we will code a full example using dummy data to see how K-means clustering works.

Getting started

Basically, we only need to create the Maven project for this chapter, add the class, and then code it. Considering that we are not reading data, we do not need to download anything.

How to do it...

1. Let us fire up a console and type in the following command:

```
mvn archetype:create -DarchetypeGroupId=org.apache.
maven.archetypes -DgroupId=com.packtpub.mahoutcookbook
-DartifactId=chapter08
```

2. Now, remove the Java class created by default (`App.java`) by right-clicking on the class name of the folder and choosing **Delete** from the menu items.
3. Now add, as usual, a new class called `DummyKmeans`, as we have seen, in the recipes in *Chapter 7, Spectral Clustering in Mahout*. At the end, add the dependencies to the Mahout source code we downloaded. You should arrive at a NetBeans project structure as follows:

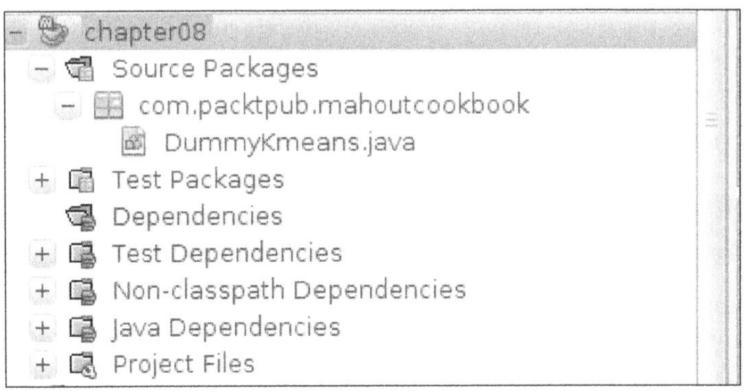

4. Now add the following code inside the `main` method of the `DummyKmeans` class:

```
//generate sample dummy vectors
generateSamples(sampleData, 400, 1, 1, 3);
generateSamples(sampleData, 300, 1, 0, 0.5);
generateSamples(sampleData, 300, 0, 2, 0.1);

//create the first cluster vectors
List<Vector> randomPoints = RandomSeedGenerator.
chooseRandomPoints(points, k);
List<Cluster> clusters = new ArrayList<Cluster>();

// associate the cluster with the random point
int clusterId = 0;
```

```
for (Vector v : randomPoints) {
  clusters.add(new Cluster(v, clusterId++));
}
// execute the kmeans cluster
List<List<Cluster>> finalClusters = KMeansClusterer.
clusterPoints(points, clusters, new EuclideanDistanceMeasure(), 3,
0.01);

// display final cluster center
for(Cluster cluster : finalClusters.get(finalClusters.size() - 1))
{
  System.out.println("Cluster id: " + cluster.getId() + " center:
"+ cluster.getCenter().asFormatString());
}
```

5. By running the class file, you should get the following output:

```
Output - chapter08 (run)
1.0: [23.227, 1.010, 16.983] belongs to cluster 2
1.0: [19.013, 15.370, 20.551] belongs to cluster 1
1.0: [8.561, 31.876, 26.411] belongs to cluster 1
1.0: [13.572, 23.204, 15.323] belongs to cluster 1
1.0: [37.289, 17.842, 31.788] belongs to cluster 4
1.0: [12.043, 8.260, 39.585] belongs to cluster 4
1.0: [22.055, 14.583, 18.032] belongs to cluster 2
1.0: [8.353, 8.074, 15.010] belongs to cluster 1
1.0: [35.512, 6.651, 22.281] belongs to cluster 2
1.0: [36.362, 26.580, 12.805] belongs to cluster 0
1.0: [4.491, 11.518, 8.797] belongs to cluster 1
1.0: [18.919, 10.876, 1.584] belongs to cluster 2
1.0: [23.727, 25.317, 20.823] belongs to cluster 3
1.0: [28.573, 39.552, 28.693] belongs to cluster 3
1.0: [20.700, 16.097, 5.924] belongs to cluster 2
1.0: [33.271, 30.925, 27.009] belongs to cluster 3
1.0: [18.489, 2.574, 36.413] belongs to cluster 4
BUILD SUCCESSFUL (total time: 1 minute 17 seconds)
```

How it works...

Basically, the K-means algorithm works in the following three steps:

1. The algorithm starts with some n-dimensional vectors representing points in *n*-dimensional space.
2. As input, we also have a set of *k* vectors representing the centroids of the clusters.
3. With a loop, the cluster vectors are moved until a minimum threshold or a number of iterations have been done.

The initial centroids can be chosen from some initial points or randomly. The power of the K-means algorithm is due to the fact that even if we choose random initial centroids, we have an output. Using a 10,000 foot view of the algorithm, we perform the following steps:

1. Input a number of centroids.
2. Assign all the data points to one of these centroids.
3. The centroids are recalculated.

Steps 2 and 3 are repeated until a good estimation is reached (no more improvement is possible) or a number of iterations have been reached.

In this case, a picture is worth a 1,000 words as is the following one:

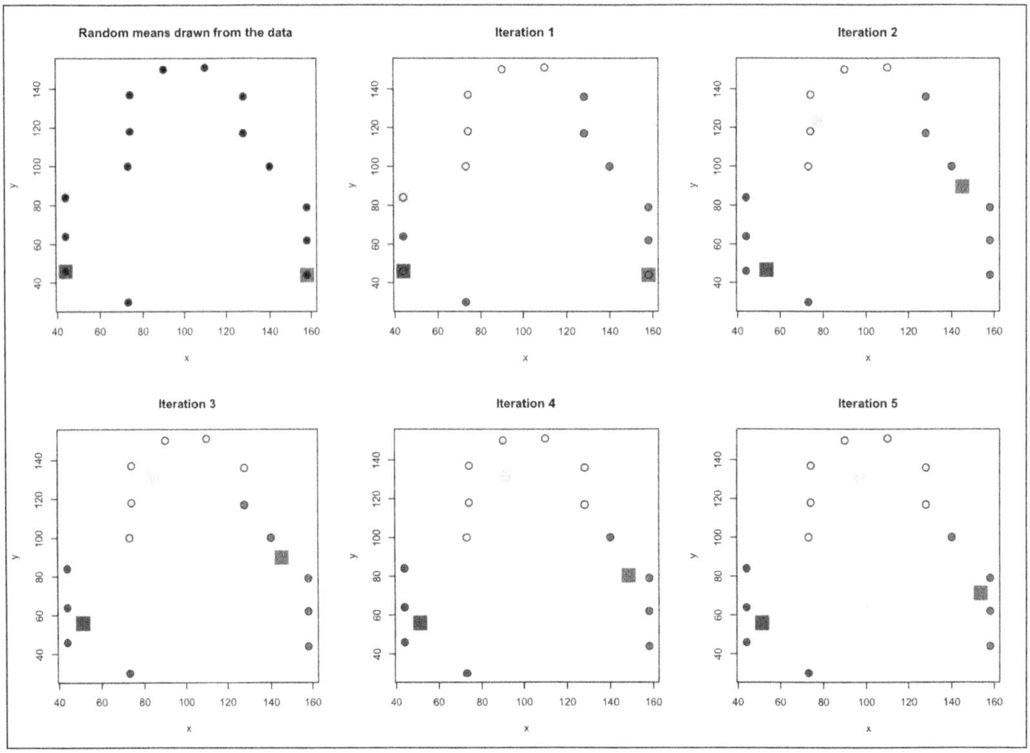

As you can see, we are dealing with 2D sized vectors (the circle dots) while the centroid clusters are the three square points. At every iteration, the centroids move themselves, so they are re-estimated, until the convergence.

Our dummy example works in the same way. We first create a random set of vectors. This is done by the `generateSamples` method, whose code is as follows:

```
public static void generateSamples(List vectors, int num,double mx,
double my, double sd) {
for (int i = 0; i < num; i++) {
   sampleData.add(
        new DenseVector(new double[] {UncommonDistributions.rNorm(mx,s
d),UncommonDistributions.rNorm(my, sd)}));
        }
    }
```

Then, the method accepts a list and for a predefined number of times, it adds (at every iteration) a point whose coordinates are calculated using a random Gaussian norm, with values between the two maximum values.

The method itself is called three times, as we want to build three sets of points that could be clustered with the following parameters:

```
generateSamples(sampleData, 400, 1, 1, 3);
generateSamples(sampleData, 300, 1, 0, 0.5);
generateSamples(sampleData, 300, 0, 2, 0.1);
```

So, we have a total of 1,000 points divided into three clusters. You might have noticed that we also create a limitation on the random min/max value to be taken, because we would like to have a concentrated cluster so that the iterations do not take so long to complete.

Next, we create the centroid vectors that contain three randomly chosen center points. The code to create them is as follows:

```
List<Vector> randomPoints =
  RandomSeedGenerator.chooseRandomPoints(points, k);
```

Notice that we decide how many final cluster centroid points we should have before starting the computational task.

Next, we initialize the clusters vectors with the initial chosen random points, by simply using the following code:

```
List<Cluster> clusters = new ArrayList<Cluster>();
int clusterId = 0;
for (Vector v : randomPoints) {
  clusters.add(new Cluster(v, clusterId++));
}
```

So, we have some `out` clusters that are initialized with the `randomPoints` objects. Then, we have the core of our analysis done using the simple code:

```
List<List<Cluster>> finalClusters =
  KMeansClusterer.clusterPoints(points, clusters, new
  EuclideanDistanceMeasure(), 3, 0.01);
```

The whole job is handled by Mahout's `KMeansClusterer` object using the `clusterPoints` method. The algorithm basically works with the following parameters:

- It is the initial set of points
- It clusters the initialized random chosen centroids
- It is the distance to be used for evaluation if a point is near to a cluster centroid
- It is the number of clusters to form, which is `3` in this case
- It is the threshold value to be used to define the end of the computation, which is `0.01` in this case

The output is the set of centroids that can be printed to the standard console using the last part of our code:

```
// display final cluster center
for(Cluster cluster : finalClusters.get(finalClusters.size() - 1)) {
  System.out.println("Cluster id: " + cluster.getId() + " center:
    "+ cluster.getCenter().asFormatString());
}
```

The K-means algorithm has been demonstrated to find the final clusters in a very fast way. It can also be used by changing the number of clusters. In our example, we used three clusters, but you can also try this with more clusters. As a rough way to estimate the number of clusters based on the initial number of points, you can use the following rule of thumb:

$$k <= \sqrt{\frac{n}{2}}$$

Where *n* is the number of points and *k* is the number of clusters to be generated. So, for example, if you are using a million points, your first step should be to use *707* as the value of *k*, so that your first run will create 707 clusters. The preceding calculation gives the following result:

$$k <= \sqrt{\frac{1000000}{2}} = \sqrt{50000} = 707,01$$

Obviously, the number of clusters is an integer one, so we choose the first integer number, which is 707.

The other important variable is `EuclideanDistanceMeasure`, which is the way to find the proximity of one point to the cluster centroids. We have already seen in the previous chapter how this distance is calculated. We would like to point out that Mahout also provides another way to calculate distances:

- The distance between two vectors of double value respectively x_i and y_i, is referred to as **SquaredEuclideanDistanceMeasure**; the formula for this is as follows:

$$d(x,y)=(x_1-y_1)^2+(x_2-y_2)^2+\ldots+(x_{1n}-y_n)^2$$

- The **ManhattanDistanceMeasure** is calculated as:

$$d(x,y)=|x_1-y_1|+|x_2-y_2|+\ldots+|x_n-y_n|$$

- The **CosineDistanceMeasure** is calculated as:

$$d(x,y)=\frac{\sum_{i=1}^{n}x_iy_i}{\sqrt{\sum_{i=1}^{n}x_i^2}\sqrt{\sum_{i=1}^{n}y_i^2}}$$

- The **TanimotoDistanceMeasure** is calculated as:

$$d(x,y)=\frac{\sum_{i=1}^{n}x_iy_i}{\sum_{i=1}^{n}x_i^2+\sum_{i=1}^{n}y_i^2-\sum_{i=1}^{n}x_iy_i}$$

- The **WeightedDistanceMeasure** is calculated as:

$$d(x,y)=\sqrt{\sum_{i-1}^{n}\left(\frac{x_i}{s_i}-\frac{y_i}{s_i}\right)^2}$$

As an exercise, you change the code to see how different the final clusters are, if you uses different distances.

Before continuing with the next recipe, we also need to consider that we choose the initial values of the cluster at random. This seems a very poor performance approach when dealing with juggernaut datasets. A simple way to choose the centroid that we have tested is the following one: for every data point find the min and max of every coordinate *i*. Then, distribute your initial centroid by distributing the number of the *i* position from the min to the max value. So, for example, if you have 1,000,000 dataset points with five observed values, we could choose 707 centroids as the total number. Then, let us take the first value in position one of every dataset point. Finding *h* equals to the max-min value of all the numbers in position one. Then, call *m=h/707* to create 707 initial centroids such that the first one has its first *i*th coordinate min, then the second vector *h*, the third one *2h*, and so on. The final result is that you will have to create a lattice of 7070 points that you can use as first centroids. We refer you to the cookbook code of this chapter for an example class.

We only detail the expression of the first three. For `CosineDistance`, we suggest the Tanimoto distance at the following links: `http://reference.wolfram.com/mathematica/ref/CosineDistance.html` and `http://en.wikipedia.org/wiki/Jaccard_index#Tanimoto_Similarity_and_Distance`.

Clustering traffic accidents using K-means

In this recipe we will give you a full approach to the K-means clustering using a real dataset.

Getting ready

To get started, let us first prepare our environment. So, as usual, we create the `$WORK_DIR` console variable and download our real dataset.

Let us open up a terminal window and type in the following series of commands:

```
export WORK_DIR=/mnt/new/traffic
cd $WORK_DIR
wget http://fimi.ua.ac.be/data/accidents.dat.gz
tar -xvzf http://fimi.ua.ac.be/data/accidents.dat.gz
```

So, we have the file `accidents.dat` downloaded and decompressed ready to be used. By opening it, we can see the following entries:

```
1 2 3 4 5 6 7 8 9 10 11 12 13 14 15 16 17 18 19 20 21 22 23 24 25 26 27
28 29 30 31
2 5 7 8 9 10 12 13 14 15 16 17 18 20 22 23 24 25 27 28 29 32 33 34 35 36
37 38 39
7 10 12 13 14 15 16 17 18 20 25 28 29 30 33 40 41 42 43 44 45 46 47 48 49
50 51 52
```

```
1 5 8 10 12 14 15 16 17 18 19 20 21 22 24 25 26 27 28 29 30 31 41 43 46
48 49 51 52 53 54 55 56 57 58 59 60 61

5 8 10 12 14 15 16 17 18 21 22 24 25 26 27 28 29 31 33 36 38 39 41 43 46
56 62 63 64 65 66 67 68

7 8 10 12 17 18 21 23 24 26 27 28 29 30 33 34 35 36 38 41 43 47 59 63 66
69 70 71 72 73 74 75 76 77 78 79
```

This dataset of traffic accidents is obtained from the **National Institute of Statistics** (**NIS**) for the region of Flanders (Belgium) for the period 1991-2000. More specifically, the data is obtained from the Belgian "Analysis Form for Traffic Accidents", which should be filled out by a police officer for each traffic accident that occurs with injured or dead casualties on a public road in Belgium. In total, 340.184 traffic accident records are included in the dataset.

For a full description of every variable involved, we refer you to the original paper by *Karolien Geurts* available at `http://fimi.ua.ac.be/data/accidents.pdf`. We warn you that if you would like to use this dataset, it is mandatory to cite the author.

Moving on, we are now ready for the interesting part: we are going to use the K-means clusters algorithm to determine clusters of the accidents to get the points where some accidents happen more frequently.

How to do it...

1. Open up NetBeans and add a new class with a `main` method to the `chapter08` Maven project we created in the previous recipe. The code creation window should be the following one:

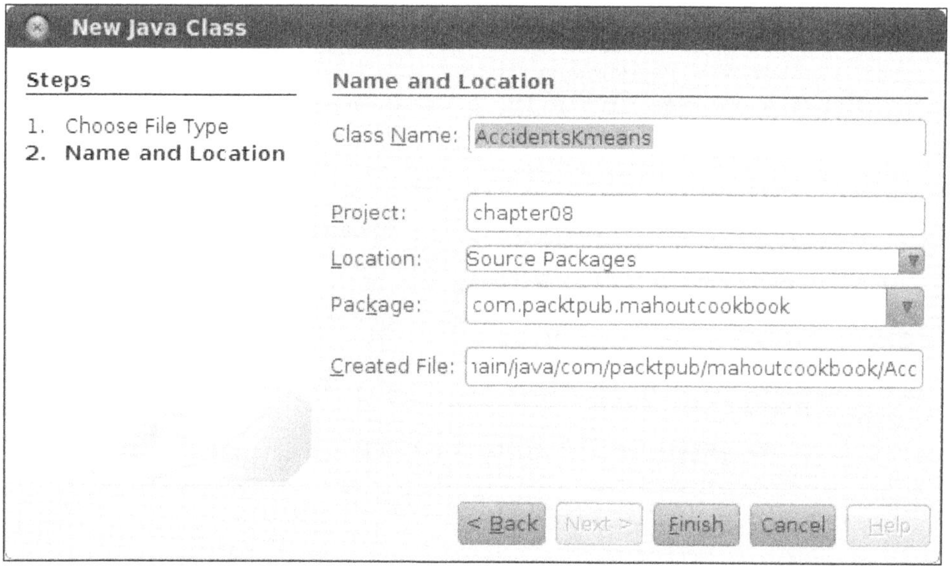

2. Now we need to add the following code into the class:

```
List<Vector> sampleData = new ArrayList<Vector>();
String accidentsFile =  "/mnt/traffic/accidents.dat";
BufferedReader br = new BufferedReader(new
FileReader(accidentsFile) );

String line;
int rows = 0;
while ((line = br.readLine()) != null)
{
  rows++;
  String[] svalues = line.split("\\s+");
  double[] dvalues  = new double[svalues.length];

  sampleData.add(new DenseVector(dvalues));

}
int k = (int) Math.round(Math.sqrt(rows/2));
List<Vector> randomData = new ArrayList<Vector>();

for (int i = 0; i < k;i++)
{
  randomData.add(sampleData.get(i) );
}
List<Cluster> clusters = new ArrayList<Cluster>();

int clusterId = 0;
for (Vector v : randomData) {
  clusters.add(new Cluster(v, clusterId++,
WeightedEuclideanDistanceMeasure ()));
}

List<List<Cluster>> finalClusters = KMeansClusterer.
clusterPoints(sampleData, clusters,new
WeightedEuclideanDistanceMeasure (), 3, 0.01);
for(Cluster cluster : finalClusters.get(finalClusters.size() - 1))
{
    System.out.println("Cluster id: " + cluster.getId() + "
center: " +
    cluster.getCenter().asFormatString());
}
```

The output should be like the following:

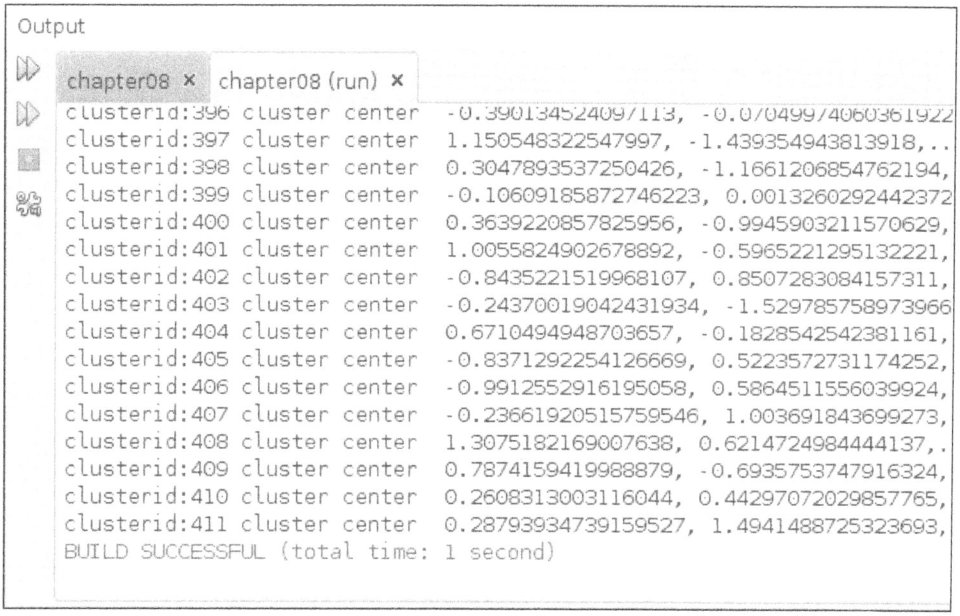

```
Output
chapter08 × chapter08 (run) ×
clusterid:396 cluster center -0.390134524097113, -0.070499740603619 22
clusterid:397 cluster center 1.150548322547997, -1.439354943813918,..
clusterid:398 cluster center 0.3047893537250426, -1.1661206854762194,
clusterid:399 cluster center -0.10609185872746223, 0.0013260292442372
clusterid:400 cluster center 0.3639220857825956, -0.994590321157062 9,
clusterid:401 cluster center 1.0055824902678892, -0.5965221295132221,
clusterid:402 cluster center -0.8435221519968107, 0.8507283084157311,
clusterid:403 cluster center -0.24370019042431934, -1.529785758973966
clusterid:404 cluster center 0.6710494948703657, -0.1828542542381161,
clusterid:405 cluster center -0.8371292254126669, 0.5223572731174252,
clusterid:406 cluster center -0.9912552916195058, 0.5864511556039924,
clusterid:407 cluster center -0.23661920515759546, 1.003691843699273,
clusterid:408 cluster center 1.3075182169007638, 0.6214724984444137,.
clusterid:409 cluster center 0.7874159419988879, -0.6935753747916324,
clusterid:410 cluster center 0.2608313003116044, 0.44297072029857765,
clusterid:411 cluster center 0.28793934739159527, 1.4941488725323693,
BUILD SUCCESSFUL (total time: 1 second)
```

How it works...

Basically, we only recode the previous example using some tricks. The first one is to transform the input value into a format—the vector one that can be handled by Mahout.

First of all, we read the file line by line, and convert every line that represents our *n*-dimensional point in the cluster into a series of double coordinates:

```
String accidentsFile =  "/mnt/traffic/accidents.dat";
BufferedReader br = new BufferedReader(new FileReader(accidentsFile)
);

String line;
int rows = 0;
while ((line = br.readLine()) != null)
{
  rows++;
  String[] svalues = line.split("\\s+");
  double[] dvalues  = new double[svalues.length];

  sampleData.add(new DenseVector(dvalues));

}
```

We also store the total number of observations, that is, the number of points in our *n*-dimensional dataset, and then calculate using our rough estimation of the final number of clusters.

So, it is time to create the initial set of random points. In the previous recipe, we coded them randomly, while in this case, we decide to assign to them to the first *k* observations of our input file:

```
int k = (int) Math.round(Math.sqrt(rows/2));
List<Vector> randomData = new ArrayList<Vector>();

for (int i = 0; i < k;i++)
{
  randomData.add(sampleData.get(i) );
}

List<Cluster> clusters = new ArrayList<Cluster>();

int clusterId = 0;
for (Vector v : randomData) {
  clusters.add(new Cluster(v, clusterId++,
WeightedEuclideanDistanceMeasure ()));
}
```

Next, we evaluate everything using the same code with the only difference being that now we can re-run the same code using `WeightedEuclideanDistanceMeasure` as a measure of similarity.

We invite you to experiment with how the cluster changes using different distance measures.

See also

- The accidents dataset is fully described at `http://fimi.ua.ac.be/data/accidents.pdf`

K-means clustering using MapReduce

Until now, we have seen K-means used in a sequential way, but as usual, the power of Mahout is the implementation done for the algorithm using the MapReduce paradigm.

In this example, we will code a fully K-means based analysis using MapReduce.

Getting ready

We only need to add the following class to our existing `chapter 08` Maven project; the class will be named as follows:

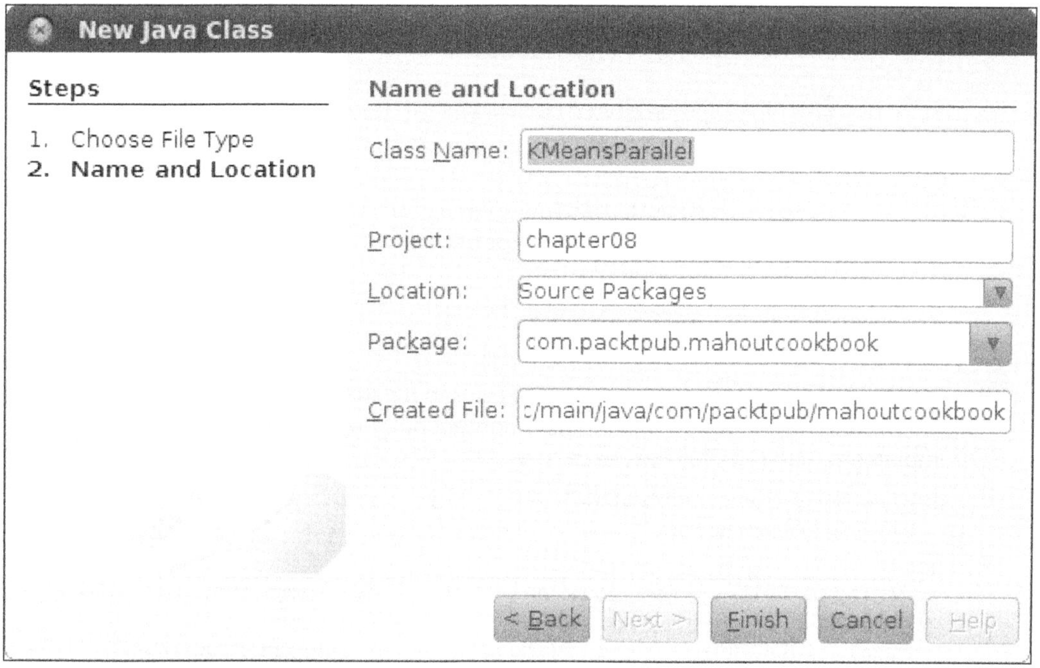

How to do it...

We will now code a complete example in Java to undertake a K-means cluster analysis using the MapReduce framework:

1. Add the following code into the `main` method:

```
public static void main(String[] args) throws Exception {
        Configuration conf = new Configuration();

        // setting mapping and reducers
        conf.setInt(JobContext.NUM_REDUCES, 1);

        conf.setInt(JobContext.NUM_MAPS, 4);

        conf.set("numCluster", "5");
        conf.set("numAuxCluster", "500");
```

```
        Job job = new MRSJob(conf, "KMeansParallel");

        job.setOutputKeyClass(IntWritable.class);
        job.setOutputValueClass(Clusters.class);

        job.setMapperClass(KMeansMapper.class);
        job.setReducerClass(KMeansReducer.class);

        job.setInputFormatClass(TextInputFormat.class);
        job.setOutputFormatClass(TextOutputFormat.class);

        FileInputFormat.addInputPath(job, new Path(args[0]));
        FileOutputFormat.setOutputPath(job, new Path(args[1]));

        job.waitForCompletion(true);
}
```

2. For the remaining code, we invite you to refer to the book's code. We only cite the interesting methods that are implemented into the mapper; the mapper implementation is as follows:

```
public void map(LongWritable key, Text value, Context context)
  throws IOException, InterruptedException {

  // Input format: one data point per line, components delimited
by spaces
  final List<Double> doubleValues = new ArrayList<Double>();
  final StringTokenizer tk = new StringTokenizer(value.
toString());
  while(tk.hasMoreElements()) {
    final String token = tk.nextToken();
    doubleValues.add(Double.parseDouble(token));
  }

  double[] dv = new double[doubleValues.size()];
  for(int i=0; i<doubleValues.size(); i++) {
    dv[i] = doubleValues.get(i);
  }
  DenseVector dvec = new DenseVector(dv);
  DenseVectorWritable sample = new DenseVectorWritable(dvec);

  // add sample to local auxiliary clusters
  this.cache.addSample(sample);

  // first k points are chosen as initial centroids
  if (nextCentroidToInit < k) {
    this.clusters.set(nextCentroidToInit, new Cluster(sample,
```

```
sample));
    this.nextCentroidToInit += 1;
  } else if (nextCentroidToInit == k) {
    // send initial centroids to reducer
    context.write(new IntWritable(0), this.clusters);
    this.nextCentroidToInit += 1;
  }
}
```

The reducer implementation is as follows:

```
protected void reduce(IntWritable key, Iterable<Clusters> valu
es,ReduceContext<IntWritable, Clusters, IntWritable, Clusters,
Clusters> context) throws IOException, InterruptedException {

  // Merge the list of clusters into one set of clusters
  Clusters results = null;
  for(Clusters clusters : values) {
    if( results == null ) {
      results = clusters;
    } else {
      results.merge(clusters);
    }
  }

  Double error = results.getMSE();

  LOG.info("Last error " + lastError + ", current error " +
error);

  if (lastError < Double.MAX_VALUE &&
      error <= lastError + epsilon &&
      error >= lastError - epsilon) {
    // MSE has changed by less than epsilon: Emit final result
    context.write(new IntWritable(0), results);
    LOG.info("Final result written.");
  } else {
    // MSE has changed by more than epsilon: Send recomputed
preliminary clusters to mappers to start a new
    // iteration
    this.lastError = error;
    results.computeNewCentroids();
    context.restream(results);
    LOG.info("Preliminary result restreamed.");
  }
}
```

How it works...

As we have already discussed the parallelization of Mahout, the K-means algorithm is done using the MapReduce paradigm. We will provide a brief description of how the MapReduce implementation works at a higher level.

Every Mahout MapReduce job involves two steps. In the map we perform the following actions:

1. Read the cluster centers into memory from a sequence file as we saw in *Chapter 3, Integrating Mahout with an External Datasource*.
2. Iterate over each cluster center for each input key/value pair.
3. Measure the distances and save the nearest center that has the lowest distance to the vector.
4. Write `clustercenter` with its vector to the filesystem.

In the reduce step (we get associated vectors for each center), we perform the following actions:

1. Iterate over each value vector and calculate the average vector. (Sum up each vector and divide each part by the number of vectors we received.)
2. This is the new center, save it into a `SequenceFile`.
3. Check the convergence between `clustercenter` that is stored in the key object and the new center. If they are not equal, increment an update counter.

Run this whole thing until nothing is updated anymore. The reduce step will end because the iteration of the error does not last forever if the mean is under the defined threshold.

As a basic initial step, you need to create the cluster and the sample data in a sequence file so that it can be handled both by the mapper as for the reducers. You might have noticed that we choose the following as the number of clusters:

```
conf.set("numCluster", "5");
```

However, you are free to modify the code according to your own needs.

Using K-means clustering from the command line

By following what we have done in *Chapter 7, Spectral Clustering in Mahout*, we will now create a fully K-means clustering algorithm, but as the algorithm works with similarity matrices, we need to create them.

Getting ready

To do this, let us first create the input and output folders. So open up the command-line terminal and type in the following command:

```
export WORK_DIR=/mnt/kmeans
mkdir $WOKR_DIR/reuters-out-seqdir
mkdir $WOKR_DIR/reuters-out
```

We have many folders because we need to transform the original files into sequence files that can be manipulated by the K-means cluster implementation done by Mahout.

Now type in the following command:

```
cd $WORK_DIR
```

Then download the `reuters` dataset into the folder by typing the following `wget` command:

```
wget http://kdd.ics.uci.edu/databases/reuters21578/reuters21578.tar.gz -o
${WORK_DIR}/reuters21578.tar.gz
```

Now, it is time to extract everything using the following command:

```
tar xzf $WORK_DIR/reuters21578.tar.gz -C $WORK_DIR/reuters-sgm
```

This will create a folder called `reuters-sgm` inside the `$WORK_DIR` folder, which you set up previously with the following contents:

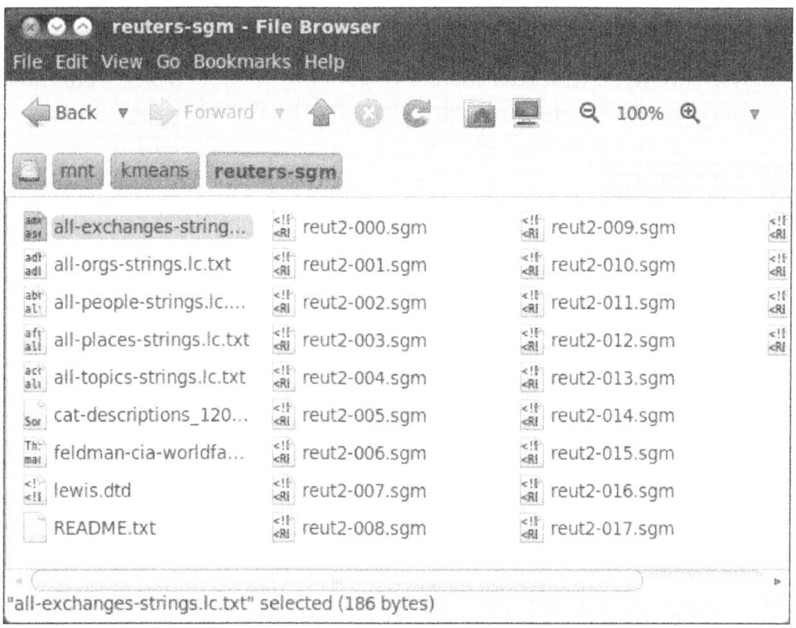

Before continuing, a word on where this dataset comes from. The `reuters` dataset contains some documents that were assembled and indexed with categories by personnel from Reuters Ltd. This is very old and so is often used in data mining research. As you can see, the core data of the documents is contained in the `.sgm` files that display such kind of content:

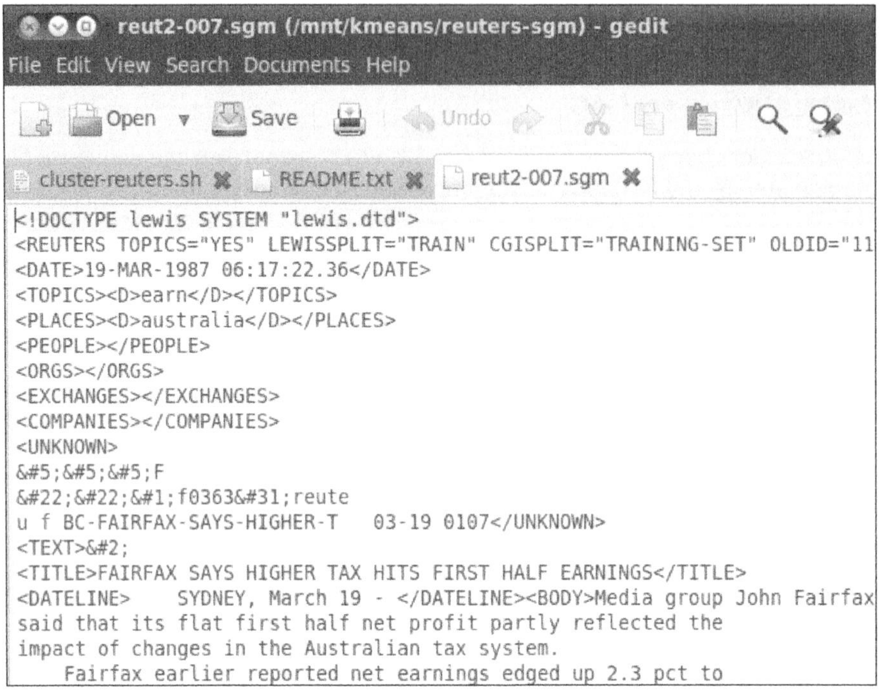

```
<!DOCTYPE lewis SYSTEM "lewis.dtd">
<REUTERS TOPICS="YES" LEWISSPLIT="TRAIN" CGISPLIT="TRAINING-SET" OLDID="11
<DATE>19-MAR-1987 06:17:22.36</DATE>
<TOPICS><D>earn</D></TOPICS>
<PLACES><D>australia</D></PLACES>
<PEOPLE></PEOPLE>
<ORGS></ORGS>
<EXCHANGES></EXCHANGES>
<COMPANIES></COMPANIES>
<UNKNOWN>
&#5;&#5;&#5;F
&#22;&#22;&#1;f0363&#31;reute
u f BC-FAIRFAX-SAYS-HIGHER-T   03-19 0107</UNKNOWN>
<TEXT>&#2;
<TITLE>FAIRFAX SAYS HIGHER TAX HITS FIRST HALF EARNINGS</TITLE>
<DATELINE>    SYDNEY, March 19 - </DATELINE><BODY>Media group John Fairfax
said that its flat first half net profit partly reflected the
impact of changes in the Australian tax system.
    Fairfax earlier reported net earnings edged up 2.3 pct to
```

From this document, we need to create the corresponding sequence files that represent the affinity matrix, which is needed as the starting point for the K-means algorithm.

How to do it...

To summarize, the steps involved in this algorithm are as follows:

1. Get the dataset.
2. Convert the input in to sequence file format.
3. Calculate the vectors' data points converting text occurrence to number.
4. Run the K-means algorithm.

A detailed analysis of this algorithm is as follows:

1. To create the sequence files, you need to invoke the following command from the command line:

```
mahout org.apache.lucene.benchmark.utils.ExtractReuters $WORK_DIR/
reuters-sgm $WORK_DIR/reuters-out
```

   The command output should be the following:

```
Running on hadoop, using /home/hadoop-mahout/hadoop-1.0.4/bin/
hadoop and HADOOP_CONF_DIR=
MAHOUT-JOB: /home/hadoop-mahout/NetBeansProjects/trunk/examples/
target/mahout-examples-0.8-SNAPSHOT-job.jar


13/05/10 17:25:28 WARN driver.MahoutDriver: No org.apache.lucene.
benchmark.utils.ExtractReuters.props found on classpath, will use
command-line arguments only
Deleting all files in /mnt/kmeans/reuters-out-tmp
13/05/10 17:25:31 INFO driver.MahoutDriver: Program took 3568 ms
(Minutes: 0.0594833333
```

   The corresponding new folder content should look like the following screenshot:

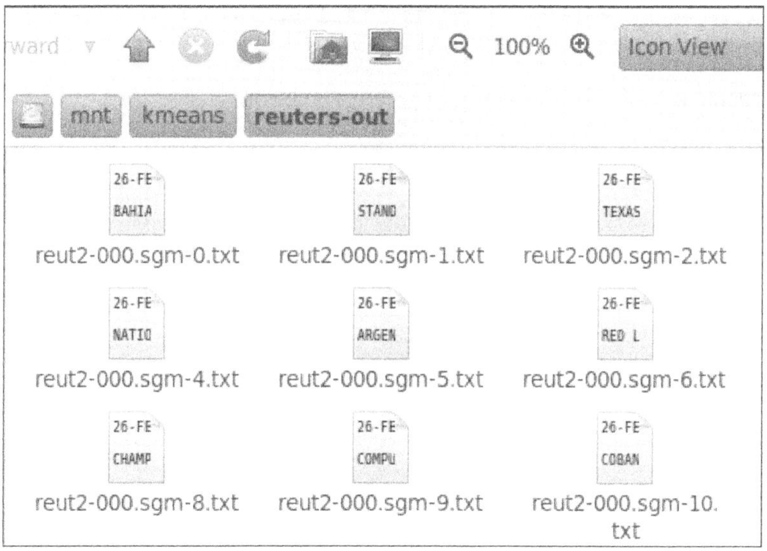

2. The command dumps the content of the sequence files into the `.txt` files. A single file displays the content:

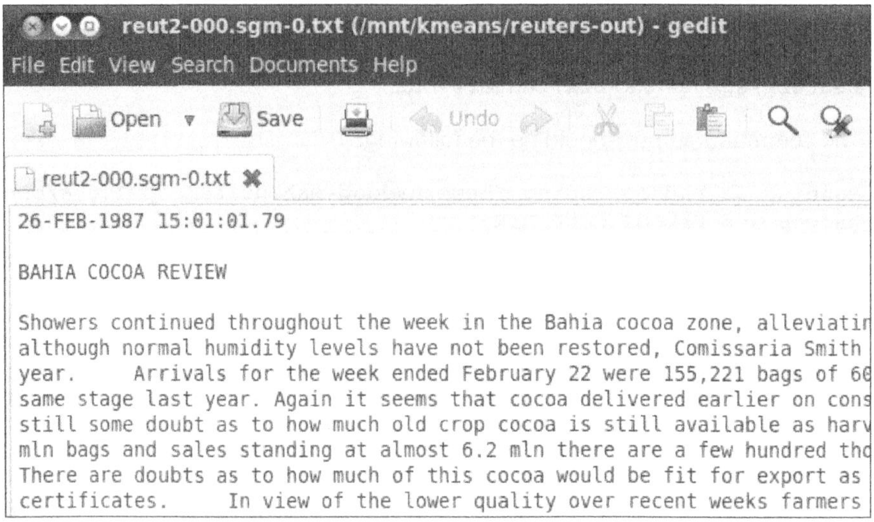

3. Now that we have disassembled the whole corpus into separate files, it is time to give the command to create the sequence files based on the corpus we already extracted:

```
mahout  seqdirectory -i $WORK_DIR/reuters-out -o $WORK_DIR/
reuters-out-seqdir -c UTF-8 -chunk 5
```

The result is now saved in the `reuters-out-seqdir` directory.

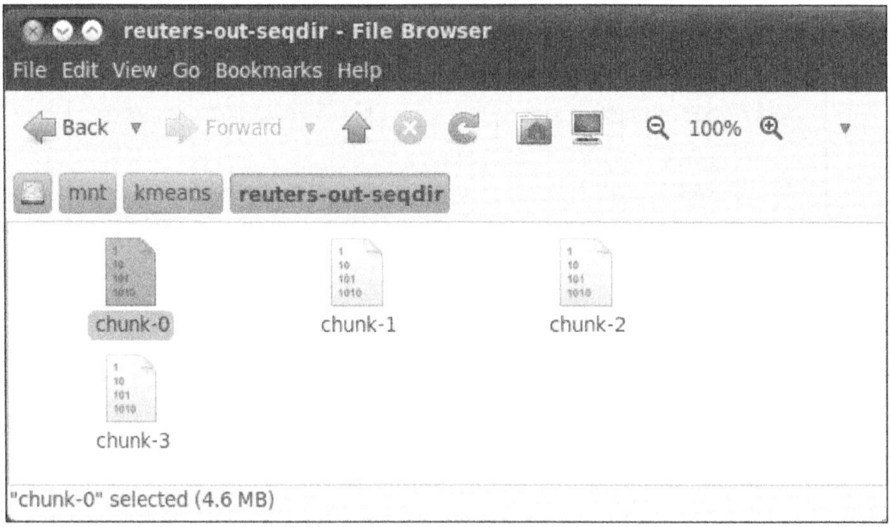

4. Now that we have created the files, we can start with the interesting part. Basically, we need to give the following command:

```
mahout seq2sparse -i $WORK_DIR/reuters-out-seqdir/ -o $WORK_DIR/
reuters-out-seqdir-sparse-kmeans --maxDFPercent 85 --namedVector
```

We will create the sparse vector files that one can see in the following screenshot:

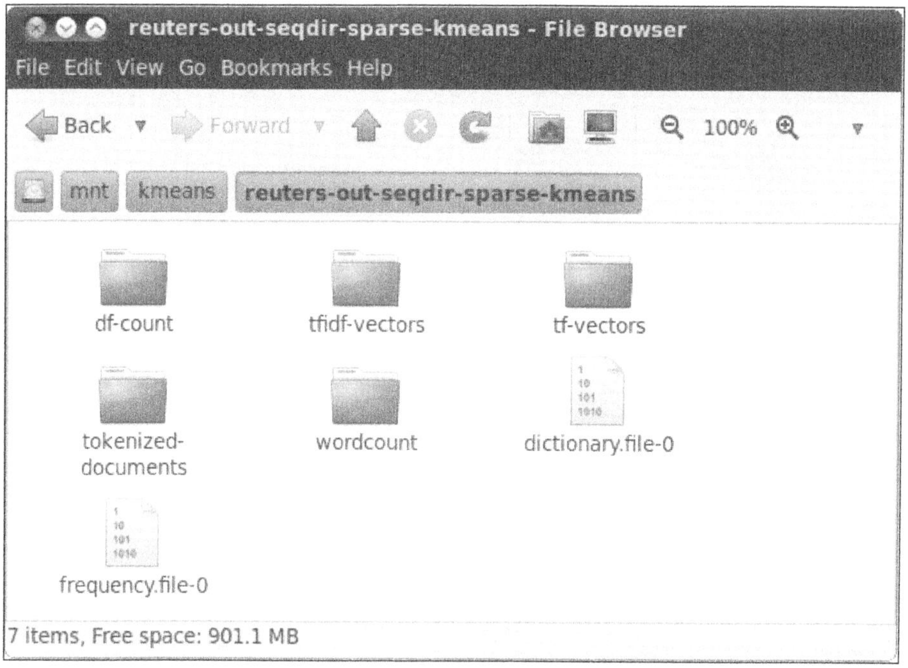

5. Now we have everything we need to conduct our analysis using K-means. The core of the analysis is done by implementing the following command:

```
mahout kmeans -i $WORK_DIR/reuters-out-seqdir-sparse-kmeans/tfidf-
vectors/     -c $WORK_DIR/reuters-kmeans-clusters   -o $WORK_DIR/
reuters-kmeans

-dm org.apache.mahout.common.distance.CosineDistanceMeasure

-x 10 -k 20 -ow
```

The result is a sequence file created in `$WORK_DIR/reuters-kmeans`:

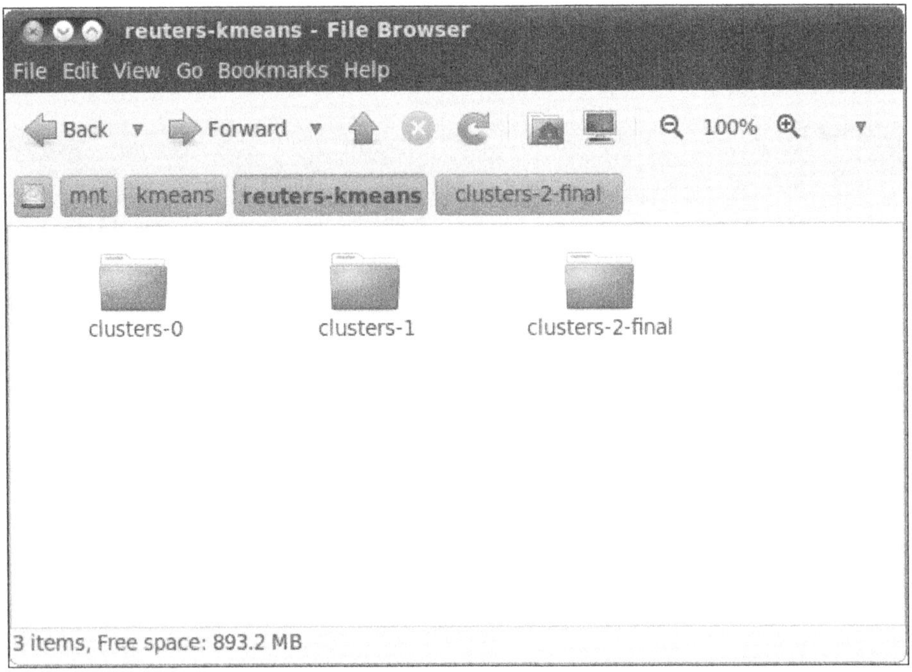

6. Finally, you would like to see the final result, we have:

```
mahout clusterdump
-i $WORK_DIR/reuters-kmeans/clusters-*-final
-o $WORK_DIR/reuters-kmeans/clusterdump
-d $WORK_DIR/reuters-out-seqdir sparse-kmeans/dictionary.file-0
-dt sequencefile -b 100 -n 20 --evaluate -dm org.apache.mahout.
common.distance.CosineDistanceMeasure -sp 0
--pointsDir $WORK_DIR/reuters-kmeans/clusteredPoints
```

How it works...

Before describing the computational steps involved, we define the following symbols involved:

- **Raw data matrix** (**R**): This is the *(k xn)* dimensional data that the user is interested in clustering.
- **Similarity matrix** (**S**): This a *k* X *k* transformation of **R** that shows how "related" each point is, pairwise. This "relation" function can be anything from pixel intensity to radial Euclidean distance.

- **Adjacency/Affinity matrix (A)**: This also is a *k* X *k* transformation, but this time a transformation of **S** by applying the *k*-nearest neighbor filter to build a representation of the graph (or, for a fully-connected graph, *A* = S). This matrix is critical to our calculations.
- **Diagonal degree matrix (D)**: This is also *k* X *k*, formed by summing the degree of each vertex and placing it on the diagonal.
- **Normalized and symmetric Laplacian matrix (L)**: This is formed in an operation with **A** and **D**. This is the matrix that we will perform Eigen-decompositions on.
- **Matrix of eigenvectors of L (U)**: Using eigenvectors, we'll perform K-means clustering on their components.

Now that we have all the symbols defined, we can describe the K-means algorithm a little better. The steps involved are as follows:

- Preprocessing data
- Constructing adjacency matrix
- Constructing diagonal degree matrix
- Constructing normalized Laplacian
- Performing Eigen-decomposition
- Performing K-means clustering

The pre-processing phase is done by constructing the similarity matrix S using a relation function from the raw data matrix R. The relation function describes the edge between two dimensional nodes in terms of a graph. By using S, we construct the adjacency matrix that describes the links between vertices represented by the similarity matrix. Again, do not forget that in this case, the matrix is formed by `0` and `1`, and that matrix A is equal to S in the case where each node of the graph is connected to all the other ones.

Once you have built the adjacency matrix, it is time to construct the diagonal degree matrix. This step is probably the most straightforward: simply sum up the degrees of each vertex, and place the value along the diagonal. We need to remember that the degree of a node/vertex on a matrix is the number of edges it has.

Up to now, starting from R, we have built in sequence S, A, and D, and now we build another Laplacian matrix using the linear algebra definition that states:

$$L = \frac{1}{\sqrt{D}} A \sqrt{D}$$

Performing eigenvalues' decomposition starting from L is the next step. We build up a new matrix U where the columns are the eigenvectors of the matrix L. Mathematics has proved that this matrix can always be constructed.

We are now ready to perform a K-means cluster analysis; this is done by using the rows of the U matrix to construct a new matrix that affects the previous one.

This is a more complicated example, but in any case, it can be used as a demonstration of a real-world data mining task for text clustering.

We start with the `reuters` dataset, but the *Getting ready* section can be ported without a major effort for any kind of text document.

See also

- Refer to `http://www.win-vector.com/blog/` for more information on some of the most interesting uses

9

Soft Computing with Mahout

We will cover the following recipes in this chapter:

- Frequent Pattern Mining with Mahout
- Creating metrics for Frequent Pattern Mining
- Using Frequent Pattern Mining from Java code
- Using LDA for creating topics

Introduction

After the previous long run on clustering algorithm, we now move on algorithm and devote our discussions to data-mining and rule extraction purposes. Let's get straight to work!

Frequent Pattern Mining with Mahout

One of the first presented cases to demonstrate the data mining value was introduced back in the 70s, in trying to extract the rules for presenting items to sell based on the knowledge acquired from previous buying patterns.

So in this recipe, we will detail a full example on how to extract rules in order to find the pattern of customers buying items.

Let us start as usual by preparing our working environment.

Getting ready

As usual, the starting point for our analysis is to get a dataset. Let us open up a terminal window and type in the following commands:

```
export WORK_DIR=/mnt/fpm
mkdir -p $WORK_DIR
cd $WORK_DIR
wget http://fimi.ua.ac.be/data/retail.dat
```

The file that we get is shown in the following screenshot:

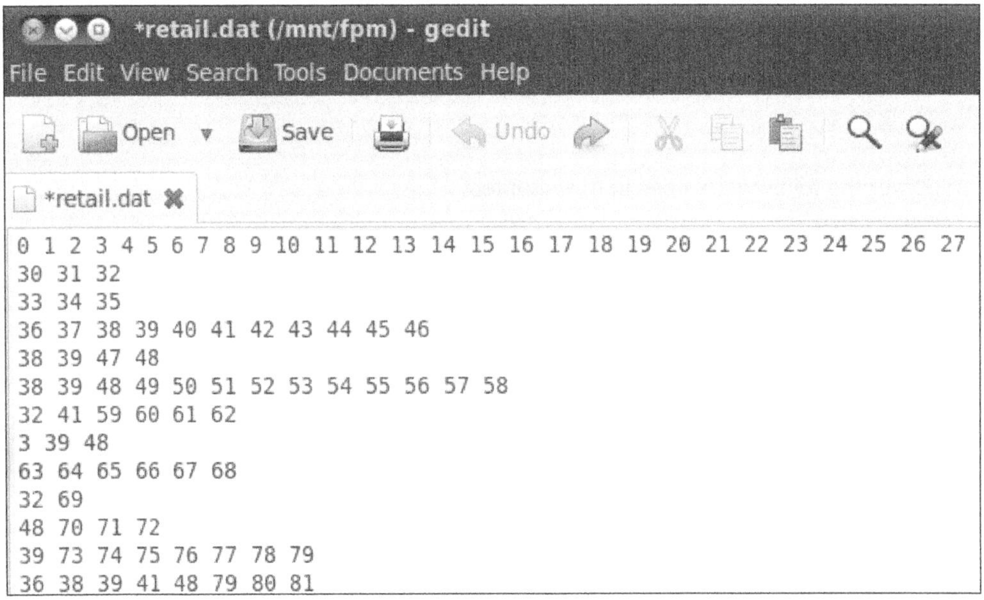

The file can be interpreted in the following way. The first row is a set of 30 items for sale. Every other row is a single transaction (that is, a bill) asserting how many of these items have been bought in that single transaction.

So, for example, the first row states that the buyer has to buy **30** pieces of item **0**, **31** of item **1**, and so on.

The input can be used just as it is, but other input formats should be managed and arranged before being mined by Mahout.

How to do it...

We basically need to launch the Frequent Pattern Mining algorithm on this dataset to create an output sequence file.

The command line in this case is a simple one, so type the following command into an open console:

```
mahout fpg -i $WORK_DIR/retail.dat  -o patterns -k 50 -method mapreduce
-regex ['\ '] -s 2
```

The computational task output will be something like the following screenshot:

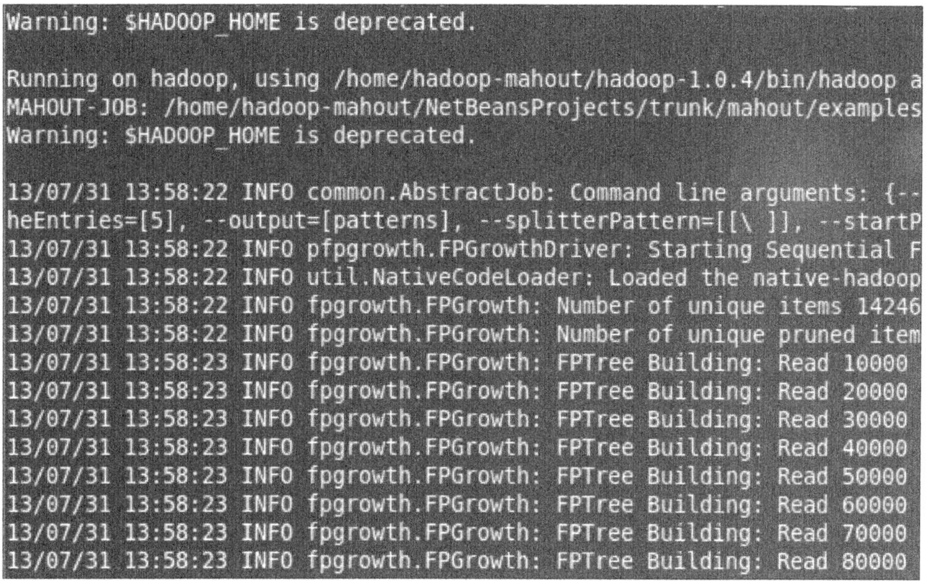

The result is a sequence file called with the suffix `patterns`. To see the content, you should type a command like the following:

```
mahout seqdumper -i $WORK_DIR/patterns -o patterns.txt
```

A portion of the output file will look like the following screenshot:

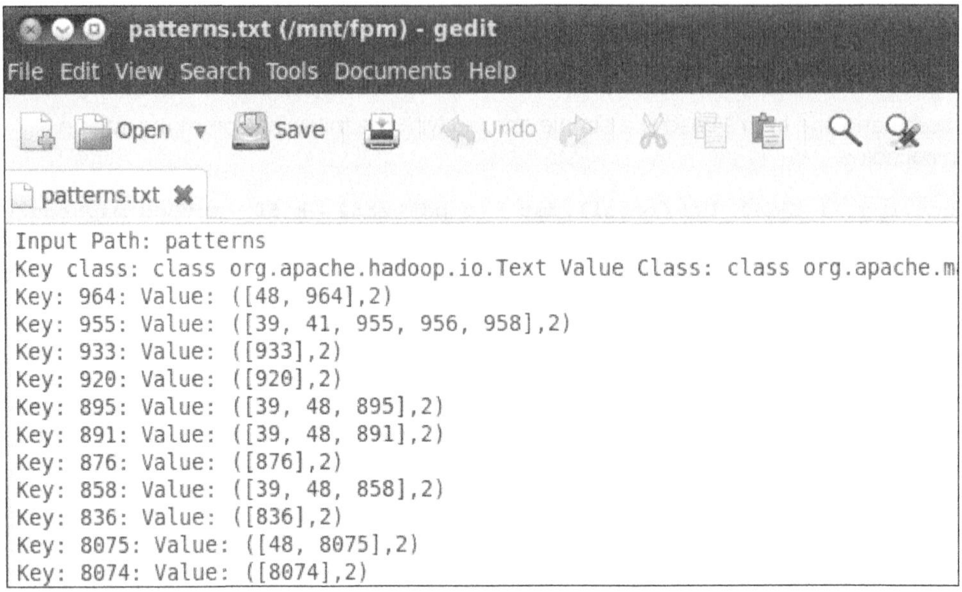

How it works...

The algorithm for Frequent Pattern Mining basically works with only one step if we use it from the command line. We have an input file (`retail.dat`) that is parsed line by line by explicitly declaring the separators between the different values. A list of useful command-line parameters is as follows:

- `-i`: This is the input folder containing the input files
- `-o`: This is the output folder
- `-k`: This is the maximum number of items to mine (the default is 50)
- `-regex`: This is the regular expression to split every line
- `-method`: This tells us to use the sequential or MapReduce implementation
- `-s`: This is the minimum number of times a transaction should be present

As we discussed earlier, the input file should have a predefined format, that is, every line is a transaction that contains a number of the items contained in a single transaction.

So for example, if we talk about a store selling items, we have a total number of items `N` and a number of transactions `M`. A line of the input file will be as follows:

```
0,1,0,3,4
```

For item 1, we have 0 total occurrences in the transaction, that is, we did not buy it. We buy one item 2 and three occurrences of item 4, and so on. If we buy a single occurrence of every item, we should have one line, all composed with the number one.

So every line is a transaction and each transaction is formatted as a list of numbers indicating the number of items purchased and their positions indicating the specific item.

The algorithm that is basically the implementation is presented in the paper `http://infolab.stanford.edu/~echang/recsys08-69.pdf`. The algorithm works by using a divide and conquer strategy. In the first part, it creates a list of frequency items ordered by their frequency in descending order, so from the most frequent item present in all transactions to the one that is least present. The second part is the recursive construction of the so-called Frequent Pattern Tree or FP-tree. The FP-tree is a particular type of graph structure where we have a principal node (sometimes called the root node) and all the other nodes are edged with this principal one. We will detail FP-Tree's behavior better in the *How it works...* section.

The file obtained by running the algorithm using the MapReduce implementation provides a folder named **patterns** contained inside the files shown in the following screenshot:

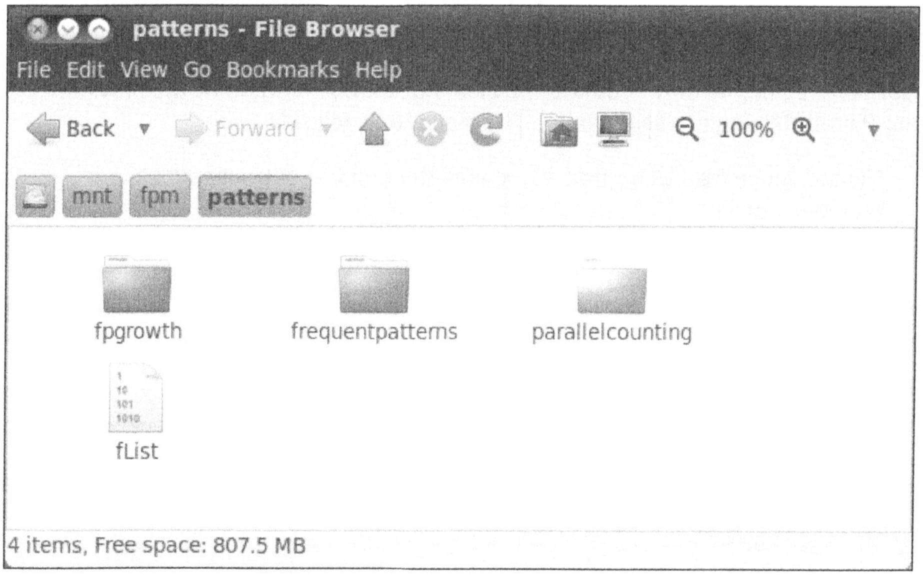

The results are described as follows:

- **fList**: These are sequence files that contain the occurrence of the item for every item inside the transaction database
- **part-***: These files inside the `frequentpatterns` folder contain a sequence file whose content we saw in the earlier screenshot

Considering the result sequence file, it should be read as follows. Consider the first line, which in our case is the following:

```
Key: 0: Value: ([0],26), ([39, 0],14), ([39, 48, 41, 32, 616, 0,
1314],2), ([39, 41, 0,])
```

It describes the number of associations found between item `0` and others within the whole transaction database. So `([0],26)` means that the item `0` appears in `26` transactions. The `([39,0],14)` confirms that the item `0` coupled with the item `39` appears in `14` transactions, and so on.

Obviously, without any metrics to understand the correlations between the data, the output does not have much meaning. In the next recipes, we will see some common metrics to help us understand all the results.

Creating metrics for Frequent Pattern Mining

We will code a full set of metrics to evaluate a Frequent Pattern Mining file.

Getting ready

To prepare our recipe, we only need the two files that were generated by the previous Frequent Pattern Mining run as the input. The files are as follows:

- The sequence file `fList` that associates the number of transactions to a key/value format
- All the files contained in the `frequentpatterns` folder

The resulting sequence files could be split into many files. So before proceeding, we need to merge all of them into one.

The result could be split into more sequence files depending on the initial size of the transaction dataset; hence, we need to merge them. This is not the case here, so we will simply use both the generated files. If you need to merge files into the Hadoop filesystem, use the following console command:

```
hadoop fs -getmerge patterns/frequentpatterns destination.seq
```

We also need to create the skeleton with Maven and a class called `FrequentPatternMetrics` that can be used for general purposes. The final NetBeans Maven project structure should look like the following screenshot:

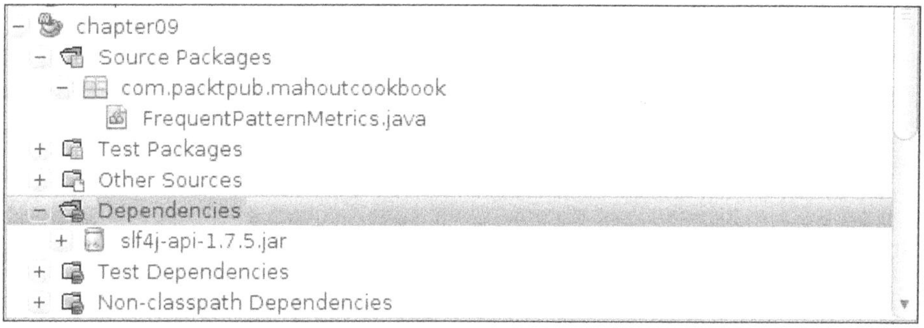

How to do it...

We are now ready to code a general purpose class that can be used to evaluate the output of the file created by the Mahout Frequent Pattern Mining. The full code of the `main` method can be seen in the following code:

```
    public static void main(String[] argv) throws IOException
    {
        FrequentPatternMetrics fpm = new FrequentPatternMetrics();

        fpm.set_FREQUENCY_ITEM_LIST("/mnt/fpm/patterns/fList");
        fpm.set_FREQUENCY_ITEM_PATTERNS("/mnt/fpm/patterns/
frequentpatterns/");
        fpm.readFrequency();
        fpm.readFrequentPatterns();
        fpm.OutputPatterns()
    }
```

For the full code, we refer the reader to the book's code. A simple run will give the following output:

```
[item 0] => item 456 : supp=0.045, conf=0.324, lift=0.002,
conviction=1.701
```

This means people who buy item `0` are usually willing to buy item `456`, and so on.

How it works...

Prior to proceeding with our code, we need to provide some background math for the metrics used to obtain our result. The search for meaningful metrics for Frequent Pattern Mining is still an object of research as we do not have an optimal metric for every case (See, for example, `http://www.textedu.ru/tw_files2/urls_6/147/d-146938/7z-docs/5.pdf` for a good survey) However, a standard set of metrics to evaluate the association between patterns has a good research history, so they can be used as a first port of call to find association rules. Let us define some of these standard metrics.

From now on, let *X* be a general set of items, *N* the total number of transactions, then we can define the following:

SUPPORT(X) is the proportion of transactions containing the set *X*. This is defined by the following math formula:

$$SUPPORT(X) = \frac{M}{N}$$

Here, *M* is the number of transactions containing the set *X*.

CONFIDENCE(X, Y) is the proportion of transactions containing *X* and *Y*, so referring to the previous *SUPPORT* equation, we can define it as:

$$CONFIDENCE(X,Y) = \frac{SUPPORT(X \cup Y)}{SUPPORT(X)}$$

These are very basic metrics but moving on, we have two more interesting ones in particular:

LIFT(X,Y) is formulated as:

$$LIFT(X,Y) = \frac{SUPPORT(X \cup Y)}{SUPPORT(X) \cdot SUPPORT(Y)}$$

The formula is slightly different from the *CONFIDENCE* one because in the second case, we hypothesize the fact that a transaction that contains *X* is independent of the fact that the same transaction contains *Y*.

Last, we have the *CONVINCTION* equation that is the ratio of the expected frequency that *X* occurs without *Y*.

To code our class, we choose, according to the standard Java OOP, to code some properties that will be used within the whole code to undertake standard operations. The properties themselves are as follows:

```
String  FREQUENCY_ITEM_LIST = "";
String  FREQUENCY_ITEM_PATTERNS = "";
Configuration configuration;
FileSystem fs;
Reader rd;
private static final Logger log = LoggerFactory.getLogger(FrequentPatt
ernMetrics.class);
int transactionCount;
double minSupport;
double minConfidence;
Map<Integer, Long> frequency;
```

So we have the full path name to the frequency files containing the frequency of every item and the `patterns` file output by the Mahout FPM algorithm. We also use a Hadoop reader as we need to read these files. However, the most interesting parts are the `minSupport` and `minConfidence` intervals that describe the minimum level for the support value and the confidence value. This is to help us decide which associations are meaningful for our analysis.

Our class steps are as follows:

- Read the frequency items file
- Read the frequency patterns file and compute the support and confidence values for the set of items involved in the transaction, for every single transaction
- Output the results according to the `minSupport` and `minConfidence` intervals

Every time we need an `ArrayList`, `Map`, `Hashmap`, or any other structure to handle data, we decide to declare it as an internal private property, nonaccessible from outside the class itself. We initialize every internal property under the constructor of the class itself to avoid a possible null pointer exception as shown in the following code. The constructor is pretty self-explanatory:

```
public  FrequentPatternMetrics()
{
  FREQUENCY_ITEM_LIST = "";
  FREQUENCY_ITEM_PATTERNS = "";
  configuration = new Configuration();
  int transactionCount = 0;
  int minSupport = 0;
  int minConfidence = 0 ;
  frequency = new HashMap<Integer, Long>();
}
```

Then we code an `Init` method to set values on everything that we need for our computation:

```
public void Init() throws IOException
{
  log.info("init process");
  fs = FileSystem.get(configuration);
  FREQUENCY_ITEM_LIST = "/mnt/fpm/patterns/fList";
  FREQUENCY_ITEM_PATTERNS = "/mnt/fpm/patterns/frequentpatterns/";
  GetTransactionCount();
  minSupport = 0.04;
  minConfidence = 0.4;
}
```

In the `Init()` method, we also called the `GetTransactionCount` method that basically initializes the `transactionCount` property that will be needed in the rest of the code; again the method is pretty easy:

```
private void GetTransactionCount() throws IOException
{
  LineNumberReader reader  = new LineNumberReader(new FileReader("/
mnt/fpm/retail.dat"));
  String lineRead = "";
  while ((lineRead = reader.readLine()) != null) {}
  transactionCount =  reader.getLineNumber();
  reader.close();
}
```

Things have now become more interesting; first we need to load the frequency from HDFS for every item using sequence files methods. So we code the following method:

```
private void ReadFrequencies() throws IOException {
  rd = new SequenceFile.Reader(fs, new Path(FREQUENCY_ITEM_LIST),
this.configuration);
  Text key = new Text();
  LongWritable value = new LongWritable();
  while(rd.next(key, value)) {
    log.info("find key " + key.toString() + " with value : " + value.
get());
    frequency.put(Integer.parseInt(key.toString()), value.get());
  }
}
```

Then we need to compute the frequent patterns:

```
private void readFrequentPatterns() throws IOException {
  rd = new SequenceFile.Reader(fs,new Path(this.FREQUENCY_ITEM_
PATTERNS), configuration);
  Text key = new Text();
  TopKStringPatterns value = new TopKStringPatterns();
  while(rd.next(key, value)) {
    long firstFrequencyItem = -1;
    String firstItemId = null;
    List<Pair<List<String>,Long>> patterns = value.getPatterns();
    int i = 0;
    for(Pair<List<String>,Long> pair: patterns) {
      List itemList = pair.getFirst();
      Long occurrence = pair.getSecond();
      if (i == 0) {
        firstFrequencyItem = occurrence;
  firstItemId = itemList.get(0).toString();
      } else {
        double support = (double)occurrence / transactionCount;
        double confidence = (double)occurrence / firstFrequencyItem;
        List listWithoutFirstItem = new ArrayList();
        for(Object itemId: itemList) {
          if (!itemId.equals(firstItemId)) {
            listWithoutFirstItem.add(itemId);
          }
        }
        long otherItemOccurrence = frequency.get(0);
        double lift = (double)occurrence / (firstFrequencyItem *
otherItemOccurrence);
        double conviction = (1.0 - (double)otherItemOccurrence /
transactionCount) / (1.0 - confidence);
        i++;
    }
  }
  rd.close();
}
```

This is so that at the end, we have the `listWithoutFirstItem` object of type `ArrayList` containing the frequent patterns.

Using Frequent Pattern Mining from Java code

In this recipe, we will give a full working example using the Frequent Pattern Mining Mahout-cabled algorithms for performing a retail rule extraction.

Getting ready

As usual, we set a working folder and download a test dataset that we will use during the recipe. To create the working folder, we give the following commands:

```
export WORK_DIR=/mnt/fpmjava
mkdir -p $WORK_DIR
cd $WORK_DIR
```

Now we download a dataset of transactions from a grocery store provided by professor *Marina Marski* on her website `http://csci.viu.ca/~barskym/`. To download the file type into a bash shell, use the following command:

```
wget http://csci.viu.ca/~barskym/teaching/DM_LABS/LAB_7/data.zip
```

Once unzipped, you should find a file called `marketbasket.csv`.

The structure of the CSV file is as shown in the following screenshot:

A	B	C	D	E
Hair Conditioner	Lemons	Standard coffee	Frozen Chicken Wings	98pct. Fat Free Hamburger
0	0	0	0	0
0	0	0	0	0
0	0	0	0	0
0	0	0	0	0
0	0	0	0	0
0	0	0	0	0
0	0	0	0	0
0	0	0	0	1
0	0	0	0	0
0	0	0	0	0
0	0	0	0	0
0	0	0	0	0
0	0	0	0	0
0	0	0	0	1

The first row enumerates all the items sold by the grocery store. Then every row represents a transaction. In the preceding screenshot, you can see that the eighth bill has one fat-free hamburger, and so on.

The whole dataset has 1361 transactions that we will analyze using the Frequent Pattern Mining algorithm.

Before proceeding, we will add a new class called `FrequentMiningPatternJava` inside the previously created `Maven` project. Thus, we have the following folder structure:

Lets now move on to the coding part.

How to do it...

Essentially, we recode the previous chapter's recipe, but in this case we also add a few data transformations. Our class essentially performs the following steps:

1. Read all the items' descriptions.
2. Read all the transactions and compute a list.
3. Run the Frequent Pattern Mining algorithm.
4. Output the results.

So let us start with the first easy method that reads the first line of our `marketbasket.csv` file and load it into an `ArrayList` called `items` of string objects to get all the item names. The code is pretty simple as we will see next:

```
private void readItemsName() {
  if (items != null)
    items.clear();
  log.info("adding items name");
  BufferedReader br = null;
  String line = "";
  String cvsSplitBy = ",";
  items = new ArrayList<String>();
  try {
    br = new BufferedReader(new FileReader(cvsFileName));
    line = br.readLine();
    String[] itemss = line.split(",");
    for(int i=0;i<itemss.length;i++)
    {
```

```
         log.info("adding item " + itemss[i]);
         System.out.println("adding item " + itemss[i]);
         items.add(itemss[i]);
       }
     } catch (FileNotFoundException e) {
       e.printStackTrace();
     } catch (IOException e) {
       e.printStackTrace();
     } finally {
       if (br != null) {
         try {
             br.close();
         } catch (IOException e) {
             e.printStackTrace();
         }
     }
     }

   }
```

We need to load every transaction into a `Map` object, also detailing the items involved in the single transaction; this will create an `Arraylist` of objects called `transaction`. The following code details the process:

```
private void readTransactions()
{
        if (transactions != null)  transactions.clear();
        log.info("adding transactions");
        BufferedReader br = null;
        String line = "";

        try {
                br = new BufferedReader(new FileReader(cvsFileName));
                line = br.readLine();
                while ((line = br.readLine()) != null) {
            // use comma as separator
      String[] itemsintransaction = line.split(",");
                        ArrayList<String> ar = new
ArrayList<String>();
                        for (int i = 0; i <  itemsintransaction.
length; i++)
                        {
                            if (Integer.
parseInt(itemsintransaction[i]) > 0 )
                            {
```

```
                                                ar.add(items.get(i));
                                            }
                                        }
                                        if (ar.size() > 0)
                                        {
                                            log.info("adding a transaction of " +
    ar.toString());
                                            transactions.add( new Pair(ar,1L) );
                                        }
                }
                  } catch (FileNotFoundException e) {
                          log.error(e.getMessage());
                  } catch (IOException e) {
                          log.error(e.getMessage());
                  } finally {
                          if (br != null) {
                                  try {
                                          br.close();
                                  } catch (IOException e) {
                                          log.error(e.getMessage());
                                  }
                          }
                  }
    }
```

As you must have noticed, basically, we parse line by line (except the first one) from the `marketbasket.csv` file that contains the transactions. In this case, considering that the full item list is always fully initialized, we split every line into an array of string containing zeros and ones. Then we looped this array and every time we found a quantity, it means that in the transaction, if the item in position `i` has been bought, we add it to our transactions. Then we add the resulting transaction to our `transactions` object by specifying a default `minSupport` value for every transaction, that is, `1L`. You should have noticed that some transactions do not involve any item of the grocery, so insert only valid transactions within the code:

```
if (ar.size() > 0)
{
  log.info("adding a transaction of " + ar.toString());
  transactions.add( new Pair(ar,1L) );
}
```

Using the `slf4j` logging library, we also provide some logging to let the users see the soundness of the transactions loaded during computation. We can see something like the following screenshot:

```
adding a transaction of [ Diet Cola]
adding a transaction of [ Lettuce]
adding a transaction of [ Hair Conditioner,  Dishwasher Detergent,  Diet
adding a transaction of [ Orange Juice,  Bologna,  Bananas]
adding a transaction of [ Chocolate Bar,  Paper Plates]
adding a transaction of [ Honey Roasted Peanuts,  Peaches,  Soft Tissue]
adding a transaction of [ Cream Soda]
adding a transaction of [ Hair Conditioner,  98pct. Fat Free Hamburger,
adding a transaction of [ Ranch Dip]
adding a transaction of [ Smoked Turkey Sliced,  Plums,  Chocolate Chip
adding a transaction of [ Frozen Chicken Wings,  Sugar Cookies,  Onions,
adding a transaction of [ Columbian Coffee]
adding a transaction of [ Peach Shampoo,  Toilet Paper]
adding a transaction of [ Hair Conditioner,  98pct. Fat Free Hamburger,
adding a transaction of [ Frozen Sausage Pizza]
adding a transaction of [ Orange Flavored Fruit Bars]
```

Just to see that everything is correct, we computed the frequencies and output them using the logging framework:

```
private void findFrequencies() {
  frequencies = fps.generateFList(transactions.iterator(), (int)
minSupport);
   for (Pair<String, Long> frequency : frequencies)
   {
     log.info("frequency of item : " + frequency.toString() + " up to "
+ transactions.size()  );
   }
}
```

The result should flow on the output console, as shown in the following screenshot:

```
frequency of item : ( Eggs,167) up to 1260
frequency of item : ( White Bread,162) up to 1260
frequency of item : ( 2pct. Milk,149) up to 1260
frequency of item : ( Potato Chips,133) up to 1260
frequency of item : ( 98pct. Fat Free Hamburger,127) up to 1260
frequency of item : ( Hot Dogs,126) up to 1260
frequency of item : ( Sweet Relish,116) up to 1260
frequency of item : ( Onions,109) up to 1260
frequency of item : ( Toothpaste,108) up to 1260
frequency of item : ( Cola,106) up to 1260
frequency of item : ( Wheat Bread,105) up to 1260
frequency of item : ( Toilet Paper,101) up to 1260
frequency of item : ( Hamburger Buns,97) up to 1260
frequency of item : ( Pepperoni Pizza - Frozen,94) up to 1260
frequency of item : ( Domestic Beer,92) up to 1260
```

Then we need to set up two objects required for the MapReduce implementation to work, the `updater` and the `output` objects respectively. To ensure the code is as compact as possible, we implement all the methods required for the two objects.

The updater is a `StatusUpdater` object, so only the `update` method has been overridden to provide some logging info. The whole initialization part is handled by the `initUpdater` method.

```
private void initUpdater()
{
  updater = new StatusUpdater() {
    public void update(String status) {
    log.info("updater :" + status);
    }
  };
}
```

More interesting is the implementation of the `output` object that is done in the `createOutput()` method.

```
private void createOutput() {
    output = new OutputCollector<String, List<Pair<List<String>,
Long>>>() {

      @Override
      public void collect(String x1, List<Pair<List<String>, Long>>
listPair) throws IOException {
    StringBuffer sb = new StringBuffer();
    sb.append(x1 + ":");
    for (Pair<List<String>, Long> pair : listPair) {
    sb.append("[");
      String sep = "";
      for (String item : pair.getFirst()) {
      sb.append(item + sep);
      sep = ", ";
      }
      sb.append("]:" + pair.getSecond());
    }
    log.info("createOutput:  " + sb.toString());
    }
  };
}
```

This method basically only overrides the `collect` method to output some information. As a result, during computation of the `output` object, the `collect` method will output some info like the output shown in the following screenshot:

```
updater :Bottom Up FP Growth
updater :Bottom Up FP Growth
updater :Bottom Up FP Growth
updater :Bottom Up FP Growth
updater :Bottom Up FP Growth
updater :FPGrowth Algorithm for a given feature: 250
updater :FPGrowth Algorithm for a given feature: 251
updater :FPGrowth Algorithm for a given feature: 252
updater :FPGrowth Algorithm for a given feature: 253
updater :FPGrowth Algorithm for a given feature: 254
 createOutput  Cheese Flavored Chips:[ Cheese Flavored Chips]:8[ 2pct.
```

Finally, we come to the interesting part of the algorithm itself, calling the Frequent Pattern Mining algorithm. The code that does the whole elaboration is only one single line:

```
fps.generateTopKFrequentPatterns(
            transactions.iterator(),
            frequencies,
            minSupport,
            k,
            null,
            output,
            updater);
```

As we can see, all the values set or initialized are used as parameters.

In this case, we did not store the output on a `Map` object to save it as a sequence file. To do this, we need to change the implementations on the `output.collect` method. One possible change could be the following:

```
@Override
        public void collect(String key, List<Pair<List<String>,Long>>
value) {
          for (Pair<List<String>,Long> v : value) {
            List<String> l = v.getFirst();
            results.put(Sets.newHashSet(l), v.getSecond());
          }
        }
```

The result is declared as follows:

```
Map<Set<String>,Long> results = Maps.newHashMap();
```

As a last word, we have only detailed a little bit better how the Frequent Pattern Mining algorithm works.

The core of the algorithm is a data structure called Frequent Pattern Tree (FP-tree), that in the language of mathematics is an undirected simple graph that is connected and any two vertices are always connected with a simple path. The FP-tree is represented as follows:

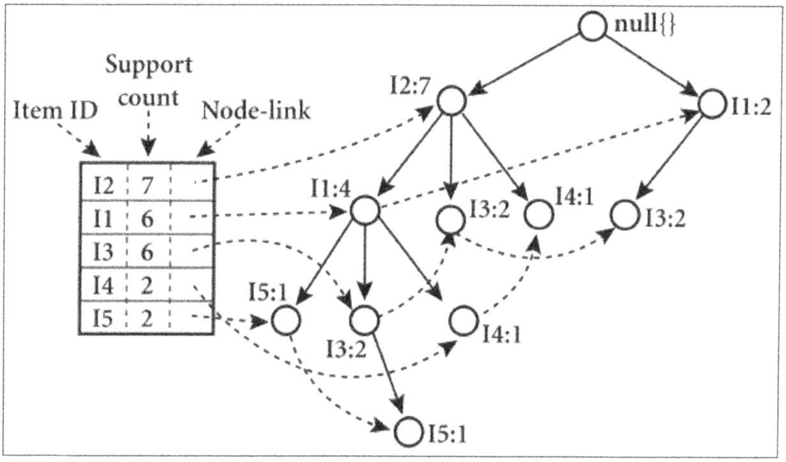

Starting from the initial dataset, we create a tree where every node represents an item and the edges between nodes represent the fact that if item `i` is present in one transaction with item `j`, then there is an edge between `i` and `j` connecting them.

The FP-tree is also characterized by the following properties: the root node is the one that is null and every other node is described by the following three fields:

- **Item name**: This is the name of the items
- **Count**: This is the number of items connected
- **Link:** This will be 1 if the next node contains the same item name and 0 otherwise

The whole algorithm works with the FP-Tree in a two-stage operation:

- Building the FP-tree
- Growing the tree to find association rules

The procedure for growing the tree is: scan the FP-tree, and for every `i` node consider that the subtree having the `i` node as the root node and generate another pattern by adding a new node whose fields are defined using the `minSupport` input value. So the algorithm chooses the item (node) `i` and considers all the other nodes that are connected, that is, have common transactions with item `i`. For a full reference of the method, we cite the seminal paper by *Jiawen Han* available at `http://www.cs.uiuc.edu/~hanj/pdf/dami04_fptree.pdf`.

Obviously, we did not let MapReduce enter the theory right now. Only for reference, we cite the following: `https://blog.antecons.net/2012/11/11/mapreduce-and-frequent-patterns/`.

Using LDA for creating topics

In this recipe, we will code a full command-line example of topic extraction from text using the **LDA** (**Latent Dirichlet Allocation**) algorithm.

The LDA algorithm was first used to extract topics from documents but can be generalized to find new unobserved topics from observed data.

Getting ready

To get started, we need (as usual) a dataset for testing purposes. In this case, we will use the usual Reuters e-mail dataset. The steps involved prior to applying the LDA learning algorithm are as follows:

1. Convert the whole dataset into the `SequenceFile` format.
2. Create weighted vectors from the sequence file.

Let us start by downloading the Reuters archive for our analysis. So open up a terminal window and type in the following command:

```
export WORK_DIR=/mnt/new/lda
mkdir $WORK_DIR
mkdir $WORK_DIR/input
mkdir $WORK_DIR/sequencefiles
mkdir $WORK_DIR/vectors
mkdir $WORK_DIR/ouput
mkdir $WORK_DIR/reutersfinal
cd $WORK_DIR
```

So, we have the folder structure shown in the following screenshot:

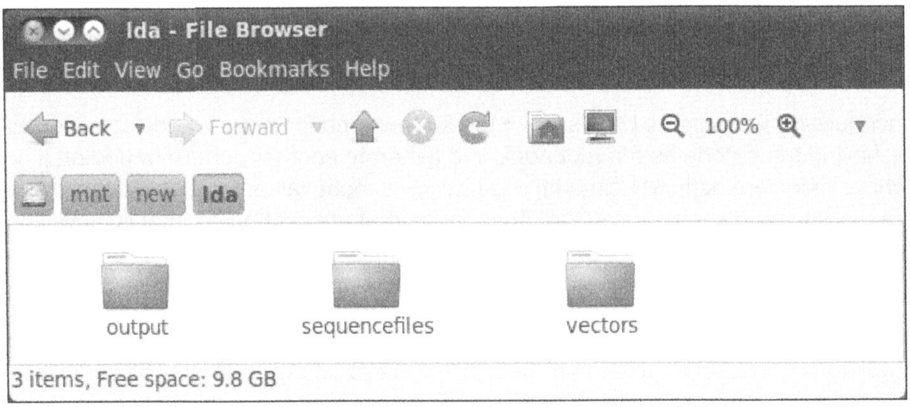

Now we need to download and decompress the Reuters archive. To do this, in your `$WORK_DIR` folder, type in the following command:

```
wget http://kdd.ics.uci.edu/databases/reuters21578/reuters21578.tar.gz

tar xvzf reuters21578.tar.gz -C $WORK_DIR/input
```

Now the folder should appear as shown in the following screenshot, where the whole Reuters dataset is extracted into the `input` folder:

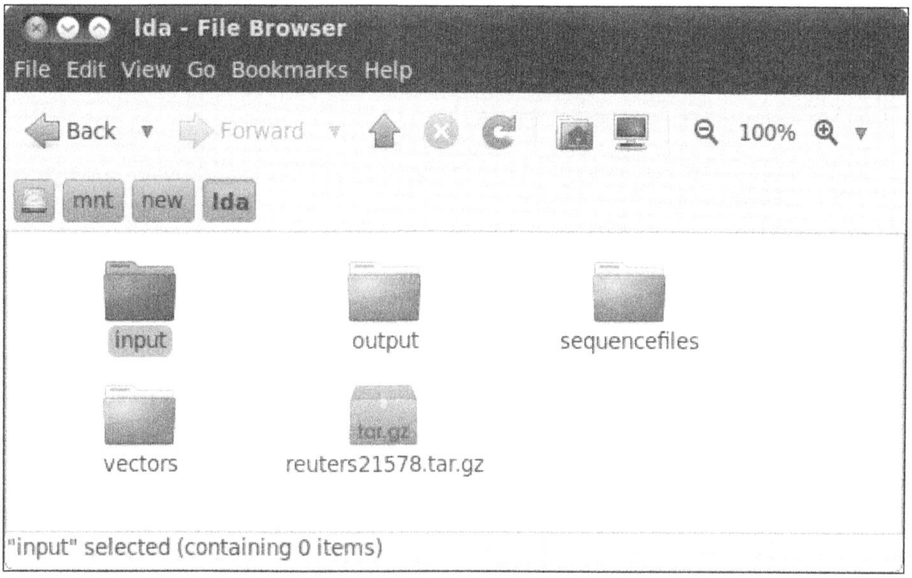

We are now ready to conduct our analysis with some preprocessing tasks.

How to do it...

Prior to proceeding with the LDA algorithm, we need to do three major preprocessing tasks:

1. Creating a sequence file from the documents.
2. Constructing the vectors for the weights.
3. Applying the LDA algorithm.

So prior to proceeding from the `$WORK_DIR` folder, type the following command:

```
mahout  org.apache.lucene.benchmark.utils.ExtractReuters $WORK_DIR/input
$WORK_DIR/reutersfinal
```

This utility will extract the Reuters e-mail in a text file format . We use the `ExtractReuters` class object specifically created for this purpose. The content of a single file is something like the following screenshot:

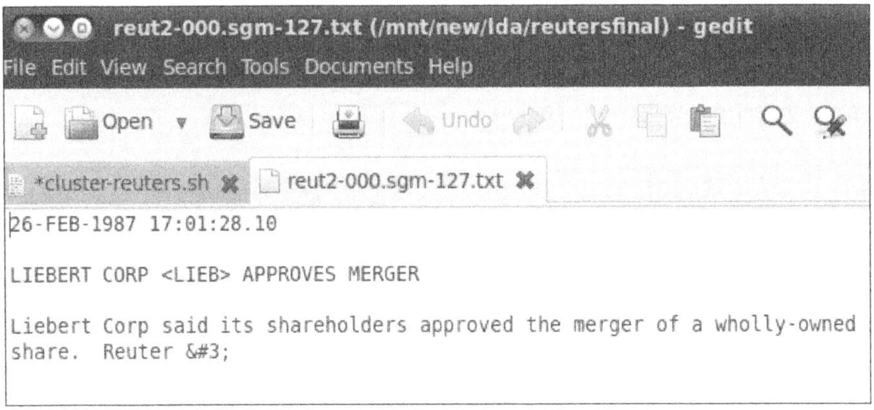

Now that we are ready, we could proceed by creating the `sequencefiles` from this text file. The `seqdirectory` command to be used is:

```
mahout seqdirectory -i $WORK_DIR/reutersfinal -o $WORK_DIR/sequencefiles/
-c UTF-8 -chunk 5
```

This will create the sequence file inside the new folder, `sequencefiles`. To see the file content and how it is organized, we need to type the following command:

```
mahout seqdumper -i ./part-m-00000 -o part-m-00000.txt
```

The result is something like:

```
Input Path: part-m-00000
Key class: class org.apache.hadoop.io.Text Value Class: class org.apache.
hadoop.io.Text
Key: /reut2-000.sgm-301.txt: Value:  2-MAR-1987 04:45:57.78
Key: /reut2-012.sgm-635.txt: Value:  2-APR-1987 12:14:08.24
```

Then, from this sequence file, we need to calculate the weight as we did in *Chapter 5, Stock Market Forecasting with Mahout*, to have the sequence file vector's point ready to be analyzed by the LDA. So our last preprocessing step gives the following commands:

```
mahout seq2sparse -i $WORK_DIR/sequencefiles/ -o $WORK_DIR/vectors/  -wt
tf
mahout seq2sparse -i $WORK_DIR/sequencefiles/ -o $WORK_DIR/vectors/  -wt
tf
```

Now that we have the sparse vectors sequence inside the `vectors` folder, as shown in the following screenshot, we can move on with the core algorithm.

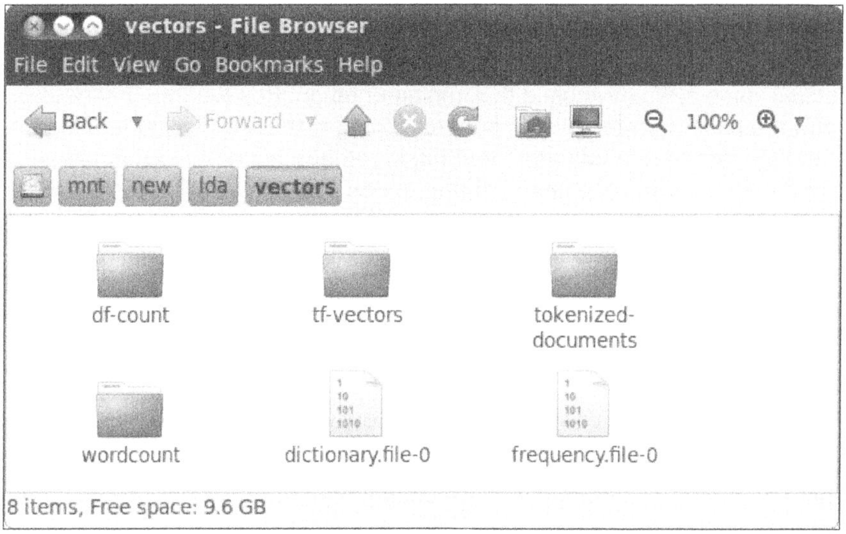

Now we are ready to give our analysis command, which is as follows:

```
mahout cvb -i $WORK_DIR/reuters-out-matrix/matrix  -o $WORK_DIR/reuters-
lda -k 20 -ow -x 20  -dict $WORK_DIR/reuters-out-seqdir-sparse-lda/
dictionary.file-*  -dt $WORK_DIR/reuters-lda-topics  -mt $WORK_DIR/
reuters-lda-model
```

The output will result in the folder named `$WORK_DIR/reuters-lda` as a sequence file object.

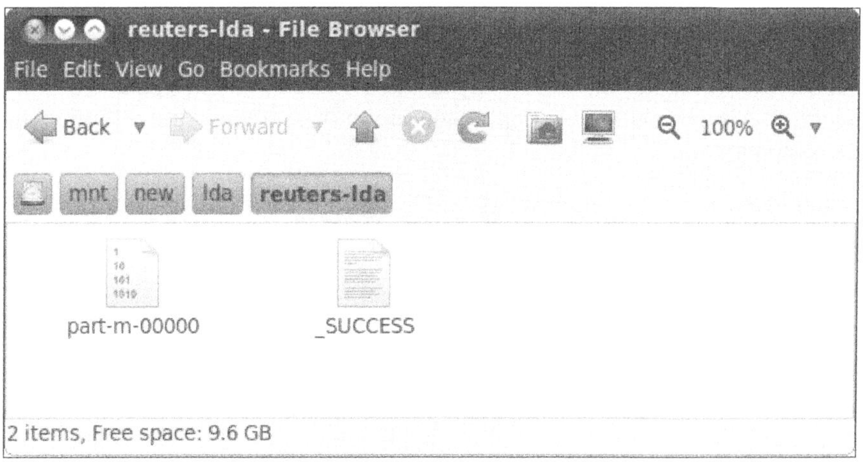

It is now time to understand what we have done.

How it works...

Prior to proceeding with how the Mahout Latent Dirichelet Algorithm works, we need to first let readers know that apart from being based on the MapReduce paradigm, the Mahout LDA implementation has been deprecated in favor of the Collapse Variation Bayes LDA algorithm. So in the actual version, we have used this implementation. However, we first need to explain generally how the base algorithm works prior to moving to the Mahout implementation. The algorithm best fits for text analysis and information retrieval considering that when it was first presented in the journal *Machine Learning*, it was applied to extract topics from a known corpus of documents. So let us start with the simple version of LDA.

Suppose you have a set of documents and a fixed number of topics to discover, and you would like to learn the topics of each document and the number of words belonging to each topic.

The steps for the algorithm are as follows:

1. First go through every document and for every word, assign it to a random chosen topic.
2. This first rough classification will give us the requested number of topics even if it is totally random.

To improve this mapping, we proceed as follows:

1. For each word `w` in a document `D`, compute two quantities: the proportion of words in the document that are currently assigned to topic `t` and the proportion of assignments to topic `t` over all documents that come from this word `w`.
2. Reassign the word `w` to a new topic `t2` with probability that the new topic `t2` generates word `w`. So it makes sense to reassign it.
3. Repeat the previous steps until some limit has been reached or until a maximum error level is reached.

All these steps involve the use of a dictionary to find the appropriate words and to evaluate the frequency. This is why we need to do the analysis prior to creating the dictionary using the `sparse2seq` command.

Mahout implements a modified version of the LDA algorithm, the Collapsed Variation Bayes LDA. The original paper can be found at `http://machinelearning.wustl.edu/mlpapers/paper_files/NIPS2006_511.pdf`.

The power of the algorithm relies on the fact that the computational part can be approximated in a good way. As the name suggests, the algorithm uses the Bayesian inference to estimate the probability of a word to be associated with a topic.

The main computational tasks are performed using the following command line.

```
mahout cvb -i $WORK_DIR/reuters-out-matrix/matrix  -o $WORK_DIR/reuters-
lda -k 20 -ow -x 20  -dict $WORK_DIR/reuters-out-seqdir-sparse-lda/
dictionary.file-*  -dt $WORK_DIR/reuters-lda-topics  -mt $WORK_DIR/
reuters-lda-model
```

The command-line parameter needs a more detailed description:

- The `input` folder is where the input job relies
- The `output` folder is where the sequence file will be created
- The `K` parameter is the number of topics to generate
- The `X` parameter is the maximum number of words to aggregate into a topic
- The `-ow` directive instructs to remove the final output if it exists
- The `-dict` tells you where the dictionary is located (the `output` folder)
- The `-dt` is the output path for the document training
- The `-mt` is the model topic folder

Once the computation is completed, to see the results, you can use the `ldatopics` tool provided by Mahout. The command is pretty easy:

```
mahout ldatopics \
    -i <input vectors directory> \
    -d <input dictionary file> \
```

Obviously in this example, we mimic the LDA on text mining. The algorithm works well both with structured and unstructured text, and it has been successfully used in other prediction tasks. We suggest the reader takes a look at the Scirus website to see the field of applications.

We also suggest the reader tries different topics and number of words per topic to evaluate which is the best solution.

10
Implementing the Genetic Algorithm in Mahout

In this last chapter we will deal with a very well-known type of algorithm called the genetic algorithm, also referred to as GA. It can extract information from a dataset using algorithms that mimic the natural world.

In particular, we will see the following recipes:

- Setting up Mahout for using GA
- Using the genetic algorithm over graphs
- Using the genetic algorithm from Java code

Introduction

In this chapter, we will cover the examples contained in a previous Mahout version and not the one that we use in the whole book. The reason is mostly pedagogical as we want to show the possibilities offered by Mahout's evolutionary algorithm framework. So we will review in a deeper manner the examples that are contained and are available to the reader through Apache License.

Setting up Mahout for using GA

Before proceeding, you should know that for this recipe, we are going to use an older version of the evolutionary algorithm. The first MapReduce implementation of genetic algorithm in Mahout was done using an external framework. But in the current version of Mahout Version 0.8—the one we have used throughout the whole book—this support has been withdrawn.

To do this, we need to reset the development environment to let the reader use this kind of algorithm. This first recipe is divided into two steps:

- Downloading the correct revision of the Mahout developing environment
- Compiling and testing it

For compatibility with what has been done until now, we will use NetBeans, even if it is possible to use `git` and `maven` from the command line.

Getting ready

To start, first of all, fire up NetBeans, then go to the menu and choose **Team** | **git** | **clone** and enter the following details in the form:

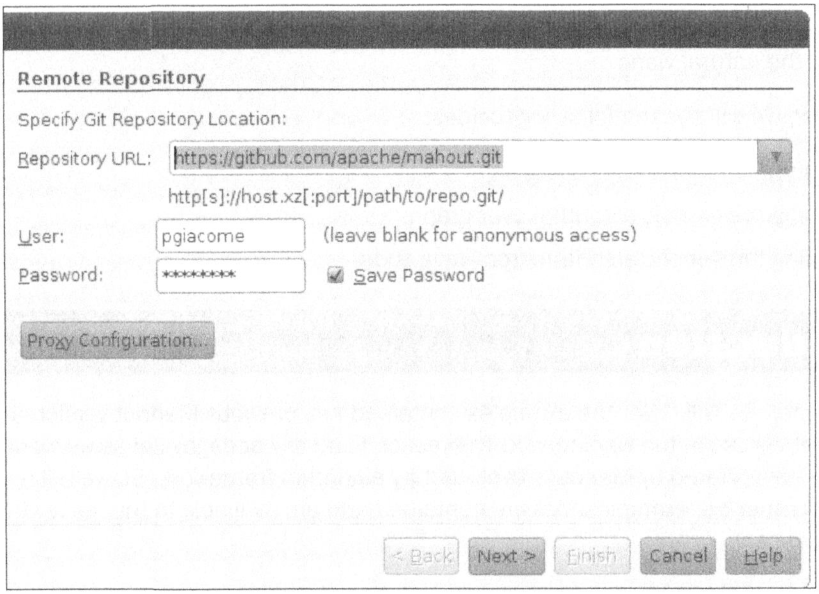

> It is strongly suggested to register at GitHub (`www.github.com`), as this is the official supported versioning system for the Apache Mahout framework.

Select the Mahout version you want to use; in this case, it is 1.0—the latest one that supports the GA implementation:

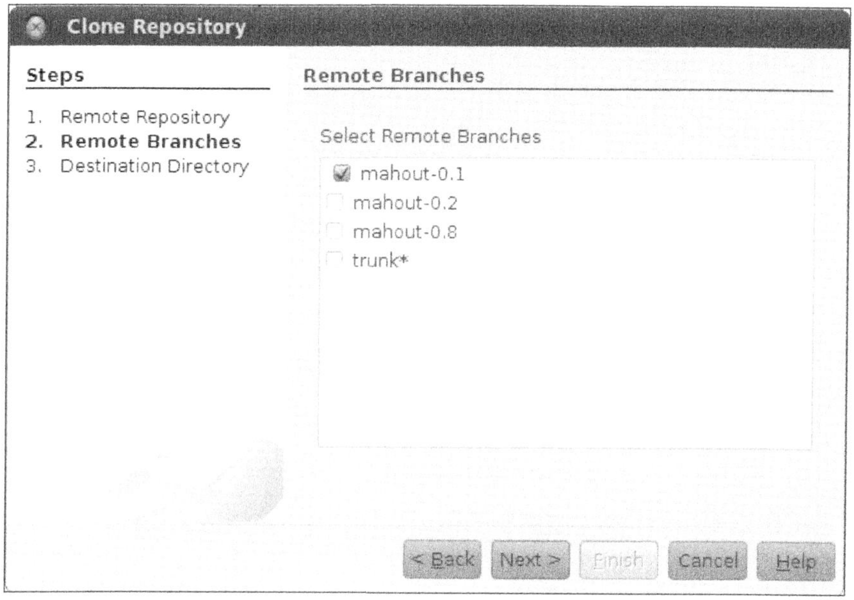

Then in the window that appears, enter the local folder where you want to clone the remote repository; in our case, enter `mahout0.1` to distinguish it from the current Mahout folder we used in *Chapter 1, Mahout is Not So Difficult!*, for Version 0.8 of Mahout.

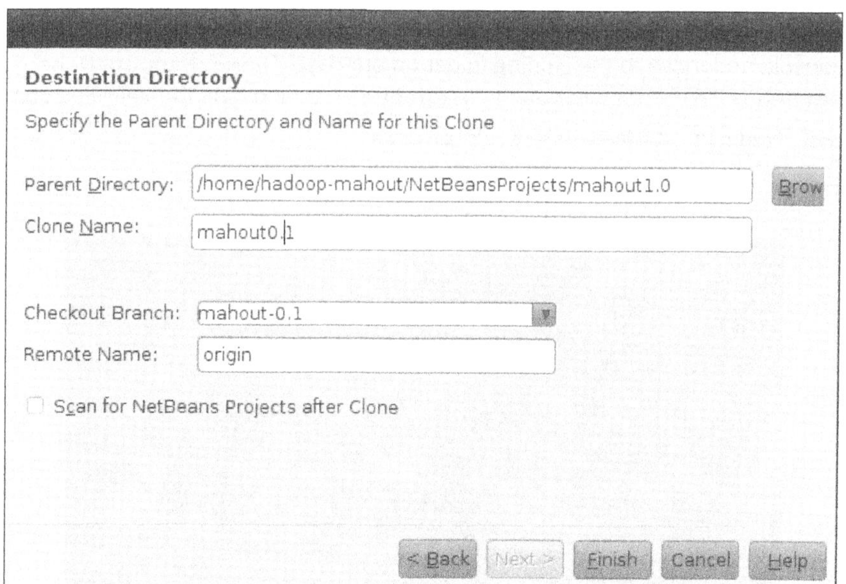

By clicking on the **Finish** button, after a while the output window should display the following lines:

```
Output - mahout0.1 - /home/hadoop-mahout/NetBeansProjects/mahout1.0/mahout0.1
Tag    : mahout-0.4
Result : NEW

Tag    : mahout-0.5
Result : NEW

Tag    : mahout-0.6
Result : NEW

Tag    : mahout-0.7
Result : NEW

Tag    : mahout-0.8
Result : NEW

setting up remote: origin
git branch --track mahout-0.1 origin/mahout-0.1
git checkout mahout-0.1
==[IDE]== Oct 7, 2013 1:49:41 PM Cloning... finished.

Search Results  Output
```

We will now proceed with the compilation part.

How to do it...

1. In the cloning local folder, we have the Maven main `pom.xml` file that can be compiled. To compile it from the command line, just open up a terminal console and move to the cloning folder (in our case `/home/Hadoop-Mahout/NetBeansProjects/mahout1.0/mahout1.0`) and type the following command:

   `mvn install -Dmaven.test.skip=true`

2. This will output the following lines:

```
[INFO] ------------------------------------------------------------------------
[INFO] Reactor Summary:
[INFO]
[INFO] Mahout Build Tools ................................ SUCCESS [2.402s]
[INFO] Apache Mahout ..................................... SUCCESS [0.419s]
[INFO] Mahout Math ....................................... SUCCESS [8.148s]
[INFO] Mahout Core ....................................... SUCCESS [12.527s
[INFO] Mahout Integration ................................ SUCCESS [0.812s]
[INFO] Mahout Examples ................................... SUCCESS [14.878s
[INFO] Mahout Release Package ............................ SUCCESS [0.019s]
[INFO] ------------------------------------------------------------------------
[INFO] BUILD SUCCESS
[INFO] ------------------------------------------------------------------------
[INFO] Total time: 39.544s
[INFO] Finished at: Mon Dec 02 14:47:43 CET 2013
[INFO] Final Memory: 31M/172M
[INFO] ------------------------------------------------------------------------
```

3. If you want NetBeans to compile and create all the JAR files required, you should go to the **Main** menu and choose **File** | **Open Project**, locate the folder used to clone the project and then click on the **Open project** button as follows:

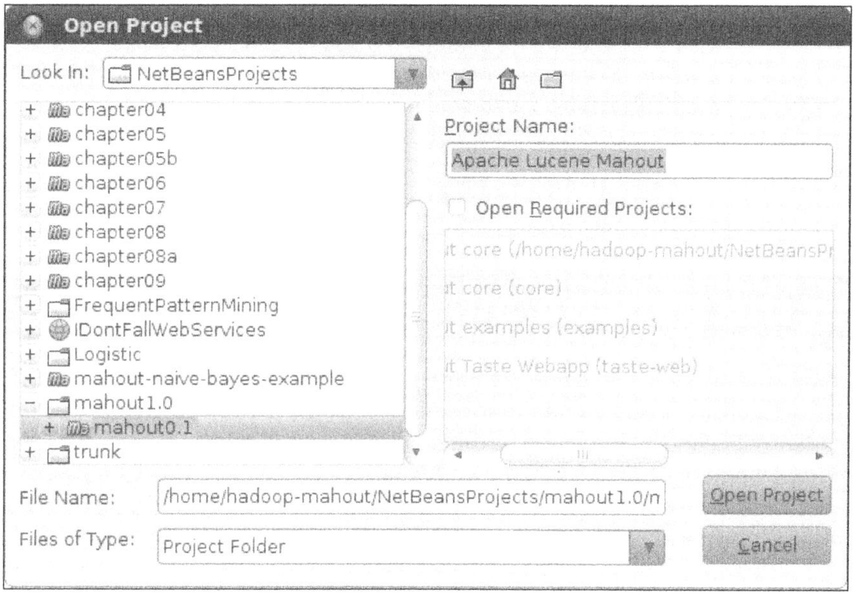

4. Once opened, the project can be compiled by right-clicking the mouse button and by choosing the **Clean and Build** menu item as follows:

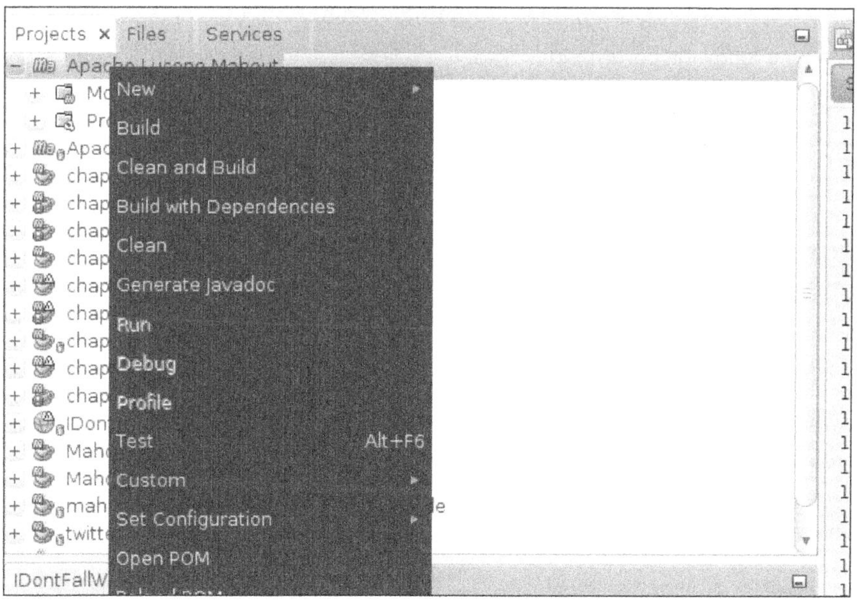

After finishing here, we have a fully functional Mahout 0.1 release that also contains the GA examples.

> One last word: the careful reader should have noticed that in the command line we skipped the testing phase, but while using NetBeans we do the testing. Obviously, if you want to avoid full testing, it can be done. For reference, see `http://stackoverflow.com/questions/6074752/in-netbeans-7-how-do-i-skip-testing-and-add-maven-additional-parameters-when-bui`.

Using the genetic algorithm over graphs

In this section, we will use GA to solve the famous **Traveling Salesman Problem** (**TSP**). Imagine, you are a traveling salesman that has to visit some cities that are connected by street. A generic city can be connected to the remaining with different streets. Traveling from one city to the other has a cost depending on the street you choose. The TSP tries to find the cheapest route to visit all of the cities. The problem can be restated for every graph, for example, the routers network and the link between sites.

Getting ready

Basically, we have everything set up by the previous recipe, but as in this recipe we will use the command-line utility, we need to be sure that the `$MAHOUT_HOME` environment variable is configured to point to the right folder. So prior to proceeding, we need to launch the command line and give the following command:

```
export $MAHOUT_HOME=/home/Hadoop-Mahout/NetBeansProjects/mahout1.0/
mahout1.0
```

You should accordingly change it to the folder where you saved the git distribution.

How to do it...

To test the implementation of GA for the TSP, we need to be on the same terminal console where we set up the `$MAHOUT_HOME` environment variable. Perform the following steps:

1. Type in the following command:

   ```
   cd $MAHOUT_HOME
   ```

   ```
   mahout org.apache.mahout.ga.watchmaker.travellingsalesman.
   TravellingSalesman
   ```

The following window should appear:

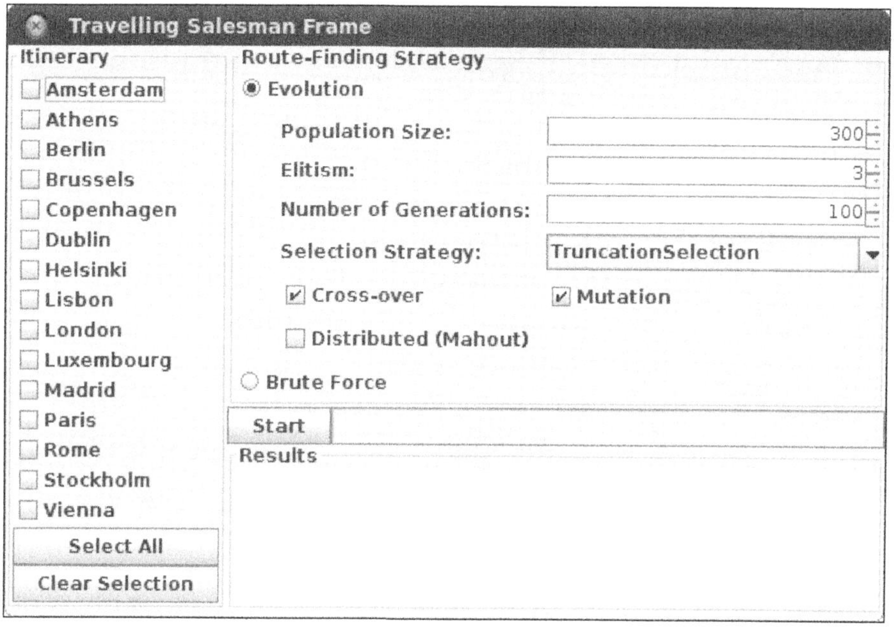

2. Now to proceed, click on the **Select All** button, and the form should look like the following screenshot:

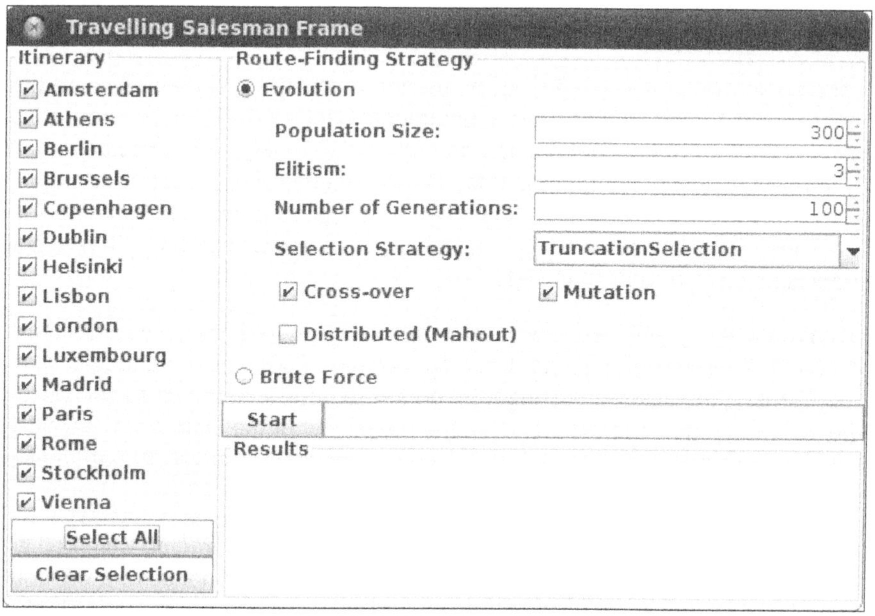

3. Now click on the **Start** button and after a while, in the **Results** panel, something like the following screenshot should appear:

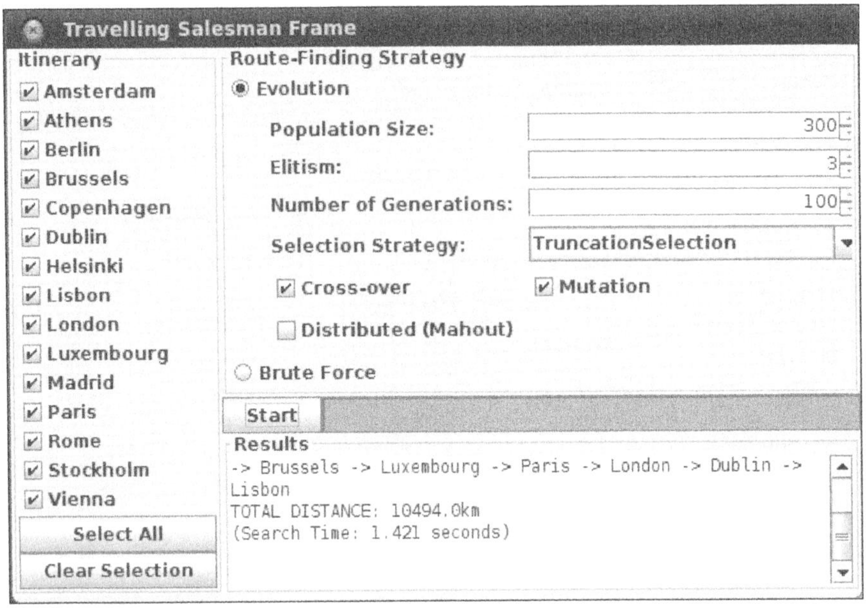

We are now ready to understand what happened.

How it works...

TSP is a very well-known problem in the graph theory, which was first defined as we know it by Hamilton during the first decade of the nineteenth century. The problem spans from Mathematics to the Complexity theory and Computer Science. Even now, its popularity is constantly increasing as it deals with the best way to walk through a graph. The problem was shown to an NP-hard, meaning that there is no existing algorithm to solve it in a polynomial time. This means that if we have n cities, it takes k time to find a solution; with $n+1$ cities, the time to find a solution is greater than $k+1$.

Mathematically speaking, let us start with an undirected weighted graph, which means a graph composed of vertices and edges. The edge between node *x* and *y* is tagged with a number representing the cost from going from node *x* to node *y*. In the classical case, we can think of the nodes as cities and the edges as the mean cost of the flight from one city to the other. Given a set of cities, the TSP consists on finding the least costly flight path that exists between the cities in the whole set.

Recall the mathematical theory behind the claim that giving an undirected weighted graph with m nodes not directly connected. What is the path between the nodes that minimize the value of the sum of all the edges?

Considering the formulation, the simplest way to solve this problem by a computer is the brute force algorithm that consists of the following computational steps:

- First find all available path from node x to node y
- For every path, compute the total cost path
- Find the minimum of this set

The brute force approach also gives the exact solution, but the really big problem is that while it is relatively easy to compute the last two steps, the first one is computationally expensive. Consider that in a graph we have n nodes, the possible number of paths could scale up to *n!*, where *n! = n(n-1)(n-2)...2*. With only 20 cities, we find that the number of a possible paths connecting to them could be 20! Believe me, this one number is very, very big. A 30-city tour would have to measure the total distance of *2.65 X 1032* different tours. Assuming a trillion additions per second, this would take 252,333,390,232,297 years. Adding one more city would cause the time to increase by a factor of 31. Obviously, this is an impossible solution.

In our recipe, we use some EU capitals as the node for our graph to find the solution to the TSP. The brute force approach can be set using the **Brute Force** radio button as follows:

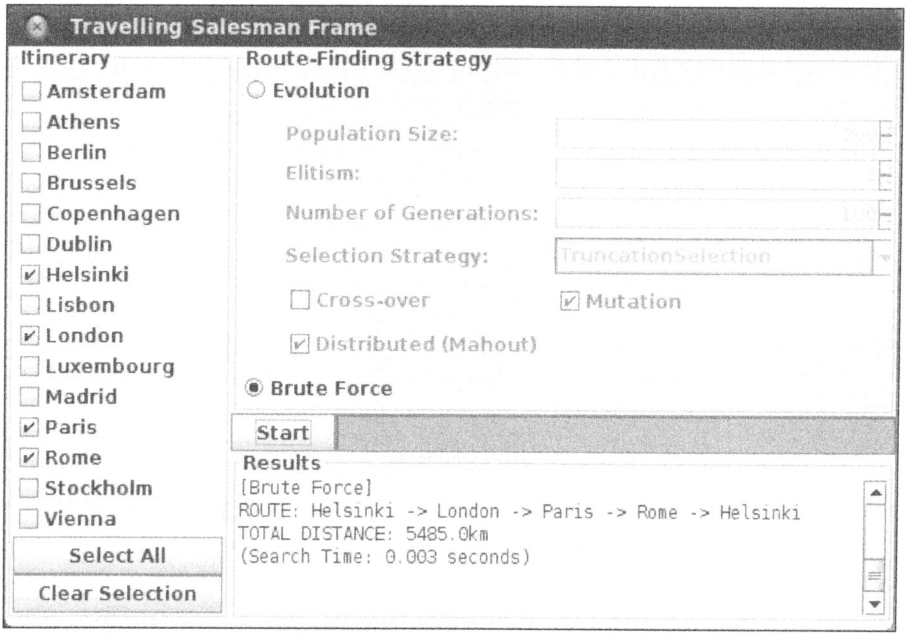

> We use only four cities, which is the minimum number allowed to test whether one can progressively increase the number of cities to see the computational time increase in non-linear progression.

Another proposed solution to the TSP algorithm is to use the evolutionary approach. The concept behind genetic and evolutionary algorithm deals with evolution.

Only for the sake of completeness, the reader could take a look at a Java brute force solution to the TSP available at `http://www.jimscode.ca/index.php/component/content/article/18-java/22-java-travelling-salesman-via-brute-force`.

The algorithm is composed by starting a population. Then a loop is started on the population. At every step of the loop, a new population is created from the previous one using a random selection of the genes that compose the previous one. Then, the new population is evaluated against an objective function to see whether the new population is better than the previous one. This loops end until a threshold value is raised or after a great amount of iterations. In our case, we need to detail the population and how it evolves, coupled with the objective function.

So, rewriting the GA implementation using the TSP language, the algorithm implementations will be formed by the following steps:

1. The population is composed of a set of semi-random generated tours from the set of cities.
2. Select two of the shortest paths from the initial population; combine them to obtain two new child tours.
3. The new child tours are inserted into the population replacing two of the longer tours. The size of the population remains the same.
4. The process is repeated until no increase in the shortness of the child path happens or until a total number of iterations are reached.
5. The difficult part is the evolution from the parent tours to the child tours by defining how they combine. We will not go too deep into the details, but the operation involves a crossover and/or mutation operation between single paths.

The windows we have seen basically allow us to choose the initial set of cities for the definition of the TSP algorithm. Then, we can choose the initial population of random chosen tours. Then we can choose respectively:

- The total number of populations to generate
- The way we mutate one child tour to the parent one by using mutation or crossover
- The elitism number—that is the maximum number of individual parents that can survive in the next generation—is appropriate for the fitting function

Besides, we can decide to use Mahout if we want to use the MapReduce implementation

This is the basic point where Computer Science meets Biology. If we have two organisms that tend to reproduce themselves, the DNA from the parents is mixed so that the newborn does not receive only the direct DNA from one of the two parents, but a mixture of them. This is the crossover action. The mutation is randomly changed in the DNA that affects the newborn, so that the blind force of mutation can donate to the next generation's organism the ability to be more adaptable to the new environment with respect to the parents that generate it.

If we translate this to the algorithm, it implies that after every new generation, a mixture of the path between the two parents' paths are recombined, plus some random changes are added. This will create a new path that could be more adaptable to minimize the total cost of the weighted edges between two cities.

For reference, we point the curious reader to the introductory text book *Introduction to Genetic Algorithms, Springer* (`http://www.springer.com/engineering/computational+intelligence+and+complexity/book/978-3-540-73189-4`).

We invite the reader to try different combinations of the parameter and above all, to test whether the brute force solution—that is, the correct one—is also best approximated by a different implementation.

Using the genetic algorithm from Java code

We are now ready to code a more complicated recipe both from the programming part as well as the theoretical background. Before proceeding, we need to set up our NetBeans environment to use the Mahout version we downloaded and Maven compiled in the previous recipe.

Getting ready

Let us start by firing up our NetBeans IDE. Then, as we did many times during the book, create a new quick-start Maven project called `chapter10`; the final result should be like the following screenshot:

Now, it is time to connect the Mahout code to get the Mahout release that contains the implementation.

From the explorer tab where we just created the new project, right-click on the Dependencies icon and the from the menu item, choose **Add Dependencies**, and then complete the form as follows:

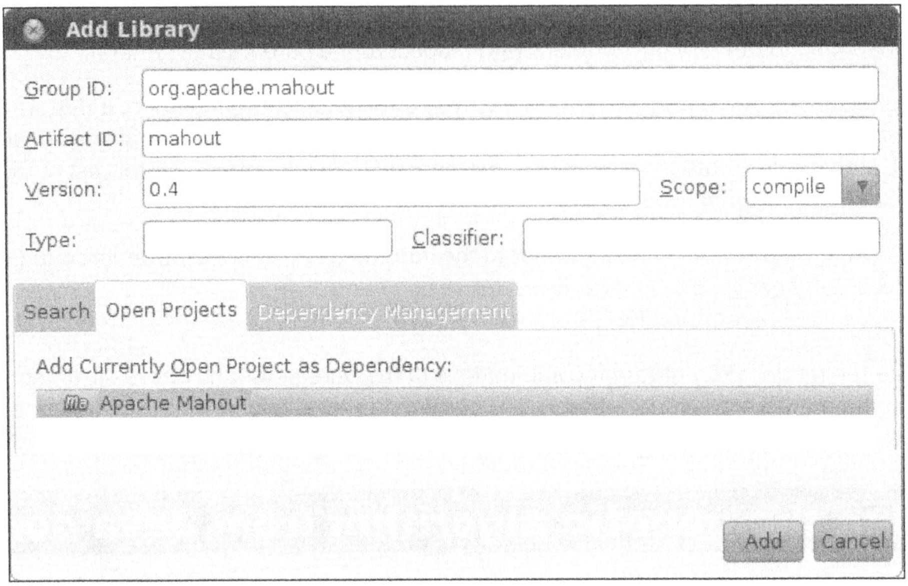

Once you have added the Mahout version, you could clean and build the whole project to obtain the following as the final result:

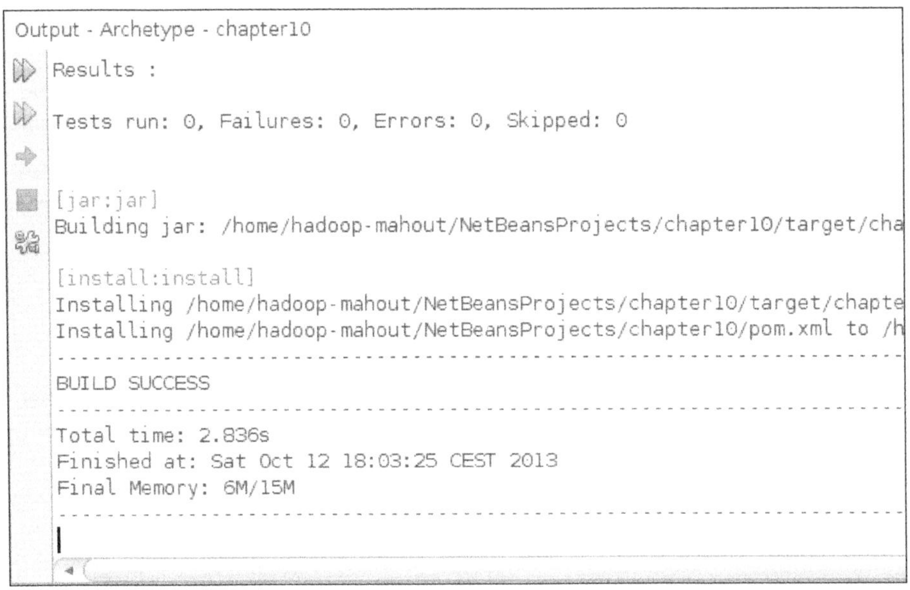

For this example, we also need to use a file as a dataset; we need to move the data from its default location to the new one.

Open up a terminal window and type the following commands:

```
export $WORK_DIR=/mnt/GA
mkdir $WORK_DIR
cd $WORK_DIR
```

Now we need to copy the file required for our analysis into this folder to have it ready to be used. With the correct `$MAHOUT_HOME` variable set, we need to type the following command:

```
cp -R $MAHOUT_HOME/examples/src/test/resources/* $WORK_DIR
```

Two files are copied: the `wdbc.infos` file, and a `wdbc` folder that contains the `wdbc.data` file. The `wdbc.infos` file has the following content:

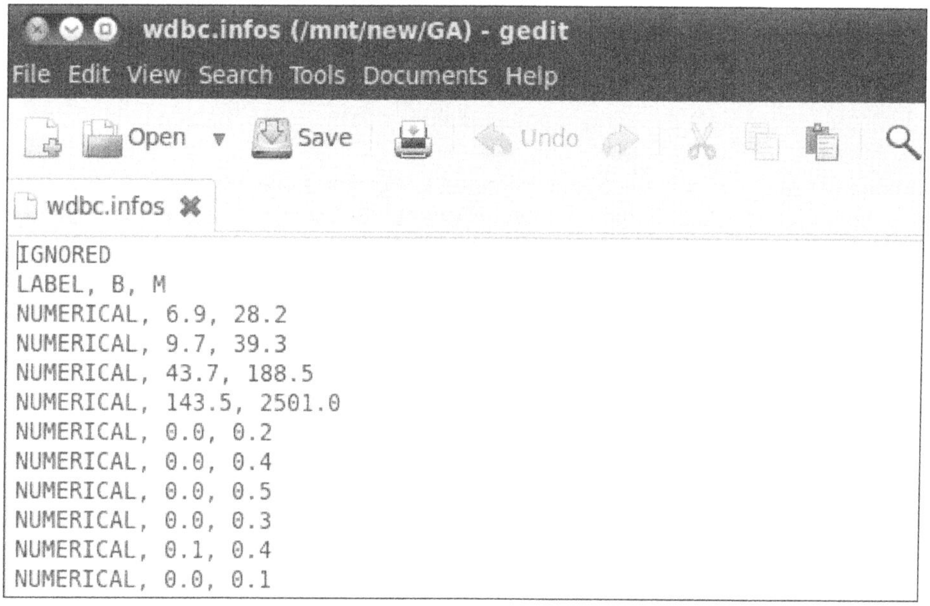

The `wdbc.data` file has the following content:

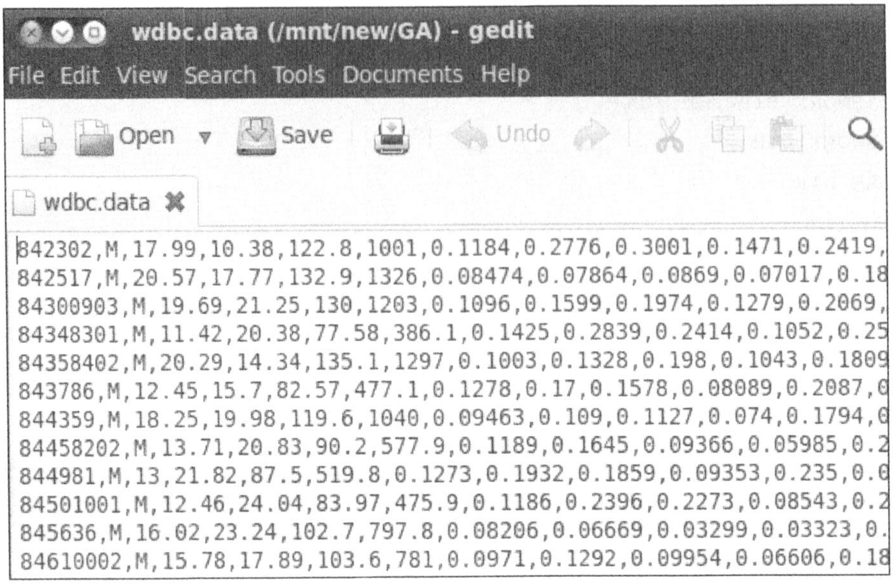

The purpose of this example is to code some classification rules over this dataset. The dataset itself has been used for classification purpose in *Chapter 7, Spectral Clustering in Mahout*. We suggest the reader refers to the recipes there or to the website that describes its attributes (`http://mlearn.ics.uci.edu/databases/breast-cancer-wisconsin/`). It is important to note that the `wdbc.infos` file that describes the content of every variable to be discrete or continuous, is not mandatory. So if you are thinking of recoding the example with another dataset, it is important to create the same file that contains the description of the columns involved.

We are now ready to move to the coding phase.

How to do it...

1. Open up the default generated `App.java` class and add the following lines inside the `main` method:

```
String dataset = "target";

int target = 1;
double threshold = 0.9;
int crosspnts = 1;
double mutrate= 0.033;
double mutrange= 0.1;
int mutprec= 0;
```

```
int popSize= 100;
int genCount= 10;

Path inpath = new Path(dataset);
CDMahoutEvaluator cdMahoutEvaluator;
CDMahoutEvaluator.initializeDataSet(inpath);

CandidateFactory<CDRule> factory = new CDFactory(threshold);

List<EvolutionaryOperator<CDRule>> operators = new ArrayList<Evolu
tionaryOperator<CDRule>>();
operators.add(new CDCrossover(crosspnts));
operators.add(new CDMutation(mutrate, mutrange, mutprec));
EvolutionPipeline<CDRule> pipeline = new EvolutionPipeline<CDRule>
(operators);

DatasetSplit split = new DatasetSplit(0.75);

FitnessEvaluator<? super CDRule> evaluator = new
CDFitnessEvaluator(dataset, target, split);
SelectionStrategy<? super CDRule> selection = new
RouletteWheelSelection();

EvolutionEngine<CDRule> engine =
new SequentialEvolutionEngine<CDRule>(factory, pipeline,
evaluator, selection, RandomUtils.getRandom());

engine.addEvolutionObserver(new EvolutionObserver<CDRule>() {
@Override
public void populationUpdate(PopulationData<? extends CDRule>
data) {
      log.info("Generation {}", data.getGenerationNumber());
}
});

Rule solution = engine.evolve(popSize, 1, new
GenerationCount(genCount));

Path output = new Path("output");

CDFitness bestTrainFit = CDMahoutEvaluator.evaluate(solution,
target, inpath, output, split);

split.setTraining(false);
CDFitness bestTestFit = CDMahoutEvaluator.evaluate(solution,
target, inpath, output, split);

log.info("Best solution fitness (train set) : {}", bestTrainFit);
log.info("Best solution fitness (test set) : {}", bestTestFit);
```

2. Then, resolve all the import issues using NetBeans' online help by pressing *Alt + Enter*:

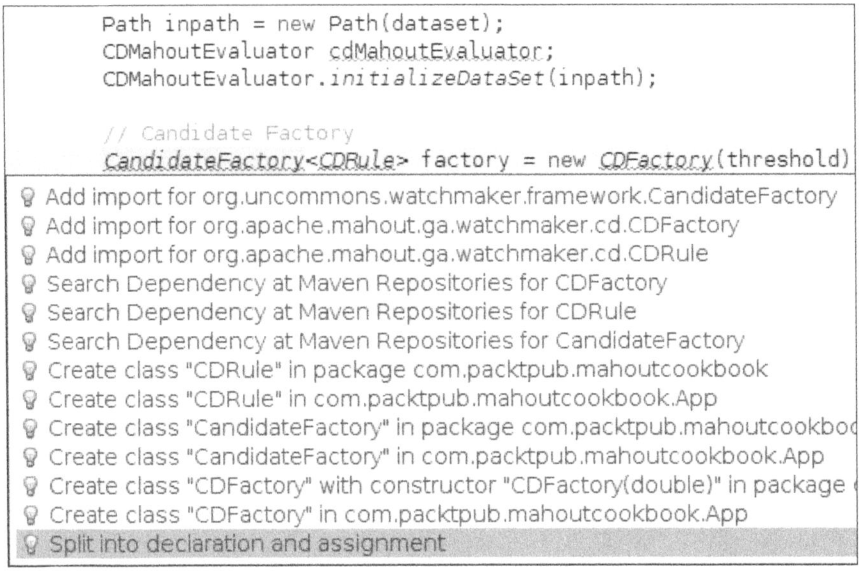

3. Then to run the example, press *F6*.

How it works...

In this example, we are using an evolutionary algorithm to extract rules of the type:

```
If <condition1> && <condition2> &&then apply
```

So basically, what the evolutionary algorithm tries to do is extract these rules from an initially random generated set of rules, where the objective function is the one that minimizes the false positive prediction.

To give an example from the seminal paper, consider a dataset that contains various variables, both discrete as well as numerical. The dataset can be defined as follows:

- Patient unique identifier
- `attribute1` (numeric)
- `attribute2` (numeric)
- ...
- `attributen` (categorical ex male/female)
- Disease (yes/no)

In this case, an evaluation rule can be the following:

```
If (
(attribute1 < 100) and (attribute1 >50)
Or
(attribute2 0.7) and (attributen = male)
)
Then
Disease = yes
```

This rule can be correct for a single line of our dataset, but there could be another line where the same rule leads to different outcomes as follows:

- **True positive**: The rule predicts that the patient has a given disease and the patient does have that disease
- **False positive**: The rule predicts that the patient has a given disease but the patient does not have it
- **True negative**: The rule predicts that the patient does not have a given disease, and indeed the patient does not have it
- **False negative**: The rule predicts that the patient does not have a given disease but the patient does have it

These are all the possible outcomes for every rule in every line of the dataset. We can therefore define the number of true positives, false positives, true negatives, and false negatives, and we indicate them respectively by the number *tp*, *fp*, *tn*, and *fn*. We can consider the quantities such as sensitivity (symbol *Se*) and specificity (*Sp*) defined respectively as follows:

$$Se = \frac{tp}{(tp + fn)}$$

$$Sp = \frac{tn}{(tn + fp)}$$

Without any advanced mathematical skill, you can understand that sensitivity represents the percentage of correct diagnoses over the subset of all the correct diagnoses.

While on the other hand, specificity is the percentage of correct negative answers (true negative means that the rules indicate no disease for the patient and the patient has no disease) over the total incorrect outcomes.

The objective function, in this case, is the product of sensitivity and specificity in formula:

$$f = Se * Sp$$

The problem in terms of the genetic algorithm can be re-stated as follows: given an initial randomly generated set of rules as with the ones we stated, find the ones that maximize the fitness function with evolution. So, this maximizes both the percentage of correct outcomes in case of positive outcomes and the correct outcomes in case of negative outcomes. Thus, the algorithm follows the following high-level pseudocode:

```
create initial random set
loop
 evaluate the whole set of rules against the main dataset
 calculate the fitness function
 generate new set of rules
 until fitness < threadshol or maxmimum number of generation reached
```

In our initial dataset, we have the following column attributes:

- ID number
- Diagnosis (*M = malignant, B = benign*)
- Radius (mean of distances from center to points on the perimeter)
- Texture (standard deviation of gray-scale values)
- Perimeter
- Area
- Smoothness (local variation in radius lengths)
- Compactness (*perimeter^2 / area - 1.0*)
- Concavity (severity of concave portions of the contour)
- Concave points (the number of concave portions of the contour)
- Symmetry
- Fractal dimension (*coastline approximation - 1*)

Our goal is to find a set of rules that we can apply to other values (that is, a new case) to diagnose whether the patient has a benign or malign tumor mass. In our case, the outcome should match the B/M switch on the second column.

In the description of the algorithm, we omit that for neural networks.

So, we transform the whole set into two main sets: the training set and the testing one. The dimension of the training is by default set to 75 percent of the whole set.

To evaluate whether the resulting set of rules is a good one, we evaluate the fitness function over the training set to see whether the final value is less than the one found over the training set. We will not enter all the algorithm details, but as we remember, it uses the MapReduce Hadoop framework. The algorithm itself has been adapted to this particular dataset, so it is not easily portable to other datasets. Instead, our goal is to provide a general view of the problem and the Mahout implementations.

The reader should not forget that the implementation of the GA has been integrated into Mahout, but it is not officially supported.

Let us start with some basic settings. In this case, we only have the initialization of the Hadoop path environment that is required:

```
Path inpath = new Path(dataset);
```

The dataset variable should be the HDFS filesystem where the `wdbc.infos` file is placed. We need to use a specific class created to evaluate the whole dataset and to initialize it:

```
CDMahoutEvaluator cdMahoutEvaluator;
CDMahoutEvaluator.initializeDataSet(inpath);
```

Do not forget that coupled with the dataset file is also the `wdbc.infos` file, which contains also the descriptions and ranges of the numerical variables involved:

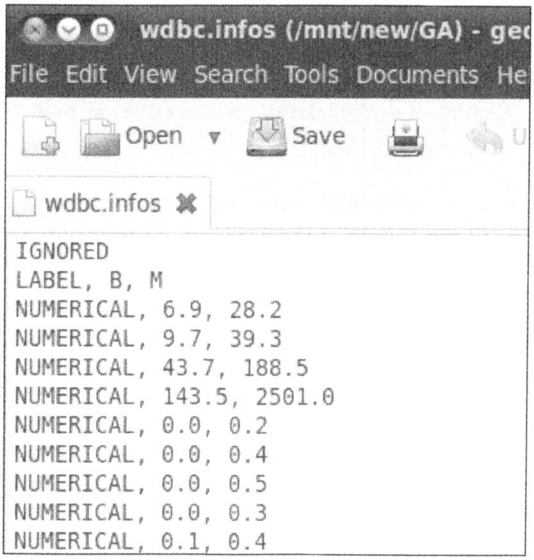

The core part of the Mahout algorithm has been coded using the Watchmaker framework (`http://watchmaker.uncommons.org/`). This framework is a high-performance framework written in Java; the framework provides some ready-to-use key features focused on genetic algorithm evolutionary strategies.

The key analysis is done using the `EvolutionEngine` Java class. The class, once instantiated, can be evolved using its `evolve` or `evolvePopulation` methods. To correctly use the evolution engine, you need to provide the correct rule and above all, the fitness function, which is the core part of the algorithm. This is the basics of how the algorithm works, but obviously in the Hadoop context, an implementation was done.

So prior to using the evolutionary schema, we create a candidate factory, which has the initial population and as a result, has a generic list of the `CDRule` objects:

```
CandidateFactory<CDRule> factory = new CDFactory(threshold);
```

`CDRule` is another object that is the logical mapping of the rule on the form:

```
if (condition1 &amp;&amp; condition2 &amp;&amp; ... ) then
 *   class = 1
 * else
 *   class = 0
```

The rules are evaluated using the following restrictions:

- For numerical attributes, the available operators are `<` and `>=`
- For categorical attributes, the available operators are `!=` and `==`

So, we have the first ingredient, that is, the population of rules to be evolved. Next, we told the engine which evolutionary operators were available for this population:

```
List<EvolutionaryOperator<CDRule>> operators = new ArrayList<Evolution
aryOperator<CDRule>>();

operators.add(new CDCrossover(crosspnts));
operators.add(new CDMutation(mutrate, mutrange, mutprec));

EvolutionPipeline<CDRule> pipeline = new EvolutionPipeline<CDRule>(op
erators);
```

Note that in this case, we use the `CDCrossover` and `CDMutation` operators—both of these objects implemented from the Mahout framework basically use the input parameter to define how the mutation from the two parent rules generate the new child rules.

A coder could also decide to implement his/her own operator. Considering that in the Mahout framework, both the `CDCrossover` and `CDMutation` operators are implemented from the Watchmaker framework abstract class `AbstractCrossover`.

Just for the matter of clarity, the `CDCrossover` operator uses the following method:

```
static void swap(CDRule ind1, CDRule ind2, int index) {

  // swap W
  double dtemp = ind1.getW(index);
  ind1.setW(index, ind2.getW(index));
  ind2.setW(index, dtemp);

  // swap O
  boolean btemp = ind1.getO(index);
  ind1.setO(index, ind2.getO(index));
```

```
        ind2.setO(index, btemp);

        // swap V
        dtemp = ind1.getV(index);
        ind1.setV(index, ind2.getV(index));
        ind2.setV(index, dtemp);
    }
```

In this case, we have two rules that act as the parents and there is one switch, which is the crossover between the rules, to mimic the possible causal mutation that can happen in nature.

We next split the dataset into the training and testing parts to arrive at the last ingredient, that is, the evaluator of the rules to find which one is suitable for surviving:

```
DatasetSplit split = new DatasetSplit(0.75);
. FitnessEvaluator<? super CDRule> evaluator = new
CDFitnessEvaluator(dataset, target, split);

SelectionStrategy<? super CDRule> selection = new
RouletteWheelSelection();
```

So, we have initialized all the elements: dataset and fitness function. It is time to use them in an evolutionary engine and launch it:

```
EvolutionEngine<CDRule> engine =
            new SequentialEvolutionEngine<CDRule>(factory, pipeline,
evaluator, selection, RandomUtils.getRandom());

        engine.addEvolutionObserver(new EvolutionObserver<CDRule>() {
          @Override
          public void populationUpdate(PopulationData<? extends
CDRule> data) {
            log.info("Generation {}", data.getGenerationNumber());
          }
        });
```

Mahout also adds an `EvolutionObserver` event to print out the number of generations every time we update the population in the logging framework. So at the end, we launch the procedure both on the training as well as on the testing dataset:

```
Rule solution = engine.evolve(popSize, 1, new
GenerationCount(genCount));
Path output = new Path("output");
CDFitness bestTrainFit = CDMahoutEvaluator.evaluate(solution, target,
inpath, output, split);
split.setTraining(false);
CDFitness bestTestFit = CDMahoutEvaluator.evaluate(solution, target,
inpath, output, split);
```

Note that `popSize` is passed as the primary parameter to the engine to be sure that in every case the procedure stops after a number of generations. It has been demonstrated (`http://citeseerx.ist.psu.edu/viewdoc/download?doi=10.1.1.105.2431&rep=rep1&type=pdf`) that increasing the number of generations does not improve the best solution too much. On the contrary, having a very large initial population tends to be a discriminant factor over the fitness function. This sounds reasonable because as the population becomes larger, there is an increase in the probability that an important genetic character is presented as one single individual.

Translating the biological term means that in our case, the larger the initial population rules—that is, the more rules I have—the more chances the evolving algorithm has to select an individual very close to the fitness factor.

We warn the reader that even if the GA is a powerful technique to find solutions to an unknown problem without a lot of background analysis, the support in Mahout has been officially discontinued. This means that you could use it at your own risk considering that the Mahout implementation depends on a third-party implementation, which is no longer supported in the current Mahout 0.8 version.

Still, there is an evolutionary algorithm of pure Mahout style implementation that is present in Mahout 0.8. It is the `EvolutionaryProcess` class that is present in the `org.apache.mahout.ep` package. The class is mainly used by the `AdaptiveLogisticRegression` class that we have already seen in *Chapter 5, Stock Market Forecasting with Mahout*.

The `EvolutionaryProcess` class has been implemented starting from the paper by Ted Dunning available online at `http://arxiv.org/abs/0803.3838`. The starting point is always the same. The class deals with a population with an initial size and a function to be optimized. The algorithm also takes an initial seed that is a state object. The constructor is highlighted as follows:

```
  public EvolutionaryProcess(int threadCount, int populationSize,
State<T, U> seed) {
    this.populationSize = populationSize;
    setThreadCount(threadCount);
    initializePopulation(populationSize, seed);
  }
```

The MapReduce implementation comes in with the method `paralledDo` that runs in parallel for all the members of the population of the same action. The method accepts the function to be applied at every state of the population.

There's more...

While you now know how to implement the evolutionary algorithm, please note that it is still in the development state and its final inclusion into the Mahout framework is still a topic of discussion in the Mahout community. We suggest that you take a look at the `dev.mahout.org` forum to see suggestions and if you have the skills to propose an implementation. For the coder who is looking for valuable GA solutions to his questions, the implementation can be done using an older version of Mahout. As usual, using the abandoned code version could lead to a bunch of potential problems. So, use it without any assurance of stability and compatibility.

Evolutionary algorithms demonstrate their power on the extraction of rules from an initial raw dataset. Apart from the medical field, they have been demonstrated to be very powerful in finding trading rules over the set of stock market index (see for reference `http://student.bus.olemiss.edu/files/conlon/others/Others/Temp/Bus669_CompInfo/Chapter%205/Genetic%20Algorithm%20-%20An%20Example%20from%20Finance/Allen%20Karjalainen%201999%20JFE.pdf`) and bankrupt prediction (`http://www.sciencedirect.com/science/article/pii/S0957417402000519`).

Index

Apache Tomcat 7 Essentials

ISBN: 978-1-84951-662-4 Paperback: 294 pages

Learn Apache Tomcat 7 step-by-step through a practical approach, achieving a wide vision of enterprise middleware along with building your own middleware along with building your own middleware servers, and administrating 24x7x365

1. Readymade solution for web technologies for migration/hosting and supporting environment for Tomcat 7
2. Tips, tricks, and best practices for web hosting solution providers for Tomcat 7
3. Content designed with practical approach and plenty of illustrations

---

Hadoop Real-World Solutions Cookbook

ISBN: 978-1-84951-912-0 Paperback: 316 pages

Realistic, simple code examples to solve problems at scale with Hadoop and related technologies

1. Solutions to common problems when working in the Hadoop environment
2. Recipes for (un)loading data, analytics, and troubleshooting
3. In depth code examples demonstrating various analytic models, analytic solutions, and common best practices

Please check **www.PacktPub.com** for information on our titles

Lightning Source UK Ltd.
Milton Keynes UK
UKOW06f1603240114

225207UK00004B/206/P

9 781849 518024